S0-CRW-502

WITHDRAWN FROM LIBRARY

WORDSWORTHIAN CRITICISM

WORDSWORTHIAN CRITICISM

A GUIDE AND BIBLIOGRAPHY

By

James V. Logan

GORDIAN PRESS
NEW YORK
1974

Originally Published 1961
Reprinted 1974

Published by Gordian Press, Inc.
By Arrangement With
Ohio State University Press

Library of Congress Cataloging in Publication Data

Logan, James Venable, 1901-
Wordsworthian criticism; a guide and bibliography.

Reprint of the 1961 ed. published by Ohio State University Press, Columbus.
Bibliography: p.
1. Wordsworth, William, 1770-1850--Criticism and interpretation--History. 2. Wordsworth, William, 1770-1850--Bibliography. I. Title.
[PR5887.3.L6 1974] 821'.7 74-7025
ISBN 0-87752-171-9

PREFACE

In the Preface to the 1961 reprinting of this book I stated that an extension of my bibliography up to the present was not warranted because of several exhaustive bibliographies that have been currently issued. These and others have continued to appear, and to add to this present edition a selection of recent material would be ludicrously superficial. Writings on Wordsworth have not diminished, and the reader needs the current bibliographies to keep up with them.

The most useful annual bibliography devoted to the Romantic period is *The Romantic Movement: A Selective and Critical Bibliography,* published in *Journal of English Literary History* 1937-49, in *Philological Quarterly* 1950-64, and in *English Language Notes* since 1965. Also of first importance is *The English Romantic Poets: A Review of Research and Criticism* (T. M. Raysor and Frank Jordan, Jr. editors, published 1950, rev. 1956, and extensively revised in 1972), which notes and discusses a variety of contributions to the literature on Wordsworth. And now there is a new, informal quarterly, a newsletter appropriately called *The Wordsworth Circle* (Marilyn Gaull, ed.) which includes notes and reviews, and a section titled "Wordsworth Scholarship: An Annual Register." Finally, the task of extending my bibliography listings to the present has been admirably done by Elton F. Henley and David H. Stam in their annotated *Wordsworthian Criticism, 1945-1964.*

Much has been written on Wordsworth since this book was first published. An outstanding achievement in research was the completion in 1949 of the new Oxford edition of the poetry, edited by de Selincourt and Helen Darbishire. Another was the publication of a new, perhaps definitive, biography by Mary Moorman. As would be expected, most of the writing on Wordsworth has been criticism and interpretation of the poetry, discussing its techniques and style, relating it to the aesthetic and spiritual streams of tendency, and penetrating into its subtle and complex thought. It would seem that the second half of the twentieth century sees Wordsworth's poetry as more needed than ever before by man in his struggle to find and hold his essential being.

February, 1973 J. V. L.

INTRODUCTORY NOTE

In Part I of this bibliographical guide I have attempted to present a body of selected Wordsworthian criticism extending from the poet's own day to the present. It has been my aim, in the chapters dealing with the contemporaries of Wordsworth, to include mostly formal criticism (which omits much from letters and private journals), my choice of material being guided by typical attitudes and prominent names. Thus the reviews of Jeffrey and of Wilson best represent the conflict of opinion for and against the poet as it appeared in the quarterlies of the first third of the nineteenth century; but also the criticism of the period includes numerous essays by writers who are outstanding literary artists. The chapters devoted to the Victorians include the writings of the men of letters who shaped the criticism of the day, and the beginnings of scholarship and research in the work of biographers, editors, and the Wordsworth Society. The later chapters on the criticism and scholarship of the twentieth century are a survey of leading trends of interpretation and of outstanding contributions.

The material in Part I will therefore be familiar to the seasoned Wordsworthian scholar, but it should be of benefit to the more general reader or to the younger student of the poet in helping him to find his bearings in the mass of literature on Wordsworth, and in enabling him more readily to proceed into his own reading and investigation. My chief task has been to select and link the material, to organize it in its chronological or topical relationships, and to determine the emphasis to give each writer. Mine is not the function of the reviewer, and minute criticism would be inappropriate, although I have provided brief critical summaries when I thought they might be of assistance in pointing up the essential problems of any given piece of criticism.

Part II, the bibliography, extends from 1850 to 1944. The items prior to the twentieth century have been selected on the basis of severe elimination. I have included only standard criticism and items of special and peculiar value. More than three-fourths of the bibliography is devoted to the twentieth century. Some books have been omitted, but I have endeavored to list not only well-recognized titles but numerous others that might be of service to a few. I have included all articles on Wordsworth (excepting reviews) in the complete files of the following learned journals: *Modern Language Notes, Publications of the Modern Language Association, Modern Philology, Philological Quarterly, Journal of English and Germanic Philology, Studies in Philology, Review of English Studies, Modern Language Review,* and *Journal of English Literary History.* A great variety of other periodicals is represented, and it is hoped that no articles of significance or of particular value, published in this century, have been omitted. *The London Times Literary Supplement* and *Notes and Queries* have presented a special problem. The letters and notes in these two publications are often of some special value but are soon buried out of sight. Yet in the course of years there accumulates much that is trivial and repetitive. Also points are queried, with tentative and speculative answers—matters that are subsequently investigated fully elsewhere and perhaps determined. The old files of *N&Q* especially contain questions on variant readings, references to, or transcripts of, newly discovered letters, and other data which have since been included in recent editions and biographies. Brief notes of this nature have usually been omitted. However, I have worked on the principle of including everything in *TLS* and *N&Q* that might conceivably be of service to someone, no matter how minute or apparently trivial the point may be.

Reviews of prominent or recent books are supplied. Not every review is included, but most of the lists are generous. In large part they have been drawn from the *Annual Bibliography of English Language and Literature* published by the Modern Humanities Research Association, and the more recent *Bibliography of the Romantic Movement* issued annually in *ELH.*

References to Wordsworth and often excellent discussions of him appear in hundreds of books and essays not specifically devoted to him. Anything approaching a complete list of such titles is impossible. My policy in selecting items of this class has been to follow the guide of Wordsworthian scholars, and to include what they have most often, in their works, found of interest and value.

It may be appropriate here to make some comment concerning earlier bibliographies of Wordsworth, and to pay my tribute to them. The only extensive bibliographies (the two books by the late T. J. Wise, *A Bibliography of Wordsworth* [1916] and *The Two Lake Poets* [1927], are limited and specialized in their service) are the catalogues of the two great collections of Wordsworth in this country, owned by Cornell University and by Amherst College: *The Wordsworth Collection,* Cornell University, 1931, and the *Supplement,* 1942; and *The Amherst Wordsworth Collection,* 1936. Both are of great value as bibliographies, and to me they have been a most helpful check list. But their contents and arrangement are determined by the collections that they describe, not by strictly bibliographical requirements. Thus a relatively small percentage of titles from twentieth-century periodicals is included; numerous "Selections" and reprints of Wordsworth's poems are listed; and the arrangement of the titles is not consistently chronological, nor do the dates always indicate the first appearance of the book or essay. Students interested in nineteenth-century American editions and reviews will find the Cornell collection especially valuable. Both catalogues have a fuller list of Victorian titles than will be found in my bibliography. But I have included titles of many articles (in the twentieth century especially) not listed in these catalogues, and throughout the bibliography I have attempted to make my selection of titles on the basis of their value to the student rather than on their fitness to be included in a collection.

I wish to express my thanks to several of my colleagues in the Department of English of The Ohio State University who have been helpful in the preparation of this book. Professor Harold R. Walley, Professor John H. Wilson, and Professor William R. Parker, members of the publications committee, read this book in manuscript and provided me with much valuable criticism. Thanks are also due to Professor Charles F. Harrold for criticism and suggestions. I am especially grateful to Professor Ruth Hughey for several readings of the manuscript as it grew and for countless helpful comments. I wish also to thank Mr. John L. Stewart, Mr. Stanley K. Coffman, and Mrs. Genevieve Tucker for their assistance in checking the files of *TLS* and *N&Q,* and the Graduate School of The Ohio State University for granting a subsidy for this work. Thanks are due to Mrs. Myra T.

McCrory for assistance in reading proof. I am heavily indebted to Miss Velma L. Carter of the Graduate School for undertaking so cheerfully and efficiently the task of preparing the manuscript for the press. It is also a pleasure to acknowledge the assistance received from Professor Earl Leslie Griggs of the Department of English, the University of Pennsylvania, who read the first draft of the chapters on Wordsworth's contemporaries. Finally, I wish to thank the Library of Amherst College, and Mr. Newton F. McKeon in particular, for the cordial hospitality shown me during parts of two very pleasant summers spent in Amherst, reading in the late Dr. Patton's splendid Wordsworth collection.

J. V. L.

ACKNOWLEDGMENTS

I am grateful to the publishers of the more recent books and articles cited for their courteous permission to quote. Thanks are due to the following: The Macmillan Company, New York, for Gingerich's *Essays in the Romantic Poets,* Beach's *The Concept of Nature in Nineteenth-Century English Poetry,* and Batho's *The Later Wordsworth;* Charles Scribner's Sons, New York, for Harper's *William Wordsworth, His Life, Works, and Influence;* The Johns Hopkins Press, Baltimore, for Havens' *The Mind of a Poet;* The Clarendon Press, Oxford, for Dicey's *The Statesmanship of Wordsworth,* Stewart's "Platonism in English Poetry" in *English Literature and the Classics,* and Garrod's *Wordsworth;* E. P. Dutton and Co., New York, for Legouis' *The Early Life of William Wordsworth;* The Graduate School, The University of Wisconsin, for Beatty's *William Wordsworth, His Doctrine and Art in Their Historical Relations;* Jonathan Cape Ltd., London, for Read's *Wordsworth;* Jonathan Cape Ltd., London, and Harcourt Brace and Co., New York, for Fausset's *The Lost Leader;* Harvard University Press, Cambridge, for Sperry's *Wordsworth's Anti-Climax;* University of California Press, Berkeley, for Miles's *Wordsworth and the Vocabulary of Emotion;* Yale University Press, New Haven, for Barstow's *Wordsworth's Theory of Poetic Diction;* University of Washington Press, Seattle, for Rader's *Presiding Ideas in Wordsworth's Poetry;* University of Michigan Press, Ann Arbor, for Campbell's and Mueschke's "Wordsworth's Aesthetic Development, 1795–1802" in *University of Michigan Publications Language and Literature;* The University of Chicago Press, Chicago, for Campbell's and Mueschke's "*The Borderers* as a Document in the History of Wordsworth's Aesthetic Development" in *Modern Philology;* Modern Language Association of America, for Stallknecht's "Wordsworth and Philosophy" in *Publications of the Modern Language Association;* University of North Carolina Press, Chapel Hill, for Weaver's "Wordsworth's *Prelude:* An Intimation of Certain Problems in Criticism," "Wordsworth's *Prelude:* The Poetic Function of Memory," "Wordsworth: Forms and Images," and "Wordsworth's *Prelude:* The Shaping Spirit," in *Studies in Philology.*

CONTENTS

I. TRENDS IN CRITICISM

II. BIBLIOGRAPHY

INDEX

PART I: TRENDS IN CRITICISM

CHAPTER ONE

EARLY PERIODICAL CRITICISM

I

In a review of the criticism of Wordsworth by his contemporaries, it is well to remember the poet's own statement: "every great and original writer, in proportion as he is great or original, must himself create the taste by which he is to be relished; he must teach the art by which he is to be seen."[1] The voluminous amount of comment on Wordsworth, recorded during his lifetime, is material for a fascinating study of this dictum.

Wordsworth was breaking new ground. He faced the strong opposition of able critics devoted to late neoclassic standards of taste. Nor was he a striking figure as the leader of a "school." He lacked personal persuasiveness, and the objectives of his poetic creed, although daring, were not sensational. Thus it was easy to miss the significance of his verse, and to ridicule him as a clumsy theorist. Moreover, in the formal explanations of his aims as a poet, prefixed to his collections, Wordsworth provoked an attack from his opponents and gave greater emphasis than was intended to certain external aspects of his art. In addition, there is an interrelationship between all his poems, a philosophic consanguinity, which excludes any one poem from being fully representative of him. Critics selecting a few poems to review were in danger of missing their ultimate interpretation. Even when they had so large a body of his verse as the 1807 volume, or later *The Excursion,* they might be excused their blind spots and confusion, since Wordsworth's poetry is infused by an abstruse and difficult philosophy, unsystematically expressed and sometimes contradictory.

A full understanding of Wordsworth comes slowly even to the modern reader who has at hand a vast body of collected information and commentary not available to readers of Wordsworth's day. It is little wonder that it required a long time for

[1] *The Letters of William and Dorothy Wordsworth, The Middle Years,* ed. E. de Selincourt, 2 vols., Oxford, The Clarendon Press, 1937, p. 130. Wordsworth attributes this statement to Coleridge.

the poet to win over his contemporaries. For twenty years he was teaching his art, he was creating the taste by which he was to be relished.

The material in this chapter and the next is arranged in approximately chronological order rather than by ideas, so that the reader may obtain some notion of the development of Wordsworthian criticism. This criticism is a living tissue fed by personal animosity, prejudice, and ignorance, or by vague enthusiasms, friendship, and spiritual and aesthetic responsiveness. It thus has a vitality, a human element, greater than is to be found in the fairer, more intelligent criticism that follows in a later day. For convenience, the criticism of the professional critics in the periodicals has been separated from the essays of the men of letters contemporary with Wordsworth. In this chapter and the next, since we are dealing with the "living word," the comments of the critics are to a large degree quoted verbatim, although much abbreviated, rather than paraphrased.[2]

Wordsworth's social views, his ability to depict nature, and his natural and spiritual philosophy are sometimes discussed by the critics, but it will be seen that for twenty years they were agitated chiefly by his manifesto of 1800: "The principal object, then, proposed in these Poems was to choose incidents and situations from common life, and to relate or describe them, throughout, as far as was possible in a selection of language really used by men."[3]

II

In spite of Wordsworth's complaints, the reception of his poetry from 1793 to the last publication of *Lyrical Ballads* in 1805 was on the whole encouraging. Except for a pert review of *An Evening Walk* and *Descriptive Sketches* in *The Monthly Review* (Oct., 1793), friendly notice was given to these early poems. On the appearance of *Lyrical Ballads* in 1798, Southey wrote an ill-advised notice in *The Critical Review* (Oct., 1798), starting the abuse of *The Ancient Mariner* and the hostility to the tenets of the brief "Advertisement." But the reviews of Wordsworth's friend, Francis Wrangham, in *The British Critic* (Oct., 1799 and

[2] For a convenient collection of reviews and private criticism, see Elsie Smith, *An Estimate of William Wordsworth by his Contemporaries, 1793–1822*, Oxford, Basil Blackwell, 1932.

[3] Preface to 1800 edition of *Lyrical Ballads, The Poetical Works of Wordsworth*, ed. Thomas Hutchinson, New York, Oxford University Press, 1933, p. 935.

Feb., 1801) were certainly cordial if not altogether understanding, and Dr. Burney's in *The Monthly Review* (June, 1799) at least recognized the importance of the book. (*The Edinburgh Review* was not founded until 1802, *The Quarterly Review* until 1809, and *Blackwood's Edinburgh Magazine* until 1817.) It was not until the publication of *Poems in Two Volumes* in 1807 that the full fury of the attack began, led by the new *Edinburgh Review*. So severe was the criticism that the poet's reputation, which had been slowly but healthily expanding during the four publications of *Lyrical Ballads*, received a shock that checked its advance ten or fifteen years. Wordsworth's poetry received many reviews from the various lesser journals, but we shall concentrate on the three leading periodicals of the day—*The Edinburgh Review, Blackwood's,* and *The Quarterly Review*—whose criticism was the most representative and influential.

Francis Jeffrey set the tone of much of the adverse criticism of Wordsworth for more than twenty years.[4] He quarreled chiefly with the poet's theory, set forth in his Prefaces, and with his practice in regard to the language and subjects of poetry, and he fell far short of understanding the poet's spiritual conception of nature. But it is hard to explain why he persevered in his attack on Wordsworth. Was it because he felt strongly the justice of his convictions regarding poetry, or because of an antipathy for Wordsworth's politics and philosophy, or because of ill nature and a delight in exercising his powers? Traces of all these motives are present.

One modern critic attributes much of Jeffrey's attitude to the editorial policies that determined in advance the position that *The Edinburgh Review* must take. Wordsworth was merely a scapegoat.[5] Some of Jeffrey's contemporaries and some recent critics have credited him with honesty, and, in varying degrees, have found his criticism of Wordsworth correct and justifiable.[6]

[4] Sperry sets the date of Jeffrey's retirement from the editorship of *The Edinburgh*, 1829, as marking the turn of the tide in Wordsworth's favor (*Wordsworth's Anti-Climax*, Cambridge, Mass., Harvard University Press, 1935, p. 110). Batho (*The Later Wordsworth*, Cambridge, Cambridge University Press, 1933) and Smith, *op. cit.*, indicate the rise of Wordsworth's popularity as early as 1820. Noyes gives a convincing argument for accepting the earlier date (*Wordsworth and Jeffrey in Controversy*, "Indiana University Publications, Humanities Series," No. 5, Bloomington, University of Indiana Press, 1941, pp. 51, 61n).

[5] Sperry, *op. cit.*, 105–9. But were not these policies formulated by Jeffrey himself?

[6] See Russell Noyes, *op. cit.*, 37 and notes. In "The Humanism of Francis Jeffrey," by Merritt Hughes (*MLR*, xvi [1921], 247) we are told that his criticism of Wordsworth "is all honest, clear-eyed criticism; and it all springs from a conviction that

But others, including Coleridge, Southey, and Crabb Robinson, stress the point that he was writing to please his readers, and "ill-natured things are said with better effect than good-natured ones."[7]

Perhaps the chief cause of the trouble was the fact that Jeffrey was incapable of understanding Wordsworth. He held a restricted standard for measuring poetry, and all verse was to be condemned that did not conform to this pattern. An advocate of common sense, he could not stomach the eccentricities of the Romantics. He believed that Wordsworth was an affected mannerist, dragging into poetry a motley band of gypsies and vagabonds who even lacked the common-sense reality of the English peasant. He did not approve of the tawdry poetic diction of the late eighteenth century, but he believed that poetry should express noble sentiment in lofty language. To this extent Jeffrey was honest, that he believed in this standard and was willing to fight to maintain it. He says, in justification of the severity of his attack on the "Lake School":

> It was precisely because the perverseness and bad taste of this new school was combined with a great deal of genius and of laudable feeling, that we were afraid of their spreading and gaining ground among us, and that we entered into the discussion with a degree of zeal and animosity which some might think unreasonable towards authors, to whom so much merit had been conceded. . . . At other times, the magnitude of these errors . . . made us wonder more than ever at the perversity by which they were retained, and regret that we had not declared ourselves against them with still more formidable and decided hostility.[8]

Yet there is more to Jeffrey's attack than can be explained solely on grounds of taste. He was clever. Few poets are more

---

Wordsworth was confounding life's plainest distinctions in the mystical mist with which he had surrounded himself for years in the solitude of the Cumberland hills."

J. M. Beatty ("Lord Jeffrey and Wordsworth," *PMLA*, xxxviii [1923], 221–35) maintains that "the classical idea of decorum was at the basis of Jeffrey's commonsense criticism and that, stripped of their thorns, many of his judgments are entirely in conformity with the opinions of modern critics." Beatty bases his defense largely on quotation of excerpts from Jeffrey, which are well selected for their apparent justness. But while many of Jeffrey's strictures are in themselves sound, detached comments do not indicate the prejudice and venom of his campaign against Wordsworth.

R. C. Bald ("Francis Jeffrey as a Literary Critic," *The Nineteenth Century and After*, xcvii [1925], 201) regards Jeffrey as the type of Romanticist that appeared just prior to *Lyrical Ballads*, as represented by Gray, Collins, and Goldsmith. Jeffrey belonged to the time when the native English genius was coming into its own again, but he was not far enough advanced to understand Lamb and Wordsworth.

[7] Southey. Quoted by Noyes, *op. cit.*, 37.

[8] *The Edinburgh Review*, xi (Oct., 1807), 215.

tempting bait to the wit than Wordsworth. Well-turned ridicule amused the readers of *The Edinburgh Review,* and Jeffrey had discovered an inexhaustible source in his tilts with the "foolish" Lake poet. It appears that most of the population of Edinburgh battened on this kind of desiccated criticism.[9] Jeffrey as a shrewd journalist played up to this taste, sometimes resorting to personal abuse worthy of the choicest critics of Pope's day. Moreover, the dapper Scotchman must have at length become unstrung by Wordsworth's refusal to be reformed. The poet was unmoved by the paltry compliments, the admonition, the fiery rebukes of the great critic, and continued solemnly to write his poetry in his own way. Little wonder Jeffrey grew violent. The critic's attempt in late life to cover his retreat is only amusing. He declared to Crabb Robinson that he was "always an admirer of Wordsworth." To which Robinson replied, "The *Edinburgh Review* had a strange way of expressing admiration."[10]

Jeffrey's first attack on the "Lake School" appeared in the first volume of *The Edinburgh Review* in a criticism of Southey's *Thalaba.*[11] The basis of his antagonism is made clear from his opening statement that the standards of poetry, like religion, were fixed long ago. The new "sect" therefore are dissenters, seducing many into an admiration of their false taste. In his criticism of *Lyrical Ballads* Jeffrey took his lead from Wordsworth's Preface. He censured the "affectation" of writing in "the ordinary language of conversation among the middling and lower orders of the people," in defiance of the obvious superiority of the language of people belonging to the higher and more cultivated classes. But worse, these poets have set out to copy the sentiments of low society, an attempt which "leads to the debasement of all those feelings which poetry is designed to communicate."

The love, or grief, or indignation of an enlightened and refined character, is not only expressed in a different language, but is in itself a different emotion from the love, or grief, or anger of a clown, a tradesman, or a market-wench. . . . The question, therefore, comes simply to be—which of them is the most proper object for poetical imitation? It is needless for us to answer a question, which the practice of all the world has long ago decided irrevocably. The poor and vulgar

[9] See Noyes, *op. cit.,* 41.

[10] *Blake, Coleridge, Wordsworth, Lamb, etc. Being Selections from the Remains of Henry Crabb Robinson,* ed. Edith J. Morley, Manchester, The University Press, 1922, p. 52.

[11] *The Edinburgh Review,* i (Oct., 1802), 63.

may interest us, in poetry, by their *situation;* but never, we apprehend, by any sentiments that are peculiar to their condition, and still less by any language that is characteristic of it.[12]

This was Jeffrey's attack on the whole school, but when he reviewed Wordsworth's *Poems in Two Volumes,* which appeared in 1807, he recognized Wordsworth, not Southey, as the leader of the fraternity.[13] Whereas earlier, in the review of *Thalaba,* Jeffrey sneered at Wordsworth in passing, without paying the compliment of even naming him, he now saw in Wordsworth his most formidable antagonist and showed a respect and fear of the poet's growing prestige.

Jeffrey observed that the *Lyrical Ballads* were popular, and deservedly so, because "in spite of their occasional vulgarity, affectation, and silliness, they were undoubtedly characterized by a strong spirit of originality, of pathos, and natural feeling."[14] However, in the mind of Jeffrey, the perversion of taste that they consciously set out to accomplish overbalanced their virtues, and he regretted that he had not dealt more severely with them. Public opinion, that may have wavered in the case of *Lyrical Ballads,* would forever renounce the whole school in condemning the 1807 *Poems.*

The critic again singled out the diction and subjects of the poems for attack.

His diction has no where any pretensions to elegance or dignity; and he has scarcely ever condescended to give the grace of correctness or melody to his versification. . . . With Mr. Wordsworth and his friends, it is plain that their peculiarities of diction are things of choice, and not of accident. They write as they do, upon principle and system; and it evidently costs them much pains to keep *down* to the standard which they have proposed to themselves. They are, to the full, as much mannerists, too, as the poetasters who ring changes on the commonplaces of magazine versification; and all the difference between them is, that . . . they have preferred furnishing themselves from vulgar ballads and plebeian nurseries.

Their peculiarities of diction alone, are enough, perhaps, to render them ridiculous; but the author before us really seems anxious to court this literary martyrdom by a device still more infallible—we mean, that of connecting his most lofty, tender, or impassioned conceptions, with objects and incidents, which the greater part of his

[12] *Ibid.,* i, 66.
[13] *Ibid.,* xi (Oct., 1807), 214.
[14] *Ibid.,* xi, 214.

readers will probably persist in thinking low, silly, or uninteresting. Whether this is done from affectation and conceit alone, or whether it may not arise, in some measure, from the self-illusion of a mind of extraordinary sensibility, habituated to solitary meditation, we cannot undertake to determine. It is possible enough, we allow, that the sight of a friend's garden-spade, or a sparrow's nest, or a man gathering leeches, might really have suggested to such a mind a train of powerful impressions and interesting reflections; but it is certain, that, to most minds, such associations will always appear forced, strained, and unnatural; and that the composition in which it is attempted to exhibit them, will always have the air of parody, or ludicrous and affected singularity.[15]

Jeffrey singled out a number of poems for ridicule. A few of his comments will suffice to illustrate this kind of criticism. *The Redbreast and the Butterfly*—"The three last lines seem to be downright raving." *To the Small Celandine*—"a piece of namby-pamby . . . which we should almost have taken for a professed imitation of one of Mr. Phillips' prettyisms." *The Beggars*—"may be taken, we fancy, as a touchstone of Mr. Wordsworth's merit. There is something about it that convinces us it is a favourite of the author's; though to us, we will confess, it appears to be a very paragon of silliness and affectation." *Ode on the Intimations of Immortality*—"the volume is wound up with an 'Ode'. . . . This is, beyond all doubt, the most illegible and unintelligible part of the publication"—a statement that is, "beyond all doubt," the most damning blunder that Francis Jeffrey ever made.

After bestowing some approbation on the sonnets, Jeffrey concludes:

When we look at these, and many still finer passages, in the writings of this author, it is impossible not to feel a mixture of indignation and compassion, at that strange infatuation which has bound him up from the fair exercise of his talents, and withheld from the public the many excellent productions that would otherwise have taken the place of the trash now before us. Even in the worst of these productions, there are, no doubt, occasional little traits of delicate feeling and original fancy; but these are quite lost and obscured in the mass of childishness and insipidity with which they are incorporated; nor can any thing give us a more melancholy view of the debasing effects of this miserable theory, than that it has given ordinary men a right

[15] *Ibid.*, xi, 217–18.

to wonder at the folly and presumption of a man gifted like Mr. Wordsworth, and made him appear, in his second avowed publication, like a bad imitator of the worst of his former productions.

We venture to hope, that there is now an end of this folly; and that, like other follies, it will be found to have cured itself by the extravagances resulting from its unbridled indulgence. In this point of view, the publication of the volumes before us may ultimately be of service to the good cause of literature . . . we think there is every reason to hope, that the lamentable consequences which have resulted from Mr. Wordsworth's open violation of the established laws of poetry, will operate as a wholesome warning to those who might otherwise have been seduced by his example, and be the means of restoring to that ancient and venerable code its due honour and authority.[16]

Jeffrey and the contributors to *The Edinburgh Review* continued their attacks on Wordsworth by means of side references in essays on other poets. In an essay on Crabbe's poetry Jeffrey points out the "childish and absurd affectations" of Wordsworth in contrast to the "manly sense and correct picturing of Mr. Crabbe."[17] He makes the surprising accusation that Wordsworth and his fraternity have not presented real, living men, but strange figments of their own invention. Again, in a review of John Wilson's *Isle of Palms and Other Poems,* Wordsworth is brought in for sharp reproval on the old score of his choice of subjects unfitted for poetry.[18] Some respect is shown for the best in Wordsworth that is absent in Jeffrey's earlier criticism. Nevertheless, Jeffrey's condemnation of Wordsworth's bad taste is sweeping rather than discriminating, and he has a way of so emphasizing his points of attack that the good qualities he concedes seem paltry in comparison. Certainly the effect of his criticism was prejudicial to any popular acceptance of Wordsworth's rightful claims as a poet.

In 1814 Jeffrey published his review of *The Excursion* with the notorious opening sentence "This will never do."[19] It is the climax of Jeffrey's long feud with Wordsworth. He had by this time lost all patience and all hope that the stubborn poet would mend his ways and write as Francis Jeffrey thought he should. The blows he struck were deadly and without mercy. The hope

[16] *Ibid.*, xi, 231.
[17] *Ibid.*, xii (April, 1808), 131.
[18] *Ibid.*, xix (Feb., 1812), 373.
[19] *Ibid.*, xxiv (Nov., 1814), 1.

of a kindly reception of *The Excursion,* pathetically entertained by the little group at Rydal Mount, was defeated by Jeffrey's worst assault.

There is much truth in Jeffrey's complaint over the prolixity of *The Excursion,* and in his comment that it lacks the strength and originality of the earlier poetry. "It is longer, weaker, and tamer, than any of Mr. Wordsworth's other productions; with less boldness or originality, and less even of that extreme simplicity and lowliness of tone which wavered so prettily, in the Lyrical Ballads, between silliness and pathos. We have imitations of Cowper, and even of Milton here, engrafted on the natural drawl of the Lakers."[20] Complaining of the tedious length and wordiness of the poem, Jeffrey concludes: "The case of Mr. Wordsworth, we perceive, is now manifestly hopeless; and we give him up as altogether incurable, and beyond the power of criticism."[21]

Jeffrey points out the evils of Wordsworth's solitary habits, and recommends that he mix more with the people who will read his poetry, and learn from them to escape the gross faults which he has for twenty years mistaken for beauties. In one facile opinion he sweeps away the entire edifice of the poem:

> The volume before us . . . we should characterize as a tissue of moral and devotional ravings, in which innumerable changes are rung upon a few simple and familiar ideas:—But with such an accompaniment of long words, long sentences, and unwieldly phrases—and such a hubbub of strained raptures and fantastical sublimities, that it is often extremely difficult for the most skilful and attentive student to obtain a glimpse of the author's meaning.[22]

In contrast to this, one recalls the overly eager young Keats who regarded *The Excursion* as one of "three things superior in the modern world."[23] The review continues with a crushing criticism of Wordsworth's "mystical morality" and of his moral and theological interpretation of nature, ridicules the style of certain passages from the poem, and makes sarcastic comments upon the choice of a pedlar as the chief spokesman of the poem.

After an equally severe review in 1815 of *The White Doe of*

[20] *Ibid.*, xxiv, 1.
[21] *Ibid.*, xxiv, 2.
[22] *Ibid.*, xxiv, 4.
[23] *The Letters of John Keats,* ed. M. B. Forman, 2 vols., Humphrey Milford, Oxford University Press, 1931, I, 86.

Rylstone, Jeffrey truly gave up all hope for the ungrateful poet and abandoned him to his evil ways, although he continued to fire a shot or two in essays on other poets.[24]

III

The Quarterly Review was founded in 1809 and was a rival of *The Edinburgh.* In respect to Wordsworthian criticism it took something of a middle position. In April, 1814, in a review of Coleridge's *Remorse,* it carried an analysis and criticism of the "Lake" poets, remarking that the poetic theory of the "school" was a matter of its own choice, but if these writers preferred to analyze minutely the smaller emotions rather than the strong and permanent feelings of the mind, they must expect the admiration of the few rather than general popularity.[25] "The majority of their readers have passed glow-worms and birds'-nests, celandines and daisies, without any emotion lively enough to be remembered; and they are surprised, unfairly perhaps, but not unnaturally, that so much sensation should be attributed to so trifling a cause."[26]

The critic points out as the creed of these writers that nature is sentient and moral.

> All the features and appearances of nature in their poetical creed possess a sentient and intellectual being, and exert an influence for good upon the hearts of her worshippers. Nothing can be more poetical than this feeling, but it is the misfortune of this school that their very excellencies are carried to an excess. Hence they constantly attribute not merely physical, but moral animation to nature.[27]

Even in disapproving, the critic has here touched on a more important aspect of Wordsworth's poetry than Jeffrey was wont to discuss.

If the reviewer seemed to admit these points grudgingly, he ventured to give some warmth of moral commendation:

> There are yet a few points of no common importance to be noticed, in which we scruple not to rank the Lake Poets above all that have gone before them. In their writings the gentle and domestic virtues of an affectionate heart are uniformly exalted above the splendid and dangerous heroism which has been too generally the theme of other poets. In their writings women are drawn, as they deserve to

[24] *Ibid.,* xxv (Oct., 1815), 355.
[25] *The Quarterly Review,* xi, 177–90.
[26] *Ibid.,* xi, 181.
[27] *Ibid.,* xi, 181.

be, lofty yet meek; patient and cheerful; dutiful, affectionate, brave, faithful, and pious; the pillars that adorn and support the temple of this life's happiness. . . . Love, with the Lake Poets, becomes what it should be, a devout spirit, purifying the soul, and worshipping God most in his most beauteous or his most noble work.[28]

In 1814 *The Quarterly* printed a review of *The Excursion* written by Charles Lamb, and thus showed itself willing to publish the opinions of a sympathetic friend of Wordsworth. Gifford, however, edited the manuscript before printing and when it appeared Lamb complained that every "warm expression is changed for a nasty cold one." Nevertheless, what remains, even if badly mutilated, is a favorable and intelligent commentary on the poem. This review will be discussed in the next chapter in connection with the men of letters who wrote on Wordsworth.

The Quarterly also reviewed the *Poems* of 1815, and *The White Doe of Rylstone*.[29] The critic warns his readers that it must not be supposed that because he admires Wordsworth's talents he approves of his entire poetical system, an opinion which he fears had got abroad. Although Wordsworth's poems "exhibit a mind richly stored with all the materials from which poetry is formed," the reviewer regrets that the poet has not used his abilities to their best advantage.[30] He possesses a true sensibility to the beauties of nature, fervid imagination, and "a most praisworthy love of simplicity both in thought and language."[31] But the old points of his theory of poetic diction are again brought forward at length against him. One point made by the critic is especially interesting, since it anticipates a somewhat similar statement of Coleridge in *Biographia Literaria*. Referring to Wordsworth's statement in the 1800 Preface that in his use of the language of humble men, he has purified it from its "real defects," the critic remarks: "if the language of low life be purified from what *we* should call its *real defects,* it will differ only in copiousness from the language of high life."[32]

It will be seen from these extracts that while *The Quarterly* did not indulge in the invective of *The Edinburgh Review,* it was lukewarm and patronizing.

[28] *Ibid.*, xi, 182.
[29] *Ibid.*, xiv (Oct., 1815), 201.
[30] *Ibid.*, xiv, 201.
[31] *Ibid.*, xiv, 201.
[32] *Ibid.*, xiv, 205. Cf. *Biographia Literaria,* ed. J. Shawcross, 2 vols., Oxford, The Clarendon Press, 1907, II, 41–42.

Blackwood's Edinburgh Magazine was founded in 1817. While *The Edinburgh Review,* through Jeffrey, led the attack against Wordsworth *Blackwood's,* largely through the contributions of John Wilson ("Christopher North"), championed him. The leading names in the journalistic criticism of Wordsworth are Jeffrey and Wilson. The writings and conversation of Professor Wilson no doubt contributed much towards the recognition of the poet's genius in the 1820's. He writes thus of himself:

> Nor are we not privileged to cherish a better feeling than pride in the belief, or rather knowledge, that WE have helped to diffuse Wordsworth's poetry not only over this Island, but the furthest dependencies of the British empire, and throughout the United States of America. Many thousands have owed to us their emancipation from the prejudices against it, under which they had wilfully remained ignorant of it during many years; and we have instructed as many more, whose hearts are free, how to look on it with those eyes of love which alone can discover the Beautiful.[33]

Wilson did not write great criticism—much of it is long-winded and tedious—but he understood, better than Jeffrey, Wordsworth's deeper purposes, he was more sensitive to the beauty of Wordsworth's natural philosophy, and he had the courage to defend the poet during the time when, in the words of Hartley Coleridge, "to admire Wordsworth . . . was to be kicked at."[34] Certainly his criticism was enlightening in its day, and should receive some prominence in the history of Wordsworthian criticism.

Like De Quincey, Wilson entertained an extravagant schoolboy admiration of Wordsworth, and at the age of seventeen wrote him a long letter which has a good deal more in it than mere juvenile worship. He later moved to Elleray, an estate on the banks of Windermere, and became a close friend and companion of the Wordsworth household. He was himself tagged a "Lake poet" by Jeffrey, and indeed his poetry is much influenced by the older man. But little by little the friendship between the two became strained. By 1820 Wilson was much less of an idolater, still commending Wordsworth's poetry, but showing a "disillusioned half contempt" for him.[35]

[33] *The Works of Professor Wilson,* ed. Ferrier, 12 vols., Edinburgh, W. Blackwood and Sons, 1865–67, X, 345.

[34] Quoted by Ferrier, *op. cit.,* V, 387.

[35] For an account of the relationship between the two men, see Alan L. Strout, "William Wordsworth and John Wilson," *PMLA,* xlix (1934), 143–83.

The youthful criticism in the letter of May 24, 1802, is interesting in that it is one of the first intelligent estimates of the psychological and moral "experiments" which had been aimed at in *Lyrical Ballads.* After opening with a glowing expression of his enthusiasm for the volume, Wilson commends as "natural" both the language and subjects of *Lyrical Ballads,* and passes to a discussion of the effect of external nature on sentiment and character, commending the poet for not being one who attempts "to write on human nature without a knowledge of the causes that affect it."[36] In other words, he sees in Wordsworth a refreshingly new psychological approach to the study of human nature.

Mention should be made of Wilson's part in instigating one of Wordsworth's important prose utterances. In a letter to *The Friend* signed "Mathetes," Wilson requested that journal to employ the pen of some great teacher to give advice on the perplexed points which, as a young man, he raises in the letter. He suggests Wordsworth as most fitted to answer his questions, and characterizes the poet thus:

> Of one such teacher who has been given to our own age you have described the power when you said, that in his annunciation of truths he seemed to speak in thunders. I believe that mighty voice has not been poured out in vain; that there are hearts that have received into their inmost depths all its varying tones; and that even now, there are many to whom the name of Wordsworth calls up the recollection of their weakness and the consciousness of their strength.[37]

Wordsworth responded to this request in his *Reply to Mathetes* which contains the central doctrines of his philosophy.[38]

Less to Wilson's credit is a curious series of three articles that appeared in *Blackwood's* in June, October, and November, 1817, at the time Wilson's friendship for the poet was becoming strained. The first pretends to be a letter written by a "Friend of Burns," assaulting Wordsworth for his "Letter Relative to a New Edition of Burns' Works." The article is a petty and insulting attack on Wordsworth's solemnity and egotism. The second letter, signed "N," defends Wordsworth as a great and good man. The third, signed "D," repeats the assault of the first. All three were really written by Wilson, an ugly piece of trickery (or

[36] Mrs. Gordon, *'Christopher North,' A Memoir of John Wilson,* Edinburgh, Thomas C. Jack, Grange Publishing Works, 1879, p. 30.

[37] *The Prose Works of William Wordsworth,* ed. A. B. Grosart, 3 vols., London, Edward Moxon, 1876, I, 307.

[38] *The Friend,* Dec. 14, 1809, and Jan. 4, 1810. See Grosart, *op. cit.,* I, 297–326.

treachery) from a recently elevated Professor of Moral Philosophy, but it is in accord with the reputation of *Blackwood's* of seeking popularity by unjust attacks (and equally unjust defenses). The whole procedure is pointless and inexcusable, and deserves mention only to show the stupid acrimony that entered into so much of the public discussion of Wordsworth. It is little wonder that he hated the press, and grew more and more dogmatic and egotistical in self-protection.

After this unpleasant episode, specimens of Wilson's mature criticism appeared in *Blackwood's* from time to time, and his intelligent and sympathetic interpretation did much to open the eyes of the public to Wordsworth's greatness. Much that he had to say has been condensed into the essay "Wordsworth," included in Ferrier's edition of Wilson's *Works*.[39] The disquisition is largely taken up with Wordsworth's moralism. The poet's optimism is noted, his "calm and self-commanding powers of the philosopher" who has an unshaken faith in the prevalence of virtue over vice and happiness over misery. Thus, with deep serenity, he gives dignity even to the meanest objects. Two things may be observed in his poetry which are almost new in English poetry and philosophy. First, "an attempt to awaken in the minds of his countrymen, certain *lumières* which they do not generally possess, and certain convictions of moral laws existing silently in the universe, and actually modifying events, in opposition to more palpable causes . . . and, secondly, a thorough knowledge of all the beauties of the human affections, and of their mutual harmonies and dependencies."[40] Wilson points out Wordsworth's idealism: his "contemplative Platonism searches for some image of perfection to admire, and perceives that the beauty of no limited being can consist in strength, but in its conformity to the moral harmony of the universe."[41] Hence the poet has no respect for mere undisciplined energy, or action that is not moral. His interest is not confined to "representing poetical objects, or moving our sympathies," but he also maintains a system of philosophical opinions, the spirit of which (unfortunately for his success) is "at variance with the philosophy at present most fashionable in this country."

After comparing Wordsworth and Milton, Wilson points

[39] Ferrier, *op. cit.*, V, 387–408.
[40] *Ibid.*, V, 392.
[41] *Ibid.*, V, 393.

out that *The Excursion* best represents Wordsworth's philosophical system, and *Lyrical Ballads* his powers "commonly called poetical . . . where pathos, imagination, and knowledge of human nature, are often presented by themselves, without any obtrusive or argumentative reference to a system. At the same time, the reverential awe, and the far-extended sympathy with which he looks upon the whole system of existing things, and the silent moral connections which he supposes to exist among them, are visible throughout all his writings."[42]

In the following summary we have a good view of Wilson's estimate of Wordsworth, which he expounded to the British public. By a comparison with Jeffrey, we may clearly see the opposite trends of criticism which had grown up by 1820.

> For our own parts, we believe that Wordworth's genius has had a greater influence on the spirit of poetry in Britain, than was ever before exercised by any individual mind. He was the first man who impregnated all his descriptions of external nature with sentiment or passion. In this he has been followed—often successfully—by other true poets. He was the first man that vindicated the native dignity of human nature, by showing that all her elementary feelings were capable of poetry—and in that too he has been followed by other true Poets, although here he stands, and probably ever will stand, unapproached. He was the first man that stripped thought and passion of all vain or foolish disguises, and showed them in their just proportions and unencumbered power. He was the first man who in poetry knew the real province of language, and suffered it not to veil the meanings of the spirit. In all these things—and in many more—Wordsworth is indisputably the most ORIGINAL POET OF THE AGE; and it is impossible, in the very nature of things, that he can ever be eclipsed.[43]

After the publication of *The Excursion,* the critics emphasized Wordsworth's ethics and philosophy. An understanding review of this nature appeared in *The Eclectic Review* (Jan., 1815), and in *The British Critic* (May, 1815), both periodicals of an ecclesiastical bent. His theory of poetry and the minor defects of some of his shorter poems, although not forgotten, were less discussed. The publication of *Peter Bell* and *The Waggoner* in 1819, although not without some applause from the public press, tended to retard this development and gave rise to a good deal of mirth on the old score of Wordsworth's ludicrous subjects and style of

[42] *Ibid.*, V, 397.
[43] *Ibid.*, V, 401–2.

writing. In May, 1820, *Blackwood's* strongly attacked the critics who for many years had persecuted Wordsworth, deliberately pouncing on all his more defective poems, and ignoring the impressive quantity of his indisputably great masterpieces. By this date the drama in the periodicals was about played out, and in spite of Jeffrey, the public was beginning to take Wordsworth seriously.

CHAPTER TWO

THE CRITICISM OF WORDSWORTH'S CONTEMPORARIES

I

Many of Wordsworth's contemporaries in the world of letters were actively engaged in literary criticism and had much to say concerning him. The memoirs and collections of letters from many hands that accumulated during the long period of his life are rich in references to him, but, with one or two exceptions, only formal criticism, intended for publication, is included here. It is a remarkable fact that of the men most representative of the criticism of Wordsworth by his fellow writers, Lamb alone shows no tincture of animosity. The others—Southey, Byron, Hunt, Hazlitt, Coleridge, Landor, De Quincey, and even Keats—are either caustic, or at one time or another permit a feeling of personal offense to influence their criticism. The association of most of the group of Romantic writers was sufficiently close to cause a clash of temperament in their criticism of each other.

The first shock came as early as 1798 in Southey's review of *Lyrical Ballads*.[1] The severity of his strictures is perhaps attributable to his quarrelings with Coleridge, and it is even possible that he thought the entire volume the work of Coleridge. At any rate, he regards as a failure the experiment in simple diction and commonplace subjects. He compares *The Idiot Boy* to a despised Flemish painting, excellent in execution but worthless in design. In regard to *The Thorn,* he declares that "he who personates tiresome loquacity, becomes tiresome himself." Some of the poems he finds pleasing, among them (fortunately for his later reputation) *Tintern Abbey.* But he pronounces *The Ancient Mariner* "a Dutch attempt at German sublimity." It should be remembered, of course, that in later years Southey expressed generous admiration of Wordsworth, calling him "the first poet of his age and country."[2]

Byron's attack on Wordsworth in *English Bards and Scotch Reviewers* (1809) is no less violent than the blows he deals on all

[1] *The Critical Review,* xxiv (Oct., 1798).

[2] Elsie Smith, *An Estimate of William Wordsworth by his Contemporaries, 1793–1822,* Oxford, Basil Blackwell, 1932, p. 144.

the other bards and critics of the day—on Scott, Southey, Coleridge, Gifford, Jeffrey, the great and the small alike. Wordsworth is called a "mild apostate from poetic rule," and both by precept and example he shows "That prose is verse, and verse is merely prose." Byron singles out *The Idiot Boy* for ridicule, and comments

> That all who view the "idiot in his glory"
> Conceive the bard the hero of the story.

Finally, those who in that age of debased taste have drawn inspiration from classic Greece, are warned not to stoop to "vulgar Wordsworth,"

> The meanest object of the lowly group,
> Whose verse, of all but childish prattle void,
> Seems blessed harmony to Lamb and Lloyd.

Less familiar is Byron's early review of the 1807 *Poems,* which shows a more open-minded attitude than his later contemptuous couplets, although perhaps it is not to be wondered at that Byron's satirical poem (born of animosity) and his critical reviews should be of a different tone. He remarks that the *Lyrical Ballads* have

> not undeservedly met with a considerable share of public applause. The characteristics of Mr. Wordsworth's muse are simple and flowing, though occasionally inharmonious verse; strong, and sometimes irresistible appeals to the feelings, with unexceptional sentiments. Though the present work may not equal his former efforts, many of them [*sic*] possess a native elegance, natural and unaffected, totally devoid of the tinsel embellishments and abstract hyperboles of several contemporary sonneteers.[3]

He gives due praise to the patriotic sonnets, and to *The Song at the Feast of Brougham Castle, Seven Sisters,* and *Affliction of Margaret.* But, echoing the popular outcry, he regrets that Wordsworth has wasted his genius on so many trifling subjects.

Certainly Byron was no friend to Wordsworth, but Leigh Hunt at least belonged to the circle of London acquaintances which included the painter Haydon.[4] Yet Hunt was no idolater,

[3] *Monthly Literary Recreations,* July, 1807. Quoted by Elsie Smith, *op. cit.,* 71. Miss Smith quotes the following from Byron's *Detached Thoughts* (1821): "In 1807, in a magazine called *Monthly Literary Recreations,* I reviewed Wordsworth's trash of the time."

[4] See G. M. Harper, *William Wordsworth, His Life, Works and Influence,* 2 vols., London, John Murray, 1916, II, 259, 261–62.

as is shown in his satire *The Feast of the Poets* (1811). He approves of much that Wordsworth's poetry stood for, but he feels that Wordsworth has not maintained his standard. He writes an extended comment on Wordsworth's theory of poetry in a long note to his satire; pokes fun at Wordsworth in the poem itself, but tempers his satire in later revisions; and in several short notes admits the poet's greatness, but laments that "he abuses that genius as Milton and Spenser never abuse it, and as to destroy those great ends of poetry, by which it should assist the uses and refresh the spirits of life. From him, to whom much is given, much shall be required."[5] Although Hunt concedes that Wordsworth stands at the head of a new and great age of poetry, "he appears to me to have made a mistake unworthy of him, and to have sought by eccentricity and by a turning away from society, what he might have obtained by keeping to his proper and more neighbourly sphere."

In his long note on Wordsworth's theory, he accepts readily the objects that Wordsworth proposes. It "is high time for poetry in general to return to nature and to a natural style," he writes, and "he will perform a great and useful work to society, who shall assist it to do so."[6] But Hunt believes that Wordsworth has failed in many of his poems to bring back a natural style and to restore to us "those healthy and natural perceptions, which he justly describes as the proper state of our poetical constitution." If Wordsworth was shocked by the popular taste for extravagant stories in verse, as he says in his Preface, how, asks Hunt, did he expect to allay this thirst by the substitution of stories of mad mothers who have murdered their babies? Does not the poet delight in "morbid abstractions" and "eremitical vagueness of sensation,—that making a business of reverie,—that despair of getting to any conclusion to any purpose, which is the next step to melancholy or indifference?"[7]

In accusing Wordsworth of substituting one kind of cheap melodrama for another, he quite misses the point. But it is interesting that he partly sees what later scholars have pointed out—a connection between the grim stories in *Lyrical Ballads* and the Gothic genre. Yet he sees not so much a literary analogy as a mistakened substitution, nor does he appear to be conscious

[5] Smith, *op. cit.*, 134.
[6] *Ibid.*, 136.
[7] *Ibid.*, 138.

of Wordsworth's original purpose in presenting these stories and his peculiar treatment of them. No sane critic today would accuse Wordsworth of employing the stories for their superficially sensational appeal. That he was attempting to achieve a deeper psychological understanding of the emotions and sensations of his Martha Rays and his Betty Foyes apparently did not occur to Hunt.

He objects to Wordsworth's theory of the language of poetry on the basis "that instead of allowing degrees and differences in what is poetical, he would have all poetry to be one and the same in point of style, and no distinction allowed between natural and artificial associations." He concludes by condemning Wordsworth for not having a better acquaintance with society, thereby missing his opportunity to do mankind a great service.

Hunt's friend, William Hazlitt, had a better acquaintance with Wordsworth and he wrote more extensively and memorably of the poet. He met him as early as 1798 when he visited Coleridge at Nether Stowey. In spite of his notoriously cantankerous nature, he brought to his criticism an intelligent understanding, and is one of the best critics of Wordsworth of the day. It is true he could not see the full scope and richness of Wordsworth's moral and philosophic poetry, but he (like other contemporary critics) had not read *The Prelude.* Our judgment today would be different if *The Excursion* were Wordsworth's only long poem. Moreover, Hazlitt knew that no critic can lay down laws to a man of genius and expect him to change his nature. And in his remarks on the ill effects on the poet's personality of years of ridicule and injustice, he has perhaps touched on the secret of that profounder change in Wordsworth, the loss of his genial faith in nature and man, which cut to the heart of his poetry in later years. Hazlitt has left us, in his essay, *My First Acquaintance with Poets* (1823), an invaluable account of Wordsworth and Coleridge as they appeared in 1798 to the eyes of a youthful zealot. Yet in mature life Hazlitt spoke scornfully of the two poets in his *Lectures on the English Poets* (1818), his opinion having been influenced by a quarrel with Wordsworth. But by 1825 his harsh views were modified, and his criticism was again more favorable.

Hazlitt published a review of *The Excursion* in *The Examiner* of August 21 and 28, and October 2, 1814. The article opens with a comparison of the poem to the scene in which it is laid—

massive, boundless, and rudimentary in its simplicity. "His mind is, as it were, coëval with the primary forms of things; his imagination holds immediately from nature, and 'owes no allegiance' but 'to the elements.'"[8] Wordsworth has created his own materials for the poem; "his thoughts are his real objects," not extraordinary incidents. Likewise, in his descriptions of human nature he avoids the unusual.

He scans the human race as the naturalist measures the earth's zone, without attending to the picturesque points of view, the abrupt inequalities of surface. He contemplates the passions and habits of men, not in their extremes, but in their first elements; their follies and vices, not at their height . . . but as lurking in embryo—the seeds of the disorder inwoven with our very constitution. He only sympathises with those simple forms of feeling, which mingle at once with his own identity, or with the stream of general humanity. To him the great and the small are the same; the nearer and the remote; what appears, and what only is. The general and the permanent, like the Platonic ideas, are his only realities.[9]

In 1818 Hazlitt delivered at the Surrey Institution a series of lectures *On the English Poets,* and published them the same year. In the lecture "On Living Poets" he devotes no little space to Wordsworth, delivering a judgment much less favorable than in his review of *The Excursion.* While he says Wordsworth is the most original of living poets, he calls him a poet of mere sentiment and denies him the constructive faculty. "He cannot form a whole . . . . He is totally deficient in all the machinery of poetry."[10] *The Excursion* is evidence of the way his lines labor, and "the poem stands stock-still." Hazlitt says there are detached beauties in the poem, but nothing equal to the best pieces in *Lyrical Ballads.* He quotes *Hart-Leap Well* in full, to illustrate the beauty and force of which Wordsworth is capable.

Hazlitt then opens up an attack on the entire "Lake school," with Wordsworth designated as its head. Influenced by the French Revolution, the group have cultivated the "simple" and "natural" to the point of impoverishment, and have leveled down their subjects to the lowest aspects of life. "They claimed kindred only with the commonest of the people: peasants, pedlars, and

[8] *Collected Works of William Hazlitt,* eds. Waller and Glover, 12 vols. and Index, London, J. M. Dent and Co., 1902–4, I, 112.

[9] *Ibid.,* I, 113.

[10] *Ibid.,* V, 156.

village-barbers were their oracles and bosom friends."[11] There follows a caustic diatribe against the egotism of Wordsworth and his lack of interest in anything but himself. Hazlitt says a great deal that is unfair. He had taken offense against the poet,[12] and had made earlier attacks, notably in a note in an article published in *The Examiner,* June 11, 1815, accusing Wordsworth of political apostasy.

In *The Spirit of the Age,* published in 1825, Hazlitt deals much more kindly with Wordsworth. Indeed, he tries (in a backhanded way) to make amends for some of the cruel thrusts he made in *English Poets,* saying they were "mere epigrams and *jeux-d'esprit,* as far from truth as they are free from malice; a sort of running satire or critical clenches."[13]

Hazlitt opens the essay by calling Wordsworth's genius "a pure emanation of the Spirit of the Age. Had he lived in any other period of the world, he would never have been heard of."[14] He repeats some of the criticisms expressed in *English Poets,* but they are not thrown out of focus by malice, or a desire to be clever, or whatever may have been their origin in the earlier work. Of Wordsworth's simplicity, Hazlitt writes:

> It is one of the innovations of the time. It partakes of, and is carried along with, the revolutionary movement of our age: the political changes of our day were the model on which he formed and conducted his poetical experiments. His Muse . . . is a levelling one. It proceeds on a principle of equality, and strives to reduce all things to the same standard. It is distinguished by a proud humility. It relies upon its own resources, and disdains external show and relief. It takes the commonest events and objects, as a test to prove that nature is always interesting from its inherent truth and beauty, without any of the ornaments of dress or pomp of circumstances to set it off. Hence the unaccountable mixture of seeming simplicity and real abstruseness in the *Lyrical Ballads.* Fools have laughed at, wise men scarcely understood them.[15]

The source and character of Wordsworth's poetry are said to be his own power of association, a significant comment. The familiar objects of nature have "become connected with a thousand

[11] *Ibid.,* V, 163.

[12] See E. L. Griggs, "Hazlitt's Estrangement from Coleridge and Wordsworth," *MLN,* xlviii (1933), 173–76; and Batho, *The Later Wordsworth,* Cambridge, Cambridge University Press, 1933, pp. 66–77.

[13] *Collected Works, op. cit.,* IV, 278.

[14] *Ibid.,* IV, 270.

[15] *Ibid.,* IV, 271.

feelings, a link in the chain of thought, a fibre of his own heart."

He has described all these objects in a way and with an intensity of feeling that no one else had done before him, and has given a new view or aspect of nature. He is in this sense the most original poet now living, and the one whose writings could least be spared: for they have no substitute elsewhere. The vulgar do not read them, the learned, who see all things through books, do not understand them, the great despise, the fashionable may ridicule them: but the author has created himself an interest in the heart of the retired and lonely student of nature, which can never die.[16]

Hazlitt contrasts the later philosophical poems with *Lyrical Ballads*. "They are a departure from, a dereliction of his first principles. They are classical and courtly. They are polished in style, without being gaudy; dignified in subject, without affectation. They seem to have been composed not in a cottage at Grasmere, but among the half-inspired groves and stately recollections of Cole-Orton."[17] Wordsworth is said to have realized Milton's wish, "and fit audience found, though few." Hazlitt doubts if *The Excursion* will ever be as popular as *Lyrical Ballads;* for "Wordsworth's mind is obtuse, except as it is the organ and the receptacle of accumulated feelings: it is not analytic, but synthetic; it is reflecting, rather than theoretical."[18]

The essay concludes with some interesting comments on Wordsworth's personality that deserve to be read along with Hazlitt's descriptions in *My First Acquaintance with Poets*. There are also remarks on Wordsworth's taste in literature and art.

Perhaps the comment of his face and voice is necessary to convey a full idea of his poetry. His language may not be intelligible, but his manner is not to be mistaken. It is clear that he is either mad or inspired. In company, even in tête-à-tête, Mr. Wordsworth is often silent, indolent, and reserved. If he is become verbose and oracular of late years, he was not so in his better days. He threw out a bold or an indifferent remark without either effort or pretension, and relapsed into musing again. . . . He sometimes gave striking views of his feelings and trains of association in composing certain passages. . . . His standard of poetry is high and severe, almost to exclusiveness. He admits of nothing below, scarcely of any thing above himself. . . . Milton is his great idol, and he sometimes dares to compare himself

[16] *Ibid.*, IV, 273.

[17] *Ibid.*, IV, 274. Coleorton was the country estate of Sir George Beaumont, frequently visited by Wordsworth.

[18] *Ibid.*, IV, 275.

with him. His Sonnets, indeed, have something of the same high-raised tone and prophetic spirit. Chaucer is another prime favourite of his, and he has been at pains to modernize some of the Canterbury Tales. Those persons who look upon Mr. Wordsworth as a merely puerile writer, must be rather at a loss to account for his strong predilection for such geniuses as Dante and Michael Angelo. We do not think our author has any very cordial sympathy with Shakespear. How should he? Shakespear was the least of an egotist of any body in the world. . . . We think, however, that if Mr. Wordsworth had been a more liberal and candid critic, he would have been a more sterling writer. If a greater number of sources of pleasure had been open to him, he would have communicated pleasure to the world more frequently. Had he been less fastidious in pronouncing sentence on the works of others, his own would have been received more favourably, and treated more leniently. The current of his feelings is deep, but narrow; the range of his understanding is lofty and aspiring rather than discursive. The force, the originality, the absolute truth and identity with which he feels some things, makes him indifferent to so many others. The simplicity and enthusiasm of his feelings, with respect to nature, renders him bigotted and intolerant in his judgments of men and things. But it happens to him, as to others, that his strength lies in his weakness; and perhaps we have no right to complain. We might get rid of the cynic and the egotist, and find in his stead a commonplace man. We should "take the good the Gods provide us:" a fine and original vein of poetry is not one of their most contemptible gifts. . . .[19]

Hazlitt maintains that the contempt and injustice with which Wordsworth had been treated by the critics and the public have spoiled his nature.

We are convinced, if he had been early a popular poet, he would have been a person of great *bonhommie* and frankness of disposition. But the sense of injustice and of undeserved ridicule sours the temper and narrows the views. To have produced works of genius, and to find them neglected or treated with scorn, is one of the heaviest trials of human patience.[20]

As a relief from the personal animosity that creeps into much even of the favorable criticism of Wordsworth, it is pleasant to turn to the friendly chat of Charles Lamb, with his freedom from ill feeling and professional conceit, and his spontaneous response to impressions as they came to him. Every reader of Lamb's let-

[19] *Ibid.*, IV, 275–78.
[20] *Ibid.*, IV, 278.

ters is familiar with his frequent comments on Wordsworth.[21] But the only formal criticism from his pen is a review of *The Excursion.*[22] When the essay appeared Lamb was outraged, as we have noted, to find that Gifford had mutilated the copy almost beyond recognition. In a letter to Wordsworth he calls the original "the prettiest piece of prose I ever writ," and says the "charm, if it had any, is all gone: more than a third of the substance is cut away, and that not all from one place, but *passim,* so as to make utter nonsense. Every warm expression is changed to a nasty cold one."[23] Unfortunately Lamb kept no copy. To get some impression of the spirit of the original review, it should be supplemented with Lamb's letters written to Wordsworth at the time.

Lamb commends the stories included in the poem, but discovers its greatest charm in the mountain setting. "We breathe in the fresh air, as we do while reading Walton's Compleat Angler."[24] He speaks of its religious creed as "expanded and generous Quakerism," which affords consolation in the promise that there are thoughts, allied to nature, which sustain the spirit when the flesh of the sufferer is broken. He considers the fourth book, "Despondency Corrected," to be the most valuable portion of the poem.

Lamb points out that Wordsworth's boldness and originality have prevented him in the past from attaining a full share of popularity. Readers, he says, are not prepared to accept a poet who thinks or feels too deeply. They reject Wordsworth's discovery of genuine passion in peasants and his elevation of them to the same level of humanity with the reader. They regard poems about children as necessarily childish. But at least in *The Excursion,* says Lamb, there is little of this sort of thing to offend.

> There is in it more of uniform elevation, a wider scope of subject, less of manner, and it contains none of those starts and imperfect shapings which in some of this author's smaller pieces offended the weak, and gave scandal to the perverse. It must indeed be approached with seriousness. It has in it much of that quality which "draws the devout, deterring the profane." Those who hate the Paradise Lost will not love this poem. The steps of the great master are discernible

[21] *The Letters of Charles Lamb,* ed. Alfred Ainger, 2 vols., London, Macmillan and Co., 1897 (first ed., 1888). See especially Letters LXXVII, CXLVI, and CXLVIII–CLII.

[22] *The Quarterly Review,* xii (Oct., 1814), 100–11.

[23] *Letters, op. cit.,* I, 281.

[24] *Quarterly Review, op. cit.,* xii, 101.

in it; not in direct imitation or injurious parody, but in the following of the spirit, in free homage and generous subjection.[25]

In contrast to the joke that Jeffrey made of the Pedlar, Lamb defends the selection of such a man for the central role, pointing out that the philosophy of the poem requires a character in humble life as its organ of expression, and drawing an apt comparison between the Pedlar and Piers Plowman.

In his letters Lamb calls *The Excursion* "the noblest conversational poem I ever read—a day in Heaven," and notes his especial fondness for the narratives.[26] He continues in the same vein of unrestrained enthusiasm, commenting on the freshness of the poem which is like pure country air. This particular virtue has not often been associated with *The Excursion* even by devout Wordsworthians; the poem is generally considered tediously didactic, even by those who find some merit in its philosophy and occasional majesty in its lines. The toiling student of today might find it interesting to recall the enthusiasm with which Lamb first turned the crisp pages of this new poem, sent him by the author before it was released for publication.

Lamb in his letters has also made a number of interesting brief comments on individual poems in the 1815 edition of the *Poems,* noting Wordsworth's revisions of previously published texts.[27] He may have made merry with the poet when he wrote that he preferred the streets of London to dales and mountaineers,[28] but Wordsworth never had a warmer and more sprightly and appreciative reader than Charles Lamb.

II

A greater friend even than Lamb was, of course, Coleridge; and the latter's criticism of Wordsworth is the most learned and analytical of all his contemporaries. There is no man to whom we would more readily listen. Many valuable comments on Wordsworth are dispersed through his collected correspondence, and a few comments are made in his *Table Talk,*[29] but his great-

[25] *Ibid.,* xii, 111.

[26] *Letters, op. cit.,* I, 271.

[27] *Ibid.,* I, 283 ff., and 286 ff. See also his observations on *Lyrical Ballads,* 1800, *ibid.,* I, 162 ff.

[28] *Ibid.,* I, 164–66.

[29] See indexes to *Letters of Samuel Taylor Coleridge,* ed. E. H. Coleridge, 2 vols., Boston, Houghton Mifflin and Co., 1895; and to *Unpublished Letters of Samuel Taylor Coleridge,* ed. E. L. Griggs, 2 vols., New Haven, Yale University Press, 1933. Also, *Coleridge's Literary Criticism,* ed. J. W. Mackail, London, Humphrey Milford, 1921; and *Miscellaneous Criticism,* ed. T. M. Raysor, Cambridge, Mass., Harvard University Press, 1936.

est body of criticism is amply elaborated in *Biographia Literaria.* The chapters on his fellow poet gather together for analysis the aspects of Wordsworth's verse most discussed by the critics—the diction and meter—with an inclusion of much of Coleridge's own system of thought, and an added summary of the "defects" and "beauties" of the poetry. Coleridge makes occasional reference to the subjects of the poems, but this is incidental to his chief concern. He believes that Wordsworth had fallen foul of the critics solely because of his theory of the language of poetry. He attempts to correct what he regards as Wordsworth's equivocal statement of that theory, and to explain its fallacies. But with all his display of reasoning, Coleridge's theory of diction is not very different from Wordsworth's. It is also remarkable that he disregards other perhaps more fundamental points in the Preface—Wordsworth's characterization of a poet, his exposition of the process of poetic creation, and his philosophic discussion of the distinction between poetry and science.

In *Biographia Literaria,* Coleridge, looking back nineteen years to the publication of *Lyrical Ballads,* explains their origin. The plan provided that he should write on incidents at least in part supernatural, but interesting because of the dramatic truth of the emotion which they evoked. Wordsworth should select incidents from ordinary life, in which he was to revive the charm of novelty, and endeavor to describe them in a language devoid of all ornament and in the words of everyday conversation. As Coleridge understood the scheme, these poems of Wordsworth's were to be an experiment, but Wordsworth added to the collection "two or three poems written in his own character, in the impassioned, lofty, and sustained diction, which is characteristic of his genius."[30] The fatal mistake was made when he published in the second edition a preface,

> in which, notwithstanding some passages of apparently a contrary import, he was understood to contend for the extension of this style to poetry of all kinds, and to reject as vicious and indefensible all phrases and forms of style that were not included in what he (unfortunately, I think, adopting an equivocal expression) called the language of *real* life. From this preface, prefixed to poems in which it was impossible to deny the presence of original genius, however mistaken its direction might be deemed, arose the whole long-continued controversy.[31]

[30] *Biographia Literaria,* ed. J. Shawcross, 2 vols., Oxford, The Clarendon Press, 1907, II, 6.

[31] *Ibid.,* II, 6–7.

Coleridge points out that the blame for Wordsworth's unpopularity lies not in his poetry, but in the poetic creed expressed in the Preface to the second edition of *Lyrical Ballads.*

> In the critical remarks, therefore, prefixed and annexed to the "Lyrical Ballads," I believe that we may safely rest, as the true origin of the unexampled opposition which Mr. Wordsworth's writings have been since doomed to encounter. The humbler passages in the poems themselves were dwelt on and cited to justify the rejection of the theory. What in and for themselves would have been either forgotten or forgiven as imperfections, or at least comparative failures, provoked direct hostility when announced as intentional, as the result of choice after full deliberation.[32]

Although disagreeing with many parts of the Preface, Coleridge says that Wordsworth's task has been useful in so far as his reformation of poetic diction was directed against figures and metaphors, originally justified by "truth of passion" and "dramatic propriety," but appropriated by modern poets for ornament and artifice. Wordsworth has done well to point out the process by which this change was affected.[33]

> I cannot likewise but add, that the comparison of such poems of merit, as have been given to the public within the last ten or twelve years, with the majority of those produced previously to the appearance of that preface, leave no doubt on my mind, that Mr. Wordsworth is fully justified in believing his efforts to have been by no means ineffectual.[34]

But the language of conversation, says Coleridge, is not the proper diction for poetry in general. Much less is the language of "low and rustic life," chosen, as Wordsworth maintained, because in that condition man speaks more emphatically, more simply, with more genuine and direct passion, and more in contact "with the beautiful and permanent forms of nature."[35]

[32] *Ibid.,* I, 51–52.

[33] These points are not in the 1800 Preface, but occur in the essay "Poetic Diction," an appendix added in 1802.

[34] *Ibid.,* II, 28.

[35] It will be noted that these statements occur near the beginning of the Preface, and refer to the experimental poems in *Lyrical Ballads.* Wordsworth did not intend to say that the language of all poetry should be drawn from the conversation of rustics. But he does affirm that the language and thoughts of such men, close as they are to the daily realities of life, are basically more permanent and "philosophic" than that frequently substituted for it by poets who "separate themselves from the sympathies of men, and indulge in arbitrary and capricious habits of expression, in order to furnish food for fickle tastes, and fickle appetites, of their own creation." (*The Prose Works of William Wordsworth,* ed. A. B. Grosart, 3 vols., London, Edward Moxon, 1876, II, 81–82.)

Now it is clear to me [writes Coleridge], that in the most interesting of the poems, in which the author is more or less dramatic, as "the Brothers," "Michael," "Ruth," "the Mad Mother," &c., the persons introduced are by no means taken *from low or rustic life* in the common acceptation of those words; and it is not less clear, that the sentiments and language, as far as they can be conceived to have been really transferred from the minds and conversation of such persons, are attributable to causes and circumstances not necessarily connected with "their occupations and abode." The thoughts, feelings, language, and manners of the shepherd-farmers in the vales of Cumberland and Westmoreland, as far as they are actually adopted in those poems, may be accounted for from causes, which will and do produce the same results in *every* state of life, whether in town or country.[36]

Coleridge takes pains to show that the beneficial influences of low and rustic life, in and for itself, are very dubious.

Coleridge agrees with Aristotle that poetry "is essentially *ideal,* that it avoids and excludes all *accident;* that its apparent individualities of rank, character, or occupation must be *representative* of a class; and that the *persons* of poetry must be clothed with *generic* attributes, with the *common* attributes of the class: not with such as one gifted individual might *possibly* possess, but such as from his situation it is most probable beforehand that he *would* possess."[37] These requirements are met in *The Brothers* and *Michael.* The characters in these poems "have all the verisimilitude and representative quality, that the purposes of poetry can require." But there are peculiarities, or *accidental* traits, in the characters portrayed in *The Idiot Boy, Harry Gill,* and *The Thorn.* The finest lines in the last poem, Coleridge adds, might have been spoken by Wordsworth in his own character. He cannot admit as valid, therefore, Wordsworth's statement that the language of the rustic (even somewhat purified) is the best for poetry. Indeed, says Coleridge,

a rustic's language, purified from all provincialism and grossness, and so far reconstructed as to be made consistent with the rules of grammar . . . will not differ from the language of any other man of common-sense, however learned or refined he may be, except as far as the notions, which the rustic has to convey, are fewer and more indiscriminate.[38]

[36] *Biographia Literaria, op. cit.,* II, 31.
[37] *Ibid.,* II, 33–34.
[38] *Ibid.,* II, 38–39.

Nor is the best part of the language derived from the objects with which the rustic communicates. It "is derived from reflection on the acts of the mind itself. It is formed by a voluntary appropriation of fixed symbols to internal acts, to processes and results of imagination, the greater part of which have no place in the consciousness of uneducated man."[39] Moreover, Wordsworth should not have used the phrase "a selection of the *real* language of men."

Every man's language has, first, its *individualities;* secondly, the common properties of the *class* to which he belongs; and thirdly, words and phrases of *universal* use. . . . For "real" therefore, we must substitute *ordinary,* or *lingua communis.* And this, we have proved, is no more to be found in the phraseology of low and rustic life than in that of any other class. Omit the peculiarities of each, and the result of course must be common to all. . . . Neither is the case rendered at all more tenable by the addition of the words, *in a state of excitement.* For the nature of a man's words, where he is strongly affected by joy, grief, or anger, must necessarily depend on the number and quality of the general truths, conceptions and images, and of the words expressing them, with which his mind had been previously stored. For the property of passion is not to *create;* but to set in increased activity.[40]

Coleridge devotes much space to the subject of meter, explaining how the language of metrical composition differs from that of prose. He examines Wordsworth's assertion that there "neither is nor can be any *essential* difference between the language of prose and metrical composition." The word *essential,* says Coleridge, in its secondary sense signifies "the point or ground of contra-distinction between two modifications of the same substance or subject." It is therefore assumed that Wordsworth denies that the "formal construction, or architecture, of the words and phrases" that constitute metrical language is essentially different from the language of prose.[41] Coleridge, interpreting Wordsworth thus, disagrees:

The true question must be, whether there are not modes of expression, a *construction,* and an *order* of sentences, which are in their fit and natural place in a serious prose composition, but would be disproportionate and heterogeneous in metrical poetry; and, vice versa, whether

[39] *Ibid.,* II, 39–40.
[40] *Ibid.,* II, 41–42.
[41] *Ibid.,* II, 47–48.

in the language of a serious poem there may not be an arrangement both of words and sentences, and a use and selection of (what are called) *figures of speech,* both as to their kind, their frequency, and their occasions, which on a subject of equal weight would be vicious and alien in correct and manly prose. I contend that in both cases this unfitness of each for the place of the other frequently will and ought to exist.[42]

He bases this contention first on the origin of meter. In a state of heightened excitement, the mind seeks a balance through the means of meter "to hold in check the workings of passion." Two conditions are required of meter. "First, that, as the *elements* of metre owe their existence to a state of increased excitement, so the metre itself should be accompanied by the natural language of excitement." Second, the conscious, voluntary effort of design should also be discerned in metrical language. Thus passion and will, "spontaneous impulse" and "voluntary purpose," must interpenetrate and form a union, "manifested only in a frequency of forms and figures of speech (originally the offspring of passion, but now the adopted children of power) greater than would be desired or endured, where the emotion is not voluntarily encouraged and kept up for the sake of that pleasure, which such emotion, so tempered and mastered by the will, is found capable of communicating."[43]

The effects of meter form Coleridge's second argument against Wordsworth's dictum. Meter, acting in and for itself, "tends to increase the vivacity and susceptibility both of the general feelings and of the attention. . . . Where, therefore, correspondent food and appropriate matter are not provided for the attention and feelings thus roused, there must needs be a disappointment felt."[44] Meter is like yeast, worthless by itself, "but giving vivacity and spirit to the liquor with which it is proportionally combined."[45] Therefore, in answer to the query why write in meter, Coleridge replies, "because I am about to use a language different from that of prose."[46]

The third argument rests on the consequent deduction that meter is "the proper form of poetry, and poetry imperfect and

[42] *Ibid.,* II, 49.
[43] *Ibid.,* II, 50.
[44] *Ibid.,* II, 51.
[45] *Ibid.,* II, 52.
[46] *Ibid.,* II, 53.

defective without metre."[47] Therefore whatever is combined with meter should be essentially poetic. And since poetic composition produces an unusual state of excitement, it "demands a correspondent difference of language."[48] The fourth argument, intimately connected with the third, is drawn from the requirement that all parts of a poem must form an organized and harmonious whole, in which the subordinate parts are assimilated to the essential and important parts. Lastly, Coleridge appeals to the example of the best poets of all ages for full evidence that there is and ought to be an essential difference between the language of prose and metrical composition.

Coleridge's interpretation of *essential difference,* on which much of his argument turns, is too philosophical and specialized to represent truly what Wordsworth meant by the phrase. Wordsworth was speaking much more loosely, but his conclusions regarding meter were not unlike Coleridge's. Nor did Wordsworth deny to poetry the use of appropriate figures, and he recognized that the tone of poetry does often differ from prose. If we examine the following statements from the Preface it will appear that Coleridge, in his arguments, has overstated the case against Wordsworth.

> By the foregoing quotation it has been shown that the language of Prose may yet well be *adapted* to Poetry; and it was previously asserted, that *a large portion* of the language of every good poem can in no respect differ from that of good Prose. We will go further. It may be safely affirmed, that there neither is, nor can be, any *essential* difference between the language of prose and metrical composition. . . . If it be affirmed that rhyme and metrical arrangement of themselves constitute a distinction which overturns what has just been said on the strict affinity of metrical language with that of prose, and paves the way for other artificial distinctions which the mind voluntarily admits, I answer that the language of such Poetry as is here recommended is, as far as is possible, *a selection* of the language really spoken by men; that this selection, wherever it is *made with true taste and feeling,* will of itself form a distinction far greater than would at first be imagined, and will entirely separate the composition from the vulgarity and meanness of ordinary life; and, if metre be superadded thereto, I believe that a dissimilitude will be produced altogether sufficent for the gratification of a rational mind. . . . for, if the Poet's

[47] *Ibid.,* II, 55.
[48] *Ibid.,* II, 56.

subject be judiciously chosen, it will *naturally,* and upon fit occasion, lead him to passions the language of which, if selected truly and judiciously, must necessarily *be dignified and variegated, and alive with metaphors and figures.* I forebear to speak of an incongruity which would shock the intelligent Reader, should the poet interweave any foreign splendour of his own with that which the passion naturally suggests; it is sufficient to say that such addition is unnecessary.[49]

The phrases that I have italicized show that Wordsworth was only saying that the better part of the language of poetry is derived from the common stock of words and constructions which are also found in prose; that poetry, under the influence of meter and animated by passion, shapes this language naturally into a style more vivid than that of ordinary prose; but that any artificial effort to attain a poetic style is to be condemned as bad taste. Indeed, in his next chapter, Coleridge concludes that perhaps, after all, Wordsworth was only disgusted by the gaudy affectations of style that were at the time regarded as poetic; that, accordingly, he temporarily narrowed his view; "feeling a justifiable preference for the language of nature and of good sense, even in its humblest and least ornamented forms, he suffered himself to express, in terms at once too large and too exclusive, his predilection for a style the most remote possible from the false and showy splendour which he wished to explode."[50]

Chapter XXI inserts into the *Biographia Literaria* a vigorous discussion of the critical journals, and eloquently comes to the defense of Wordsworth against the enmity of Jeffrey, a duty which Coleridge had for several years wished to perform. He lays down a number of broad principles which may be legitimately acted upon by the critic, and he recognizes the contribution of *The Edinburgh Review* and other journals to the improvement of the taste and the intellectual life of readers. But he has certain basic charges to make against *The Edinburgh Review,* which introduce his discussion of Jeffrey's slanderous attacks on Wordsworth.

I am referring to the substitution of assertion for argument; to the frequency of arbitrary and sometimes petulant verdicts, not seldom unsupported even by a single quotation from the work condemned. . . . Even where this is not the case, the extracts are too often made

[49] Grosart, *op. cit.,* II, 86–87. Italics (except "*essential*") mine.
[50] *Biographia Literaria, op. cit.,* II, 70.

without reference to any general grounds or rules from which the faultiness or inadmissibility of the qualities attributed may be deduced; and without any attempt to show, that the qualities *are* attributable to the passages extracted. I have met with such extracts from Mr. Wordsworth's poems, annexed to such assertions, as led me to imagine, that the reviewer, having written his critique before he had read the work, had then *pricked with a pin* for passages, wherewith to illustrate the various branches of his preconceived opinions.[51]

Coleridge is shocked and indignant over the pillorying of a fine passage from *The Excursion* as a specimen of Wordsworth's "downright ravings," and the charge of lunacy pronounced against lines which "I had analysed and found consonant with all the best convictions of my understanding; and the imagery and diction of which had collected round these convictions my noblest as well as my most delightful feelings."[52] Coleridge can only class the man who writes such slanderous criticism with the Frenchman, who, viewing the noble Moses of Michael Angelo at Rome, associated the majestic beard with a he-goat, and the horns of power with a cuckold.

The final chapter of *Biographia Literaria* sets forth the defects and the beauties of Wordsworth's poetry. The former, briefly summarized, are: frequent lapses from poetic felicity to an unimpassioned and undistinguished style; the use of too much matter-of-fact detail in descriptions; "an undue predilection for the dramatic form in certain poems"; "occasional prolixity, repetition, and an eddying, instead of progression, of thought"; and last, "thoughts and images too great for the subject."

These flaws, Coleridge says, are but occasional and he presents the excellencies with greater confidence.

The first of these excellencies is the austere purity of the poet's language, "a perfect appropriateness of the words to the meaning." Second, thoughts and sentiments have a correspondent weight and sanity, fresh like dew, from the poet's own meditative observation. Third, lines and paragraphs have a sinewy strength and originality. Fourth, images of nature are drawn with perfect truthfulness from the poet's intimate association with the spirit of what he describes. Fifth, Wordsworth unites deep and subtle thought with sensibility; he evinces a sympathy with man as man, piercing through superficial distinctions to the basic nature com-

[51] *Ibid.*, II, 90.
[52] *Ibid.*, II, 91.

mon to all. Finally, Coleridge points out the pre-eminence in Wordsworth of the imagination in its highest and strictest sense. His fancy may not always be graceful, but

> in imaginative power, he stands nearest of all modern writers to Shakespeare and Milton; and yet in a kind perfectly unborrowed and his own. To employ his own words, which are at once an instance and an illustration, he does indeed to all thoughts and to all objects
>
> . . . . . add the gleam,
> The light that never was, on sea or land,
> The consecration, and the poet's dream.[53]

Great as is the *Biographia Literaria,* the impression it gives of Wordsworth is disappointing. It is a serious misfortune that it was written after the break with Wordsworth, which occurred in 1812. The intimate understanding and oneness of mind, which Coleridge alone could have brought to an interpretation of Wordsworth the poet, had hardened. His criticism is sometimes carping and misleading. Not that he attacks Wordsworth with the bitterness of Hazlitt or that he shows a hostile or vengeful spirit; it is to the great credit of Coleridge that he exhibits no personal animosity. But the friendliness of tone is in itself disarming, and many readers unsuspectingly form their opinions from Coleridge while overlooking the alienation of spirit that has subtly altered the aspect of what Coleridge has written.

From him one does not expect the kind of criticism that an indifferent critic or lecturer might give. In 1817, the date of the publication of *Biographia Literaria,* Wordsworth needed an interpreter, a great mind and a great spirit that could cut through his petty, often irksome defects and reveal with passionate understanding the soul of the poet—his intense concern for humanity, his subtle understanding of the connection between man and nature, and his moments of spiritual exaltation when he could transcend the flesh and see into the life of things. Wordsworth has never received such an interpreter, and perhaps only Coleridge could have been the man. What a pity that *Biographia Literaria* was written seventeen years too late.

Coleridge writes lengthily and with scholastic address on Wordsworth's theories of poetic diction and meter, caviling at phrases used by the poet to express his meaning, and distorting

[53] *Ibid.,* II, 124.

the simple objectives the poet had in mind. It is the disintegration of Wordsworth's Preface that the reader remembers chiefly from Coleridge. He points out that it was not the poetry of *Lyrical Ballads* but the Preface to the second edition that got Wordsworth into trouble with the critics—yet Coleridge goes on to ring the changes on his disagreement with his fellow-poet over the theories of the Prefaces, although Wordsworth had in 1815 relegated them to an appendix. With Coleridge's equipment we look for an insight into what is far more fundamental to the poet. He says more, of course, but not so well. Nor does he finally interpret Wordsworth as a whole, or better—to use his own word—with *imagination*.

It is possible to go back to a period earlier than *Biographia Literaria* for an explanation of Coleridge's desire to correct and modify Wordsworth's theory. In a letter to Southey, dated July 29, 1802, he communicates his intention to write a volume of essays "Concerning Poetry and the characteristic merits of the Poets, our contemporaries," in which he proposes to discuss the essential nature of poetry, especially in connection with the defenses that Erasmus Darwin and Wordsworth made of their own systems of composition. He continues:

But I will apprise you of one thing, that although Wordsworth's Preface is half a child of my own brain, and arose out of conversations so frequent that, with few exceptions, we could scarcely either of us, perhaps, positively say which first started any particular thought (I am speaking of the Preface as it stood in the second volume), yet I am far from going all lengths with Wordsworth. He has written lately a number of Poems . . . the greater number of these, to my feelings, very excellent compositions, but here and there a daring humbleness of language and versification, and a strict adherence to matter of fact, even to prolixity, that startled me. . . . I rather suspect that somewhere or other there is a radical difference in our theoretical opinions respecting poetry; this I shall endeavour to go to the bottom of, and, acting the arbitrator between the old school and the new school, hope to lay down some plain and perspicuous, though not superficial canons of criticism respecting poetry. What an admirable definition Milton gives, quite in an "obiter" way, when he says of poetry, that it is "*simple, sensuous, passionate!*" It truly comprises the whole that can be said on the subject. In the new edition of L. Ballads there is a valuable appendix, which I am sure you must like, and in the Preface itself considerable additions; one on the dignity and nature of the office and character of a Poet, that is very grand, and of a sort of Verulamian power and majesty, but it is, in parts (and this is the fault, *me judice,* of all the latter half of that Preface), obscure beyond any necessity, and the extreme elaboration and almost constrainedness of the diction contrasted (to my feelings) somewhat harshly with the general style of the Poems, to which the Preface is an introduction. . . . Sara said, with some acuteness, that she wished all that part of the Preface to have been in blank verse, and *vice versâ,* etc. However, I need not say, that any diversity of opinion on the subject between you and myself, or Wordsworth and myself, can only be small, taken in a *practical* point of view.[54]

Several conclusions may be drawn from this letter. (1) It is clear that Coleridge's views on poetry were changing, and that he was eager to express his divergence from Wordsworth and to explain his own theories. But he delayed doing this until he wrote *Biographia Literaria,* although it would have been more in order in 1802 when he was still closely associated with Wordsworth. And it is thus made clear why Coleridge's discussion of Wordsworth is so largely taken up with the Preface. (2) Coleridge claimed the Preface as "half a child of my own brain . . ." Even if this be an exaggeration, his share in the origination of the theories must have been considerable. Certainly, in the conversations between the two poets, he was fully acquainted with all of the ideas and could not possibly have misunderstood Wordsworth's views. Yet when he wrote *Biographia Literaria* he professes to be unsure of the full meaning of some of Wordsworth's statements, especially as to how much of the theory was intended to apply only to the experimental poems in *Lyrical Ballads* and how much to all poetry.[55] He misinterprets one or two important points, notably Wordsworth's phrase "a selection of language really used by men," and the statement that there is no *"essential* difference between the language of prose and metrical composition." Moreover, from the tone of his criticism no one would know that he had ever shared any of the views or had had a part in their formation. (3) Likewise, it was ungenerous of Wordsworth not to have acknowledged Coleridge's part in contributing to the ideas of the Preface. Coleridge does not complain of this, and certainly the major part of the work was Wordsworth's since

[54] *Letters of Samuel Taylor Coleridge, op cit.,* I, 386–87.

[55] The chief defect of the Preface is that Wordsworth did not make this distinction as clear as he might. It is not surprising that a critic, reading hastily, would be confused, but it is surprising that Coleridge was.

he composed the Preface and it was he, not Coleridge, who was putting its theories into practice. But some acknowledgment should have been made of the conversations with his fellow-poet.

Yet it must not be forgotten that elsewhere than in *Biographia Literaria,* in letters and in conversation, no one praised Wordsworth more cordially or expounded him more profoundly than did Coleridge. Scattered references of this kind are frequent, but they form no consistent body of criticism and were, of course, not available in print to the public in Wordsworth's day. Crabb Robinson wrote of the relationship between the two men in 1812:

> Coler. was at all times a profuse eulogist of Wordsworth's poems but always with qualifications & even with objections to W.'s diction & style, which indeed he has printed. And he was *passionate* in his professions of *love* to him as a man, but these professions expressed but the feeling of the moment. Wordsworth's words might be considered as announcing his permanent convictions. . . . "But no one," said he [Wordsworth], "has completely understood me—not even Coleridge. He is not happy enough. . . ." But W. was loud in his praise of the powers of C.'s mind wh. he said was greater than those of any man he ever knew. From such a man under favourable influences anything might be hoped for. His genius he thought great, but his talents he thought still greater & it is in the union of so much genius with so much talent that he thought C. surpassed all other men. W., in a digression, remarked of himself that he had comparatively but little talent: genius was his peculiar faculty.[56]

This report refers apparently to the time of the unfortunate quarrel, and it is evidence that neither Coleridge nor Wordsworth lost wholly that mutual understanding which had once contributed so much to the thought and poetry of each.

III

Very different is the criticism of Walter Savage Landor, who revived as late as 1842 all of the spite of Jeffrey. His first criticism of Wordsworth appeared in July, 1823, in the *London Magazine.* It is presented in the dialogue "Southey and Porson" from *Imaginary Conversations.* In this dialogue the criticism is comparatively mild, for at the time Landor was something of an admirer of Wordsworth. The dialogue is continued in a second conversation between the same interlocutors, which was published in

[56] *Blake, Coleridge, Wordsworth, Lamb, etc. Being Selections from the Remains of Henry Crabb Robinson,* ed. Edith J. Morley, Manchester, The University Press, 1922, p. 49.

Blackwood's, December, 1842, and the sequel slashes Wordsworth's poetry with a two-edged sword.[57] In the first dialogue Porson suggests that some of Wordsworth's poetry is trash, that he is verbose, and that he might do well to imitate classic poetry. But Southey is suffered to defend him, and he compares *Laodamia* favorably with the writings of classic authors. Porson admits that Southey is correct in his judgment of this poem, but he points out several weak lines (which, incidentally, Wordsworth later corrected).

The second conversation, however, is written in such a spirit of ill will that it had best be read for its hard, trenchant style rather than for a fair criticism of the poet. Whatever defense of Wordsworth Southey ventures to make is weak, and serves only as points of attack for Porson. The chief interest lies in Landor's dissection of numerous lines of Wordsworth's poetry, chiefly from *Lyrical Ballads*, ridiculing their prosiness and their empty verbiage. Landor has generally chosen well for this devastating attack, and his close examination of the diction and images at least serves to quicken the critical alertness of readers who have forgotten the style in their pursuit of ideas. But a random selection of bad lines does not justify Landor's contempt for Wordsworth. It cannot be said that he contributes much that is new in his criticism, but his satire is sprightly and there are occasional flashes of illumination.

In our survey mention of De Quincey's name has long been delayed because, although he was early acquainted with Wordsworth, his chief criticism of the poetry came late. He was more intimately associated with Wordsworth in a personal way than any of the men, except Coleridge, considered hitherto. To be sure Lamb was a cherished friend with whom Wordsworth never had a serious disagreement, and the association with De Quincey was eventually marred by an estrangement. But in the early years De Quincey made long visits with the Wordsworths, was an especial favorite with Dorothy and the children, and occupied Dove Cottage after the Wordsworths left it. He saw *The Convention of Cintra* through the press—an arduous task—and was in a position to understand and interpret Wordsworth. He is best known in this connection for his autobiographic *Literary and Lake Reminiscences*, which was begun in *Tait's Magazine* in

[57] *Complete Works of Walter Savage Landor*, ed. T. E. Welby, 16 vols., London, Chapman and Hall Ltd., 1927–36, V, 139–213.

1834. Three articles of the series, devoted exclusively to Wordsworth, appeared in the issues for January, February, and April, 1839. Every biographer of the poet has made extensive use of them. They contain much intimate and personal detail, a little gossipy, Professor Harper remarks, but the fullest informal impressions we have of the poet and his family in their prime.

In September, 1845, De Quincey published in *Tait's Magazine* an essay "On Wordsworth's Poetry." He reopens the old problem of Wordsworth's diction and subjects. Of the former he concludes, as did Coleridge before him, that had Wordsworth not brought forward a theory of diction in his early Prefaces, no issue would have been raised by the poetry itself in the minds either of critics or readers. The theory has worked much against his popularity. De Quincey agrees that at the time of *Lyrical Ballads* bad taste in the language of poetry was prevalent, but he points out that Wordsworth's "experiment" in purity of diction, in the use of the language of ordinary life, was nothing new.

Spenser, Shakspere, the Bible of 1611, and Milton—how say you, William Wordsworth—are these sound and true as to diction, or are they not? If you say they *are,* then what is it that you are proposing to change? What room for a revolution? . . . if the leading classics of the English literature are, in quality of diction and style, loyal to the canons of sound taste—then you cut away the *locus standi* for yourself as a reformer: the reformation applies only to secondary and recent abuses.[58]

These statements are true enough, but De Quincey seems unaware that they are precisely what Wordsworth contended. He was not revolutionizing English poetry, but returning to the true and native style of the language. De Quincey concludes that after forty-seven years of discussion the case between Wordsworth and his critics remains unsettled, largely because neither side of the dispute has given sufficient specimens of the particular phraseology that is deemed good or bad. Therefore, "no man, in this dispute, steadily understands even himself; and if he did, no other person understands him."[59]

As to Wordsworth's subjects, De Quincey points out the

[58] *Collected Writings of Thomas De Quincey,* ed. David Masson, 14 vols., Edinburgh, A. and C. Black, 1889–90, XI, 299.

[59] *Ibid.,* XI, 300. In a "Postscript" to the essay, added in 1857, De Quincey complains that although Wordsworth lived until 1850, from indolence or lack of understanding of his own theory he never increased the original small stock of specimens that served to illustrate his theory in 1800 (*Ibid.,* XI, 323–25).

essential subtlety of his treatment. "But whosoever looks searchingly into the characteristic genius of Wordsworth will see that he does not willingly deal with a passion in its direct aspect, or presenting an unmodified contour, but in forms more complex and oblique, and when passing under the shadow of some secondary passion."[60] The fact that the multitude of superficial readers, like "romantic" young girls "dreaming of lovers," were repulsed by Wordsworth's poetry is not surprising. "This influx of the joyous into the sad, and of the sad into the joyous—this reciprocal entanglement of darkness in light, and of light in darkness—offers a subject too occult for popular criticism."[61] Rather than smiling over the simplicity of Wordsworth's subjects, De Quincey comprehends their essential complexity.

He devotes much space to a criticism of *The Excursion.* He finds the story of Margaret weakly motivated and morally perverted. He regards the Solitary as more estimable than the Pedlar, and defends the French Revolution and those who trusted in its ultimate benefits to France. He finds structural faults in the poem. "One of these defects is the *undulatory* character of the course pursued by the poem—which does not ascend uniformly, or even keep one steady level, but trespasses . . . into topics yielding a very humble inspiration, and not always closely connected with the presiding theme."[62] Wordsworth's future fame will not rest on *The Excursion,* De Quincey prophesies, but, he believes, on the earlier short poems. He gives numerous illustrations of Wordsworth's power of accurate observation in holding up the mirror to nature, an aspect of Wordsworth's poetry which he regards as more valuable than the poet's philosophic utterances.

IV

The criticism of Wordsworth in his own day reflects his span of life, from youth to age. The notices of *Lyrical Ballads* give the impression of something new, experimental, hopeful. Then ensues the long controversy over his critical theory of poetry, with the application of vulgarity and absurdity to good and bad poems alike. A pure critical attitude, even with men like Coleridge, was often obscured by the bitter taste of personal quarrels with the

[60] *Ibid.,* XI, 301.
[61] *Ibid.,* XI, 303.
[62] *Ibid.,* XI, 313. Cf. Coleridge, *vide,* p. 36.

poet. Between the heat of dogmatic journalism and personal partisanship there could be no reliable criticism of the complete Wordsworth.

But he had become an influence on the poetry and thought of his day. This is nowhere more evident than in the references of Keats to Wordsworth in his letters. At first he revered the elder poet almost to the point of worship. He speaks of him in the following manner in a sonnet written in 1816:

> Great spirits now on earth are sojourning;
> He of the cloud, the cataract, the lake,
> Who on Helvellyn's summit, wide awake,
> Catches his freshness from Archangel's wing:[63]

When Haydon proposed to send this to Wordsworth, Keats wrote: "The Idea of your sending it to Wordsworth put me out of breath —you know with what Reverence I would send my Well-wishes to him."[64] Lord Houghton writes of Keats at this time:

> It should here be remembered that Wordsworth was not then what he is now, that he was confounded with much that was thought ridiculous and unmanly in the new school, and that it was something for so young a student to have torn away the veil of prejudice then hanging over that now-honoured name, and to have proclaimed his reverence in such earnest words, while so many men of letters could only scorn or jeer.[65]

Keats regretted the injustice which Wordsworth's poetry had encountered. Speaking of the Duke of Wellington, he says: "A Man ought to have the Fame he deserves—and I begin to think that detracting from him as well as from Wordsworth is the same thing."[66]

When Keats met Wordsworth his enthusiasm was somewhat dampened by a dislike for some of the rough edges of his personality. On one occasion he seems to have been offended by the elder poet, and in February, 1818, wrote Reynolds his well-known comment on the egotism and obtrusive didacticism of Wordsworth and the "moderns."

> It may be said that we ought to read our contemporaries, that Wordsworth &c. should have their due from us. But, for the sake of a few

[63] *The Letters of John Keats,* ed. M. B. Forman, 2 vols., Humphrey Milford, Oxford University Press, 1931, I, 10.

[64] *Ibid.,* I, 12.

[65] Quoted by Forman, *op. cit.,* I, 10n.

[66] *Ibid.,* I, 35.

fine imaginative or domestic passages, are we to be bullied into a certain Philosophy engendered in the whims of an Egotist[?] Every man has his speculations, but every man does not brood and peacock over them till he makes a false coinage and deceives himself. Many a man can travel to the very bourne of Heaven, and yet want confidence to put down his half-seeing. Sancho will invent a Journey heavenward as well as any body. We hate poetry that has a palpable design upon us, and if we do not agree, seems to put its hand in its breeches pocket. Poetry should be great and unobtrusive, a thing which enters into one's soul, and does not startle it or amaze it with itself, but with its subject.—How beautiful are the retired flowers! how would they lose their beauty were they to throng into the highway crying out, "admire me I am a violet!—dote upon me I am a primrose!" Modern poets differ from the Elizabethans in this. Each of the moderns like an Elector of Hanover governs his petty state, and knows how many straws are swept daily from the Causeways in all his dominions and has a continual itching that all the Housewives should have their coppers well scoured: the antients were Emperors of vast Provinces, they had only heard of the remote ones and scarcely cared to visit them.—I will cut all this—I will have no more of Wordsworth or Hunt in particular.[67]

Keats's distaste for Wordsworth and the moderns was not lasting, but in the intensity of his feeling he expresses a comprehensible irritation at the self-contained world which is often the sphere of the romantic poet. But his personal contacts with Wordsworth were not all disagreeable. Everyone remembers Haydon's account of his merry dinner party which included, among other guests, Lamb, Keats, and Wordsworth. "It was delightful," wrote Haydon, "to see the good humour of Wordsworth in giving in to all our frolics without affectation and laughing as heartily as the best of us."[68] Keats refers several times in his letters to visits with Wordsworth when he was in London.

There are numerous quotations from Wordsworth in Keats's letters, random lines that show how thoroughly he had read the elder poet. He was not always sympathetic with some of Wordsworth's homely subjects, and he enjoyed his friend Reynolds' burlesque of *Peter Bell.* But he called *The Excursion* a thing "to rejoice at." Benjamin Bailey reports the exceeding delight Keats took in the *Intimations Ode,* how he was never weary of repeating it.[69]

[67] *Ibid.*, I, 103–4.

[68] *Autobiography and Memoirs of Benjamin Robert Haydon,* ed. Tom Taylor, 2 vols., London, Peter Davies, 1926, I, 269.

[69] *Letters of John Keats, op. cit.*, I, 74n.

Keats's best-known criticism of Wordsworth is in his long letter to Reynolds, dated May 3, 1818. It is mostly concerned with his great desire for increasing knowledge and wisdom:

An extensive knowledge is needful to thinking people—it takes away the heat and fever; and helps, by widening speculation, to ease the Burden of the Mystery.[70]

In this search after humanity and wisdom he writes thus of Wordsworth and Milton:

My Branchings out therefrom have been numerous: one of them is the consideration of Wordsworth's genius and as a help, in the manner of gold being the meridian Line of worldly wealth, how he differs from Milton. And here I have nothing but surmises, from an uncertainity whether Miltons [*sic*] apparently less anxiety for Humanity proceeds from his seeing further or no than Wordsworth: And whether Wordsworth has in truth epic passion, and martyrs himself to the human heart, the main region of his song. In regard to his genius alone—we find what he says true as far as we have experienced and we can judge no further but by larger experience—for axioms in philosophy are not axioms until they are proved upon our pulses. . . . I will return to Wordsworth—whether or no he has an extended vision or a circumscribed grandeur—whether he is an eagle in his nest, or on the wing. And to be more explicit and to show you how tall I stand by the giant, I will put down a simile of human life as far as I now perceive it; that is, to the point to which I say we both have arrived at. Well—I compare human life to a large Mansion of Many Apartments, two of which I can only describe, the doors of the rest being as yet shut upon me. The first we step into we call the infant or thoughtless Chamber, in which we remain as long as we do not think. We remain there a long while, and notwithstanding the doors of the second Chamber remain wide open, showing a bright appearance, we care not to hasten to it; but are at length imperceptibly impelled by the awakening of the thinking principle within us—we no sooner get into the second Chamber, which I shall call the Chamber of Maiden-Thought, than we become intoxicated with the light and the atmosphere, we see nothing but pleasant wonders, and think of delaying there for ever in delight. However among the effects this breathing is father of is that tremendous one of sharpening one's vision into the heart and nature of Man—of convincing one's nerves that the world is full of Misery and Heartbreak, Pain, Sickness and oppression—whereby this Chamber of Maiden Thought becomes gradually darken'd and at the same time on all sides of it many doors are set open—but all dark—all leading to

[70] *Ibid.*, I, 152.

dark passages. We see not the balance of good and evil. We are in a Mist. We are now in that state—We feel the "burden of the Mystery"—To this point was Wordsworth come, as far as I can conceive when he wrote "Tintern Abbey" and it seems to me that his Genius is explorative of those dark Passages. Now if we live, and go on thinking, we too shall explore them. He is a Genius and superior [to] us, in so far as he can, more than we, make discoveries, and shed a light in them. Here I must think Wordsworth is deeper than Milton, though I think it has depended more upon the general and gregarious advance of intellect, than individual greatness of Mind.[71]

Keats then explains how the general intellectual growth through the years is responsible for what he regards as Wordsworth's deeper philosophy of human nature. He concludes:

He [Milton] did not think into the human heart, as Wordsworth has done. Yet Milton as a Philosopher, had sure as great powers as Wordsworth.[72]

Keats did not expound Wordsworth as a critic writing for the public, but in his comments we have the sensitive perception of a poet who was himself moved by Wordsworth's poetry. His observations on *Tintern Abbey* are intimately expressive of Keats's own growth and search for truth, and his apprehension of the stages of life is one of the earliest instances of a true comprehension of that poem.

The name of Crabb Robinson has been mentioned too little in these pages to do justice to his part in establishing Wordsworth's reputation as a poet in his day. Many random observations on Wordsworth's poetry may be found in his diaries and letters, but he is perhaps read more as a source of biographical information than as a critic. He did much to spread Wordsworth's fame among his large circle of acquaintances. Likewise Benjamin Haydon, in his references to Wordsworth in his *Autobiography,* indicates the esteem in which he was held by Haydon's friends in London.

In the 1830's and 1840's there was little doubt of Wordsworth's important position among the poets of the century. To some he was a philosopher and moral teacher, to others an innocent recluse who sang of simple man and nature. Among the best commentaries of this period are two essays by Wordsworth's friend, Henry Taylor, the first on Wordsworth as a philosopher,

[71] *Ibid.*, I, 153–56.
[72] *Ibid.*, I, 157.

and the second on his sonnets in contrast to *The Excursion* and his discursive poetry.[73] Of greater import was his influence and position among the rising group of Victorian writers, Tennyson and Browning, Ruskin and John Stuart Mill. Yet still unknown to the public was *The Prelude,* the best of all guides to his great years of poetic productivity.

When he died, ripe in years, honored and revered by a wide public and loved by a chosen few, he had fulfilled his early prediction that a great and original poet "must himself create the taste by which he is to be relished."

[73] In *Notes from Books,* London, John Murray, 1848. Reprinted from *The Quarterly Review,* Nov., 1834, and Dec., 1841.

CHAPTER THREE

THE VICTORIAN CRITICAL ESSAY

I

A host of Victorian essayists have written general criticism of Wordsworth. We shall first review a representative group in the approximate order of their appearance, indicating what appears to be the special contribution of each in the development of Wordsworthian criticism. It will be noted that some of these essays constitute chapters in larger books or were delivered as a series of lectures, but that they are more in the nature of the critical essay than the full length, exhaustive study. The group includes the following writers: David Masson, Walter Bagehot, J. C. Shairp, A. H. Clough, R. H. Hutton, Walter Pater, Stopford Brooke, Leslie Stephen, Matthew Arnold, Edward Caird, A. C. Swinburne, Aubrey De Vere, and John Morley. In the second section of the chapter we shall examine the salient points discussed in common by these writers.

The essay entitled "Wordsworth," by the distinguished scholar David Masson, is somewhat disappointing, but it is interesting in that it represents the effort of a sound scholar at the time of Wordsworth's death to present a well-rounded criticism against the background of the poet's completed life, and to assign him his position among English poets.[1] The essay was written three months after Wordsworth died, and represents the conventional Victorian impression of the poet. He is found wanting in humor, energy, and passion. He is more limited in intellect than the greatest of English poets. Nor does Masson regard him as a great lyric poet, but as a "bard." Wordsworth is distinguished for his calm, contemplative mind, his high degree of poetic imagination, and his great powers as a descriptive poet. Masson recognizes his influence on the succeeding poets of the century.

In 1864 Walter Bagehot published a paper entitled "Wordsworth, Tennyson, and Browning; or Pure, Ornate, and Grotesque

[1] *North British Review,* xiii (1850), 473. Reprinted in *Essays, Biographical and Critical,* Cambridge, Macmillan and Co., 1856; and in *Wordsworth, Shelley, Keats,* London, Macmillan and Co., 1874.

Art in English Poetry."[2] The emphasis here is on Wordsworth's art, not his philosophy. He is representative of "pure" art, or that which deals with universals and treats them with strict economy of detail, and great intensity. There is no decoration, no unnecessary stroke in pure art. Moreover, no detail, no matter how choice, attracts attention to itself because everything is blended into a single whole. Wordsworth is a "nearly perfect" model of pure art in the expression of sentiment, and Milton (not so perfect) in the delineation of objective character. Wordsworth's two sonnets, *The Trossachs* and *Composed upon Westminster Bridge,* are given as examples. The singleness of impression of both these sonnets is remarked upon. "Not a single expression (the invocation in the concluding couplet of the second sonnet perhaps excepted) can be spared, yet not a single expression rivets the attention."

Also there appeared in 1864 J. C. Shairp's essay "Wordsworth, the Man and the Poet," which, the author warns us, is not criticism as it is generally understood, not an attempt to "take the measure" of a great and good man and assign him his place in literature, but merely an attempt to point out some of the sources of delight that the writer has found in Wordsworth's poetry.[3] In truth, the essay has a great deal of substance, and remains today an illuminating survey of much that is fundamental to an understanding of Wordsworth. Shairp's interpretation is incomplete and lacking in critical vigor, but it ranks with the work of Stopford Brooke and Edward Caird as the best Victorian criticism of Wordsworth prior to Legouis' exhaustive study of the poet's youth. The advantage of having read *The Prelude,* denied to Masson and critics prior to 1850, is evident in Shairp's clearer idea of the poet's aims and richer source of material for discussion.

Shairp recognizes, like Masson and later Arnold, that the poet's popularity has receded since its high crest shortly before his death and seems to have reached its ebb. He points out the need of a discriminating mental history of Wordsworth and a chronological edition of his works to give the reading public a proper understanding of him. Shairp defines three epochs in his poetry: a "spring-time" of his genius, extending from 1797 to his

[2] *National Review,* xix (1864), 27. Reprinted in *Literary Studies,* 2 vols., London, Longmans, Green and Co., 1879.

[3] *North British Review,* xli (1864), 1. Revised and enlarged in *Studies in Poetry and Philosophy,* Edinburgh, Edmonston and Douglas, 1868.

leaving Dove Cottage in 1808; a "full midsummer," extending to 1818 or 1820; and finally a "sober autumn." Thus the perspective of time was rendering it possible to distinguish clearly the stages in Wordsworth's development that are now well recognized. Shairp analyzes at length the art of Wordsworth, his philosophy of nature, and his unorthodox natural religion. He perceives in this poetry the presence of a deep passion. Some biographical material is interspersed throughout the essay.

In 1877 Shairp published his book, *On Poetic Interpretation of Nature,* the last chapter of which is devoted to Wordsworth. Again, in his Oxford lectures entitled *Aspects of Poetry* (1881), he discourses on the "Yarrow" poems, and interprets with admirable effect the beauty of *The White Doe of Rylstone.*[4]

Arthur Hugh Clough, in a brief but noteworthy "Lecture on the Poetry of Wordsworth" published in his *Poems and Prose Remains,*[5] discredits the pre-eminence that Wordsworth gave to external nature; and although admitting that he is deeper than his contemporaries as a moral and philosophic poet, Clough regards Wordsworth's morality as less creditable because, as he supposes, the poet was a recluse with no worldly temptations. The chief purpose of Clough's lecture is to point out Wordsworth's achievement in style and diction, the permanent beauty of his expression. His style is paramount and herein lies his especial charm. Clough's criticism is a powerful antidote to the many detractions of Wordsworth's genius for poetic expression.

A delicate analysis of Wordsworth's art and thought is Richard Hutton's "The Genius of Wordsworth" included in his *Literary Essays.*[6] The central point of this essay is Wordsworth's spiritual frugality, which is explained by his habit of extracting much from the smallest object of his contemplation. By this practice he gives new birth to his theme, creating for it "the life of thought which it has the power to generate in his own brooding imagination."[7] He thus "redeems new ground for spirit-meditation." He takes commonplace subjects faithful to his own simple nature, and transfuses into them the spiritual light of his own mind. He dissociates these objects from their ordinary meanings and suggestions, and transmutes them into his own world of

[4] Edinburgh, David Douglas, 1877; and Oxford, The Clarendon Press, 1881.
[5] Two vols., London, Macmillan and Co., 1869.
[6] London, Strahan, 1871.
[7] *Op. cit.,* Macmillan, 1896, p. 93.

imagination and spirit. His musings are not reveries, for reverie carries the mind beyond its own boundaries. Wordsworth "neither loses himself nor the centre of his thought. He carries his own spiritual world with him, draws the thing or thought or feeling on which he intends to write, from its common orbit, fixes it, like a new star, in his own higher firmament, and there contemplates it beneath the gleaming lights and mysterious shadows of its new sphere."[8] Thus he consciously brings his imaginative force to bear upon his subjects. Hutton has written a subtle and penetrating analysis of this aspect of Wordsworth's art, but his essay on Wordsworth's genius leaves out of account much else that is essential to it.

In 1874 Pater published an essay on Wordsworth, in which he points out the profound stream of passion and thought that underlies his poetry, and the sincerity of style that illuminates his thought and compensates for his lapses into forced sentiments and diction.[9] Pater explains that to Wordsworth the presence of life in the objects of nature is not a mere rhetorical device as it is with some poets, but a literal fact. Hence his great power in describing nature. Also, he sees man as a part of nature, and his language is the speech of real men in real situations, delivered with passionate sincerity. "And so he has much for those who value highly the concentrated presentment of passion, who appraise men and women by their susceptibility to it, and art and poetry as they afford the spectacle of it."[10] Pater points out the philosophic aspect of Wordsworth's poetry, in that it deals with that which lies beneath the surface of our immediate experience. He touches on Wordsworth's sense of the continuity of time, his revival of the idea of the *anima mundi,* and his contemplative wisdom in which ideal perfection is found in *being* rather than *doing.* In summary, the essay concludes with the statement that Wordsworth believes that

> the chief aim, in life and art alike, to be a certain deep emotion; seeking most often the great elementary passions in lowly places; having at least this condition of all impassioned work, that he aims always at an absolute sincerity of feeling and diction, so that he is the true forerunner of the deepest and most passionate poetry of our own day;

[8] *Ibid.,* p. 97.

[9] "Wordsworth," *Fortnightly Review,* xxi (1874), 455. Reprinted in *Appreciations,* London, Macmillan and Co., 1889.

[10] *Appreciations,* Macmillan, 1911, p. 52.

yet going back also, with something of a protest against the conventional fervour of much of the poetry popular in his own time, to those older English poets, whose unconscious likeness often comes out in him.[11]

In 1872 Stopford Brooke delivered a series of lectures on Sunday afternoons in St. James' Chapel, which he collected and published in 1874 under the title *Theology in the English Poets.*[12] Lectures V–XIII are on Wordsworth. The theological application of the first two lectures—while in some respects true to Wordsworth—gives too much the impression that he was a preacher and not a poet. It is doubtful that Wordsworth was as conscious of God as Brooke suggests. But the greater share of the lectures deals more with the combined spiritual and material forces evident in Wordsworth's poetry than with pure theology. It is when Brooke moves into a free interpretation of *The Prelude* that the lights and shades of Wordsworth's poetic philosophy appear. In this detailed reading of *The Prelude* Brooke, more than any of the critics before Legouis, draws the picture of Wordsworth as he is most commonly interpreted today.

To begin with, Brooke points out that Wordsworth believes in an active principle in nature, that matter is animated by a soul, that nature is the "poetic impersonation of an actual Being, the form which the poet gives to the living Spirit of God in the outward world."[13] He discusses the characteristics of this life of nature, and then explains the relation nature bears to man, how each complements each, and how God through nature works on man. By means of an extended analysis of *The Prelude* Brooke explains (as many critics have since done) how Wordsworth after his return from France lost his faith in man and nature, how he became "intellectual," and how finally he was restored. The old love returned through the genial administration of nature, and the poet finally achieved a wedding of man and nature which pervaded him with a calm and profound sense of that Holy Power that "runs through all things." In contrast to the conservative interpretations of Hutton, De Vere, and other "Wordsworthians," Brooke says a good deal about Wordsworth's enthusiasm for the Revolution and liberalism, points out that nature is essentially democratic, and discusses at length the theory

[11] *Ibid.*, pp. 63–64.
[12] London, Henry S. King and Co., 1874.
[13] *Op. cit.*, "Everyman's Library," New York, E. P. Dutton and Co., 1915, p. 79.

that the basic principles of the Revolution and Christianity are one. From these premises he draws the conclusion that when Wordsworth lost his enthusiasm for revolutionary social theories he lost to a great extent his religion of man and nature, and his greatness as a poet perished.

Of a much later date are Brooke's lectures on *Naturalism in English Poetry,* delivered in 1902.[14] They include two noteworthy essays on Wordsworth. In the first, "Wordsworth the Poet of Nature," Brooke points out that Wordsworth comes close to pantheism in his idea of an infinite spirit in the universe, which he calls nature. There are three characteristics of this life of nature—joy, quietude, and the intercommunion of its love. Wordsworth's naturalism includes the idea of the marriage of the mind of man with the external world. The second lecture, "Wordsworth: Shelley: Byron," is more general, and makes the point that Wordsworth's philosophy, his high moral teaching, do not make him a poet. "It is his passionate joy in what is beautiful, his vital feeling of all that is tender, his capacity for losing himself in Nature and in man, his imagination, his power of penetrating into the heart of that concerning which he writes . . . [his] creative, forming faculty by which he can shape his subject into words which seem divine"—these are the qualities in Wordsworth that make him a great poet.[15]

One of the most significant essays of the period is Leslie Stephen's "Wordsworth's Ethics."[16] It is not only one of the best expositions of this aspect of Wordsworth's thought, but it is important in that it provoked a reply from Matthew Arnold in his famous essay on the poet. The burden of Stephen's paper is the inescapable importance of Wordsworth's philosophy in measuring the significance of his poetry. Every poetry is a philosophy; it answers the question of the how and why of man. A great poet must not only possess a nature susceptible to emotion, but he must likewise have a versatile, penetrative, and subtle intellect. Much has been said of the purely poetical side of Wordsworth's verse, but Wordsworth "is not merely a melodious writer, or a powerful utterer of deep emotion, but a true philosopher. His poetry wears well because it has solid substance. He is a prophet

[14] London, J. M. Dent and Sons Ltd., 1902.

[15] *Op. cit.,* J. M. Dent, 1920, 179.

[16] *Cornhill Magazine,* xxxiv (1876), 206. Reprinted in *Hours in a Library,* Third Series, London, Smith, Elder and Co., 1879.

and a moralist, as well as a mere singer. His ethical system, in particular, is as distinctive and capable of systematic exposition as that of Butler."[17]

The fundamental principle of Wordsworth's system is the identity which he discovers between our childish instincts and our enlightened reason. Unlike Shelley and Byron, he does not despair of the inevitable changes that take place in the individual with the years. But the great problem of life "is to secure a continuity between the period at which we are guided by half-conscious instincts, and that in which a man is able to supply the place of these primitive impulses by reasoned convictions."[18] If our instincts are spontaneous products of a nature in harmony with the universe, as, in their pure state, Wordsworth believes they are, they must, however, be interpreted by the reasoning faculty and the higher imagination of later years. This is the problem of life, to both sides of which Wordsworth gives much attention. A portion of Stephen's paper is devoted to the comfort that may be derived from this philosophy, how by means of this system of ethics the poet turns sorrow and disappointment into strength.[19]

Perhaps the most frequently read essay on Wordsworth written by the Victorians is Matthew Arnold's "Wordsworth," which served as an introduction to *The Poems of Wordsworth* chosen and edited by Arnold in 1879.[20] He asserts that almost all of Wordsworth's first-rate work was produced between 1798 and 1808. His fame reached its height between 1830 and 1840 and has since diminished in spite of the fact that his poetry has not wanted eulogists and "almost every one who has praised Wordsworth's poetry has praised it well." But to ensure a wide acceptance of his greatness among modern readers, a selection should be made of only his best verse. Above all, admiration of Wordsworth should not be confined to a few "Wordsworthians." He should be "recognized by the public and by the world."

Indeed, we are warned to beware of the "Wordsworthians"

[17] *Hours in a Library*, Third Series, *op. cit.*, 187.

[18] *Ibid.*, 196.

[19] A brief essay by Leslie Stephen, entitled "Wordsworth's Youth," was inspired by Émile Legouis' *La Jeunesse de Wordsworth*. It appeared in the *National Review*, Feb., 1897, and was promptly reprinted in *Studies of a Biographer*, 2 vols., London, Duckworth and Co., 1898.

[20] London, Macmillan and Co., 1879. The essay also appeared in *Macmillan's Magazine*, xl (1879), 193, and was reprinted in *Essays in Criticism*, Second Series, London, Macmillan and Co., 1888.

and especially those who have elevated Wordsworth's philosophy and ethics above his poetry. Arnold objects particularly to Leslie Stephen's statement that Wordsworth's " 'ethical system is as distinctive and capable of exposition as Bishop Butler's'; that his poetry is informed by ideas which 'fall spontaneously into a scientific system of thought.' . . . His poetry [Arnold continues] is the reality, his philosophy—so far, at least, as it may put on the form and habit of 'a scientific system of thought,' . . . is the illusion. . . . But in Wordsworth's case, at any rate, we cannot do him justice until we dismiss his formal philosophy."[21] He cites several instances from the poet of what the "Wordsworthians" admire in him, and affirms that the poetry will never be seen aright as long as it is extolled for its scientific system of thought.

Arnold explains that great poetry is moral in a large sense, "that poetry is at bottom a criticism of life; that the greatness of a poet lies in his powerful and beautiful application of ideas to life,—to the question: How to live."[22] In poetry these ideas must be applied to life "under the conditions fixed for us by the laws of poetic beauty and poetic truth."[23] Wordsworth deals with more of life than Burns, or Keats, or Heine, and he deals with life as a whole more powerfully. This, says Arnold, is his superiority. Wordsworth has no poetic style of his own, but "Nature herself seems . . . to take the pen out of his hand, and to write for him with her own bare, sheer, penetrating power."[24] His best poems combine "profound truth of subject with profound truth of execution."[25]

The premises of Arnold's essay are astute and fundamental (Arnold always reaches basic realities swiftly and simply), and his Introduction and *Selections* did more to popularize Wordsworth than the often tedious philosophical and ethical analyses of the poet. All who wrote in advocacy of a more poetic apprehension of Wordsworth served in giving a timely warning to the theologians and moralists who were exclusively appropriating the poet. But certainly Leslie Stephen, at least, gave full recognition to Wordsworth's poetic expression of his ethics, although he chose to write on the systematic reasonableness of his philosophy. Moreover, when Stephen says that all poetry is a philosophy, and

[21] *Essays in Criticism,* Second Series, Macmillan, 1898, 148–49.
[22] *Ibid.,* 143–44.
[23] *Ibid.,* 142.
[24] *Ibid.,* 158–59.
[25] *Ibid.,* 159.

Arnold affirms that great poetry is moral, is at bottom "a criticism of life," they are saying something of the same thing. And it is difficult to reconcile Arnold's statement that poetry answers the question "How to live" with his demand that Wordsworth cannot be properly understood until we forget his philosophy and ethics. Certainly the elements of his philosophy and his "criticism of life" are inseparable. A sharp distinction between Wordsworth the teacher and Wordsworth the poet cannot justly be made, although it is true that the dry bones of his didacticism can be exposed when we remove from his thought his "spontaneous overflow of powerful feelings."

An able general interpretation, often read by the present-day student, is "Wordsworth," by Edward Caird.[26] Without going heavily into either the poetic artistry of Wordsworth, or his philosophic didacticism, Caird presents a well-rounded sketch which discerningly points out his poetic excellencies and defects, his views of poetic diction and the function of poetry, the effect on him of the French Revolution and his political changes, his poetry of nature, his relation to Rousseau, his democratic outlook, his faith in man, and his patriotism. The special contribution of Caird is his lucid discussion of Rousseau and Wordsworth.

Among the outstanding essays by men of letters is Swinburne's "Wordsworth and Byron."[27] Like Clough and Pater, he strongly defends Wordsworth as a poet, although his admiration is far from unqualified. The paper was incited by Arnold's essay "Byron," and half of it is a fiery attack on Arnold's admiration of that poet.[28] "Be not a Wordsworthian . . . in any narrow or exclusive or sectarian sense of the term," we are advised, "but it is better to be a Wordsworthian than a Byronite."[29] Swinburne pays tribute to Henry Taylor, Leslie Stephen, and others for their exposition of Wordsworth's ethical teaching, but in a manner he is in agreement with Arnold in regretting the overemphasis given Wordsworth as a teacher. The poet himself made the same mistake. "Not that he did wrong to think himself a great teacher: he was a teacher no less beneficent than great: but he was wrong

[26] *Fraser's Magazine,* ci (1880), 205. Reprinted in *Essays on Literature and Philosophy,* 2 vols., Glasgow, James Maclehose and Sons, 1892.

[27] *The Nineteenth Century,* xv (1884), 583; 764. Reprinted in *Miscellanies,* London, Chatto and Windus, 1886.

[28] Preface to *Poetry of Byron,* 1881. Reprinted in *Essays in Criticism,* Second Series, 1888.

[29] *The Complete Works of Algernon Charles Swinburne,* eds. Gosse and Wise, 20 vols., London, William Heinemen Ltd., 1925–27, XIV, 172.

in thinking himself a poet because he was a teacher, whereas in fact he was a teacher because he was a poet."[30] When he is not didactic he has the gift of refreshing us by his perfect and pure sincerity in all his dealing with nature. As a "poet of suffering, and of sympathy with suffering, his station is unequalled in its kind."[31] While the spirit of his teaching is serene, he is not always peaceful. Swinburne admires his great patriotic poems, where his verses have "the strength of a rushing wind," and "ring like storm-swept crannies of the crags and scaurs that nursed the spirit which imbues them." He says that "Wordsworth alone could put into his verse the whole soul of a nation armed or arming for self-devoted self-defence; could fill his meditation with the spirit of a whole people, that in the act of giving it a voice and an expression he might inform and renovate that spirit with the purity and sublimity of his own."[32]

Perhaps what interest us most in Swinburne's essay are his numerous references to the authentic and essentially poetic quality of many of Wordsworth's verses. For example, speaking of *The Solitary Reaper,* he says: "And in such lines — austere, august, but sweet beyond the most polished and perfumed verse of any more obviously elaborate melodist—all the best poems representative of Wordsworth are rich enough to satisfy any taste unspoilt by too much indulgence in metrical confectionary."[33] Swinburne, with his trained ear for meter and poetic style, eloquently demonstrates Wordsworth's achievements in versification and diction. He lends little to the study of Wordsworth as seer or philosopher, but his essay is a notable one in creating a taste for the purity of Wordsworth's emotion and the artistry of much of his verse.

Aubrey De Vere was also moved by Arnold's *Selections* to write two essays on the poet, "The Genius and Passion of Wordsworth," and "The Wisdom and Truth of Wordsworth's Poetry."[34] The first shows that man, as acted on by nature, is the twofold theme of Wordsworth's poetry. The poet comes to nature, not as to a mere gallery of landscapes, but as to a prophetess, an ap-

[30] *Ibid.*, xiv, 213.
[31] *Ibid.*, xiv, 219.
[32] *Ibid.*, xiv, 237.
[33] *Ibid.*, xiv, 230.
[34] The first appeared in *Month,* xxxviii (1880), 465; xxxix (1880), 1. The second appeared in *Catholic World,* 1884. Both were republished in *Essays Chiefly on Poetry,* 2 vols., London, Macmillan and Co., 1887.

proach which cannot be cold but which by its very nature demands impassioned enthusiasm. In the second essay, De Vere illustrates the wisdom and truth of Wordsworth's poetry as they apply to man's moral and political relations, to his cultural progress, to the exterior universe, and to man's spiritual being. De Vere's essays are somewhat tedious reading, but they reaffirm the philosophic value of Wordsworth's teaching, and answer the accusation of Masson and others that Wordsworth is cold and passionless.[35]

John Morley's Introduction to the one-volume *Complete Poetical Works of William Wordsworth*[36] was very influential in forming the late Victorian opinion of Wordsworth. While it contains some admirable criticism, the essay is one-sided in interpretation. Like Arnold, Morley discounts the value of Wordsworth's metaphysics. The poet's period of Revolutionary ardor is given scant notice. The French Revolution is said to have produced the one crisis in Wordsworth's mental life, the "one heavy assault on his continence of soul."[37] Morley remarks that Wordsworth had no teachers and inspirers save nature and solitude. His great moral value is his "direct appeal to will and conduct."[38] And finally, "What Wordsworth does is to assuage, to reconcile, to fortify."[39]

II

In examining the character of the Victorian critical essay, we may seek the answer to several questions. What was the attitude of the Victorian critics toward Wordsworth, and how did it differ from that of Wordsworth's contemporaries? What remained from the criticism of the earlier period? What were found to be his characteristics as a literary artist? What did his poetry seek to teach regarding man and nature?

With the passing of time, the bitterness or partisanship that characterized even the best contemporary criticism of the poet disappeared. Likewise, he was no longer scornfully regarded as

[35] De Vere also wrote "Personal Character of Wordsworth's Poetry," read before the Wordsworth Society in 1883 and published in the *Transactions,* No. 5 (1883), and reprinted in *Essays Chiefly Literary and Critical,* London, Macmillan and Co., 1889. Also, De Vere's "Recollections of Wordsworth" was printed by Grosart in *Prose Works,* III, and was reprinted in *Essays Chiefly on Poetry.*

[36] London, Macmillan and Co., 1888.

[37] *Ibid.,* liv.

[38] *Ibid.,* lxiv.

[39] *Ibid.,* lxvi.

an eccentric, but was firmly established as one of the leading poets of the century, both in his own right and by virtue of his influence on succeeding poets. Some of the critics remarked that he was not a popular poet, a fact which gave rise to the demand by some for a complete chronological edition of his poetry, and by others for a selection of his best verse. One group sought to increase the understanding of Wordsworth by elaborate exegeses of his moral and philosophic utterances, while others interpreted the excellencies of his style, the coexistence in his verse of serenity and deep passion, the tender sympathy he felt for man, and the exalted imagination of his greatest poetry.

There remained from the days of Jeffrey traces of the controversy over his theory of diction and the subject matter of poetry, although this was no longer a matter of first importance in Wordsworthian criticism. Those who discussed the theory expressed in the Prefaces to *Lyrical Ballads* gave it only very qualified approval. It will be seen from the following discussion that the writers, whether or not they entered into the vexed matter of Wordsworth's theory, gave his poetic style serious consideration. While admitting that much of his verse is arid, they (especially such literary artists as Pater, Clough, Swinburne, and Arnold) found that he had a mode of expression well worthy the name of poetry.

Masson discusses the matter at some length. He takes hold of Wordsworth's statement that the language of common speech must be purified, which would leave us, says Masson, a very select language indeed, the sap and flower of all popular speech. The controversy between Wordsworth and Jeffrey was a contest between the old and the new. Although Coleridge and Jeffrey differ immeasurably in the spirit of their criticism,

> there is still an almost perfect coincidence in their special objections to his style. What Jeffrey attacked was chiefly the alleged childishness of much of Wordsworth's language, the babyism of his "Alice Fells," with their cloaks of "duffle grey," &c.; and it is precisely on these points that Coleridge, even while aware of his friend's more profound reason for such familiarities, expresses his dissent from him.[40]

Wordsworth's campaign for regenerating poetic style should have been effected by means of powerful example, not by precept. But Jeffrey's "This will never do" was a false augury. "Slowly and

[40] *Wordsworth, Shelley, Keats, and Other Essays, op. cit.*, 33.

reluctantly the nation came round to Wordsworth; and, if there are still many that believe in his defects and shortcomings, all admit him to have been a true poet, and a man of rare genius."[41]

Shairp makes the brief but pointed comment "that to the Edinburgh lawgiver . . . poetic originality was as a picture to a blind man's eye."[42] Seeing deep truth and beauty in many things hitherto considered unfit for poetry, Wordsworth opened up vast tracts that had been lying waste and brought them into the domain of poetry.

In this way he has done a wider service to poetry than any other poet of his time, but since him no one has arisen of spirit strong and large enough to make full proof of the liberty he bequeathed.

The same freedom . . . he won for future poets with regard to the language of poetry. He was the first who both in theory and practice entirely shook off the trammels of the so-called poetic diction which had tyrannized over English poetry for more than a century. This diction of course exactly represented the half-courtly, half-classical mode of thinking and feeling. As Wordsworth rebelled against this conventionality of spirit, so against the outward expression of it.[43]

Clough remarks that Wordsworth's theory, as directed not against style in general but against the prevalent vices of style, was useful perhaps, but his practice was far more meritorious. Wordsworth was no careless artist.

Certain it is . . . that he did bestow infinite toil and labour upon his poetic style; that in the nice and exquisite felicities of poetic diction he specially surpassed his contemporaries; that his scrupulous and pains-taking spirit, in this particular, constitutes one of his special virtues as a poet.[44]

Wordsworth achieved the harmony between thought and word, which Clough says is no light thing, for style is much more than ornamental. Likewise, Masson remarks that Wordsworth had a natural gift of rich and exuberant expression, but this gift must have been subjected early to strict classical training, and Wordsworth must have bestowed much pains on the finish of his poetry. There is "greater smoothness and beauty, and more of strict logical coherence, in Wordsworth's style than is usual even among careful poets."[45]

[41] *Ibid.*, 34.
[42] *Studies in Poetry and Philosophy*, Houghton Mifflin Co., 1882, p. 47.
[43] *Ibid.*, 64.
[44] *Poems and Prose Remains*, *op. cit.*, I, 315.
[45] Masson, *op. cit.*, 59.

Pater says of Wordsworth's meter and language:

The music of mere metre performs but a limited, yet a very peculiar and subtly ascertained function, in Wordsworth's poetry. With him, metre is but an additional grace, accessory to that deeper music of words and sounds, that moving power, which they exercise in the nobler prose no less than in formal poetry. It is sedative to that excitement, an excitement sometimes almost painful, under which the language, alike of poetry and prose, attains a rhythmical power, independent of metrical combination, and dependent rather on some subtle adjustment of the elementary sounds of words themselves to the image or feeling they convey. Yet some of his pieces, pieces prompted by a sort of half-playful mysticism, like the *Daffodils* and *The Two April Mornings,* are distinguished by a certain quaint gaiety of metre, and rival by their perfect execution, in this respect, similar pieces among our own Elizabethan, or contemporary French poetry. . . . He drew something too from the unconscious mysticism of the old English language itself, drawing out the inward significance of its racy idiom, and the not wholly unconscious poetry of the language used by the simplest people under strong excitement—language, therefore, at its origin.[46]

Swinburne, we have seen, has pointed out the poetic eloquence of Wordsworth, and tells us that at times he achieves a music educed "from the simplest combinations of evidently spontaneous thought with apparently spontaneous expression."[47] Arnold admits that Wordsworth has no "assured and possessed poetic style," but he has something equivalent, an expressiveness such as we find in the line from *Michael,* "And never lifted up a single stone." At his best, nature seems to take the pen and write for Wordsworth, so that there is truth of execution as well as truth of subject in his poetry.

Other interesting comments on Wordsworth's artistry might be assembled, but the foregoing are sufficient to indicate the interest of the Victorians in this matter. We pass now to Wordsworth's philosophy of nature and man, an interpretation of which possibly marks the greatest advance made by the Victorian essayists. Wordsworth's two chief interests, the outward world of the senses, and the inward realm of the mind, were both understood by the critics to be his most significant subjects for poetic treatment. To quote from De Vere:

It is this blending of the inward and the outward worlds, and again the fusion of intellect with emotion, which makes the poetry of

[46] *Appreciations, op. cit.,* 58–59.
[47] *Complete Works of . . . Swinburne, op. cit.,* XIV, 240.

Wordsworth, while anything but sentimental, yet eminently the poetry of elevated sentiment. It is never dry thought; it is never irrational feeling. It comes from hidden depths of the spirit, but it weds itself in delighted sympathy with the purity and splendour of the visible universe . . . .[48]

In elucidating this view of man and nature, two questions present themselves: what does Wordsworth say about the world of the senses, the material world of nature as perceived by man? what spiritual bond exists between nature and man whereby each acts upon the other?

The part that the senses play in Wordsworth's scheme of life was less discussed by the Victorian critics than it has been since. Yet they were by no means unaware of it. Again, to quote De Vere:

Three of man's five senses are senses only, and the impressions which fall upon them terminate with them. But the senses of sight and hearing are more than mere material powers; the impressions that reach them pass through them to the intellect, which imparts to them in turn something of its own vivific might, changing mere form and colour into beauty, and mere sound into harmony. These two senses are the gates between the worlds of matter and of mind—Sacraments of Nature, feeding without intermission man's intellect and imagination. The greater part of Wordsworth's poetry celebrates the sublime ministration of the eye.[49]

Likewise Pater calls attention to Wordsworth's visual clarity, and adds a comment on his perception of sound:

Clear and delicate at once, as he is in the outlining of visible imagery, he is more clear and delicate still, and finely scrupulous, in the noting of sounds; so that he conceives of noble sound as even moulding the human countenance to nobler types, and as something actually "profaned" by colour, by visible form, or image.[50]

Shairp points out the prevalence of visual images in Wordsworth's poetry:

It would be hardly too much to say that there is not a single image in his whole works which he had not observed with his own eyes. And perhaps no poet since Homer has introduced into poetry, directly from nature, more facts and images which had not before been noted in books.[51]

[48] *Essays Chiefly on Poetry, op. cit.,* I, 222.
[49] *Ibid.,* I, 241.
[50] *Appreciations, op. cit.,* 45.
[51] *Studies in Poetry and Philosophy, op. cit.,* 11.

Here and there are such references to Wordsworth's sensuousness, but it remained for the later scholars to present this aspect of Wordsworth in relation to the philosophies of Locke and Hartley, and to give appropriate emphasis to "all that mighty world of eye and ear."

In what way did they interpret Wordsworth's idea of nature and its relation to man?

Shairp points out that after a period of overcivilization men turn from their highly strung interests to the calm, cool, equability of nature. It was in such a period that Wordsworth appeared, well fitted to lead people back to nature by the life he had led as a boy and youth among the Lakes, where he became consecrated to be the poet-priest of nature's mysteries. At that time natural objects were endeared to him by their human associations, but later were dear for their own sakes. He came to feel that nature is a living, a vital whole. It is not a dead machine, but possesses a soul of its own which exists independently of himself. This living nature is a unity, which communicates to him feelings of calmness, awe, and tenderness. These convictions, or feelings, he could not prove, but held that they were intimations coming to him direct from God. But he believed that in nature he saw "the shape and image of right reason, reason in the highest sense, embodied and made visible in order, in stability, in conformity to eternal law."[52] He made a further step in his nature philosophy.

> He discovered that in order to attain the highest and truest vision of Nature, the soul of man must not be altogether passive, but must act along with and in unison with Nature, must send from itself abroad an emanation, which, meeting with natural objects, produces something better than either the soul itself or Nature by herself could generate.[53]

Shairp points out finally that in later life Wordsworth's natural philosophy gave way somewhat to preoccupation with morality.

By reason of its specialized subject, Leslie Stephen's "Wordsworth's Ethics" excludes much of Wordsworth's nature philosophy, but some reference is necessarily made to it since our early instincts, that determine our later intellectual life, are affected by our contact with nature, if not largely derived from that source. Stephen remarks on the poet's belief in the existence of a divine order in the universe, conformity to which produces

[52] *On Poetic Interpretation of Nature,* Houghton Mifflin Co., 1882, p. 259.
[53] *Ibid.,* 261.

the beauty embodied in the external world and a correspondent virtue in man. Thus divinity reveals itself in nature; however Stephen remarks that Wordsworth neglects the evil that is in nature. "The ethical doctrine that virtue consists in conformity to nature becomes ambiguous with him, as with all its advocates, when we ask for a precise definition of nature."[54]

Pater touches on Wordsworth's conception of nature as inspirited by a universal soul.

> At other times, again, in those periods of intense susceptibility, in which he appeared to himself as but the passive recipient of external influences, he was attracted by the thought of a spirit of life in outward things, a single, all-pervading mind in them, of which man, and even the poet's imaginative energy, are but moments—the old dream of the *anima mundi,* the mother of all things and their grave, in which some had desired to lose themselves, and others had become indifferent to the distinctions of good and evil. It would come, sometimes, like the sign of the *macrocosm* to Faust in his cell: the network of man and nature was seen to be pervaded by a common, universal life . . . [55]

The fullest analysis is given by Stopford Brooke, first in the chapters on Wordsworth in *Theology in the English Poets,* and later (with some repetition) in *Naturalism in English Poetry.* Brooke explains, as a first principle, that Wordsworth conceives of an active principle in nature, each part of which has its own distinctive soul and character, and its own work to perform. This living, animate nature is in contrast with the mechanical nature of Pope and the dead nature of Cowper. Nature is a "person," not a thing, the "poetic impersonation of an actual Being, the form which the poet gives to the living Spirit of God in the outward world, in order that he may possess a metaphysical thought as a subject for his work as an artist."[56] This idea Brooke repeats in his statement that "for the sake of his art, for the sake of shaping his thought so that it should be conceived and loved by others, he embodied his idea of an infinite Spirit in the universe in the shape of a personality whom he creates and calls Nature."[57] Both these statements are unfortunate, and reveal the weakness in Brooke's interpretation. They give the impression that Wordsworth was first a theologian, full of the idea of God, and consciously built up his natural philosophy as a literary device to

[54] *Hours in a Library,* Third Series, *op. cit.,* 201.
[55] *Appreciations, op. cit.,* 56.
[56] *Theology in the English Poets,* Everyman, *op. cit.,* 79.
[57] *Naturalism in English Poetry, op. cit.,* 146–47.

present attractively his religious views. Wordsworth proceeded in the reverse direction. His naturalism led him eventually toward a realization of God, which moreover was never as distinct as Brooke supposes. It is a serious error to assert that nature, with its personality and soul, was "created" by Wordsworth.

Brooke recognizes that Wordsworth comes near to pantheism. His "life of the universe," "spirit of God," "soul which is the eternity of thought in nature," may be called so by some, Brooke remarks, but it is a pantheism which affirms God in all but which does not affirm that all includes the whole of God.

What are the characteristics of the life of nature, as Wordsworth saw them? There is first joy, which is not only symbolic, but actually the joy of God in His own creative life. Second, is nature's quietude; deep calm is at her heart. Another characteristic, which Brooke regards as perhaps the most beautiful idea that Wordsworth introduced into the poetry of nature, is "the intercommunion of all things in Nature with one another. . . . And this view of his was founded on the conviction that an infinite love flowed through the whole universe and was also its source."[58]

What is the relation that nature bears to man? First, Wordsworth draws a clear distinction between man and nature. Unlike Coleridge, he does not hold that nature lives by the projection of ourselves upon it, but it has a separate life of its own. One thing that is healthy about his poetry is that he does not willingly commit the pathetic fallacy. He "will not spoil Nature by tracing in her likeness to his own moods," a mistake which would contradict his own philosophy, because there can be no health-giving communion with nature, no receiving of *her* benefits, if she reflects only ourselves. But although different, man and nature are made to complete each other. "Each educates the other, and in their final marriage is the consummation of the perfection of the human mind and Nature."[59] This idea lies at the root of Wordsworth's philosophy, and to reveal and explain the separation but underlying unity of mind and the external world is the special work of his poetry.

But to receive nature's ministrations man must have certain qualities of character, mostly those of the child. There must be first a simple heart that loves. Our intellect, working without

[58] *Ibid.*, 153. See also *Theology in the English Poets, op. cit.*, 84–86.
[59] *Theology, ibid.*, 97.

love, misshapes the beauty of the world. It divides and subdivides, missing the living whole. There must also be reverence. But the two most important qualities are purity of heart and unworldliness of character, which nature herself teaches the child brought up under her ministrations, as the poet has shown in the early books of *The Prelude*.

Stopford Brooke combines the Victorian interest in Wordsworth's religious and moral didacticism with an account of his philosophic naturalism. It has also been mentioned that his *Theology in the English Poets* includes the best commentary on the poet's growth and development as related in *The Prelude*. However, unlike Leslie Stephen who has explained the psychological basis of Wordsworth's ethics, Brooke fails to reveal the psychology of his naturalism.

CHAPTER FOUR

THE APPEARANCE OF SPECIALIZED RESEARCH

I

It would be arbitrary to attempt a precise distinction between the material presented in the last chapter and that which we are now ready to examine, but for convenience I have separated the critical essay from the work that more closely resembles specialized studies and scholarly research. Many of the papers published by the Wordsworth Society are indeed no more than essays, and are less thorough than such studies of Wordsworth as Stopford Brooke's or Caird's. However, we are to examine the work of the Society as a whole, which was highly specialized and devoted exclusively to Wordsworth. A separate discussion of nineteenth-century biographies and editions is yet more justifiable.

The Wordsworth Society first met at Grasmere, September 29, 1880, and continued to meet annually until it disbanded after the final meeting in Westminster Abbey, July 7, 1886. To Professor William A. Knight goes the credit of founding the Society, and of guiding its course as its very active secretary. The office of president was honorary and was filled annually. Among its distinguished presidents were Matthew Arnold, James Russell Lowell, and Lord Houghton, whose addresses are preserved in the Society's *Transactions*. Robert Browning occupied the chair at the third meeting, and John Ruskin was a member. Arnold remarked in his presidential address that in the old days worn-out men entered a monastery. "Times and circumstances have changed, you cannot well enter a monastery; but you can enter the Wordsworth Society."[1]

However, its constitution expressed the following purposes of its organization.

(1) As a bond of union amongst those who are in sympathy with the general teaching and spirit of Wordsworth; (2) To promote and extend the study of the poet's works—in particular, to carry on the literary work which remains to be done in connection with the text

[1] *Transactions of the Wordsworth Society*, ed. W. A. Knight, No. 1–No. 8, 1882–87, No. 5, p. 5.

and chronology of the poems, and the local allusions which they contain; (3) To collect for preservation, and, if thought desirable, for publication, original letters and unpublished reminiscences of the poet; (4) To prepare a record of opinion, with reference to Wordsworth, from 1793 to the present time, and to investigate any points connected with the first appearance of his works.[2]

It was also proposed to issue a small volume of selections from the poet, edited by several members, to be known as the *Wordsworth Society Volume of Selections*. This was published in 1889, after the Society had dissolved. The objects proposed in (3) and (4) above were only very partially fulfilled.

Aside from the papers written by the members, the chief work of the Society was the publication in the *Transactions* of the following data:

1. Catalogue of the Rydal Mount library, reprinted from the Rydal Mount sale catalogue of 1859 (*Trans.*, No. 6, p. 195). This does not give a complete idea of the extent of Wordsworth's library, since a large number of his most valuable books had been retained by the family, but the list is the most interesting, to modern scholars, of the Society's documents. It dispels any delusions that Wordsworth owned but few books. Knight warns us that the list contains numerous bibliographical errors.

2. A list of Wordsworth's poems, "arranged in chronological order, giving (1) the Titles finally adopted by himself; (2) the text of the First Lines, as given in his last edition of 1849; (3) the precise Date of their Composition, as far as can be ascertained from a comparison of Wordsworth's own statements with the Fenwick notes, his sister's Journals, and letters by members of the family or by others; (4) the Date of their first Publication, whether in his Works or in Magazines."[3] (*Trans.*, No. 7, p. 53).

3. Bibliography of the poems of Wordsworth (*Trans.*, No. 1, second edition, amended; *Trans.*, No. 7, p. 121). This and (2) above are the work of Knight. The bibliographical notes are somewhat fuller than those Knight later published in his edition of *The Poetical Works of William Wordsworth*, but Knight's findings, especially dates, are not always accurate.

4. Bibliography of reviews and magazine articles in criticism of Wordsworth (*Trans.*, No. 5, p. 95). This was prepared by W. F. Poole of Chicago, but is not so helpful as the bibliography in Knight's edition of Wordsworth.

[2] *Ibid.*, No. 1.
[3] *Ibid.*, No. 7, iii.

5. List of letters by Wordsworth in the South Kensington Museum (*Trans.,* No. 5, p. 129).

6. A series of letters from Wordsworth to John Kenyon (*Trans.,* No. 6, p. 71), and from Wordsworth, his wife, and sister to Crabb Robinson and others (*Trans.,* No. 8, p. 81).

7. Descriptions and reproductions of five portraits of Wordsworth (*Trans.,* No. 3, p. 56, and No. 4).

It will be seen from these activities that a lively scholarly interest was growing up concerning Wordsworth. Although much of the work of the Society was not distinguished, its influence was beneficial. The papers presented before the Society are not of the first importance, but the following at least may be read with profit today.

Thomas Hutchinson, "The Structure of the Sonnets of Wordsworth" (*Trans.,* No. 2, pp. 27–31). Wordsworth's model was Milton, but he often varied the order of the rhymes, especially in his later sonnets. The paper includes tables showing irregularities.

Edward Dowden, "Wordsworth's 'Selections from Chaucer Modernised'" (*Trans.,* No. 3, pp. 47–55). Dowden commends Wordsworth's use of plain language rather than archaisms. But because "Wordsworth's modernisations of Chaucer are sufficiently good to deserve that we should know their faults," Dowden points out errors, sometimes in translation, sometimes in taste. In some instances Wordsworth's text may have been at fault. He perhaps used Urry's.

Stopford Brooke, "Wordsworth's 'Guide to the Lakes'" (*Trans.,* No. 5, pp. 25–35). Parts of the *Guide* are written in poetic prose. Some of the leading ideas of his poetry are here reiterated. There is a living Will in the universe, which has pleasure in its own doings and which harmonizes itself with man. There is a co-operative harmony between the animals and nature herself. The work of man and nature are united.

Herbert Rix, "Notes on the Localities of the Duddon Sonnets" (*Trans.,* No. 5, pp. 61–78). A detailed investigation of topographical references.

W. A. Heard, "Wordsworth's Treatment of Sound" (*Trans.,* No. 6, pp. 40–57). Wordsworth's abnormal sensitivity to sound, and the variety of meanings he attributes to sound. The study is well developed, with many quotations. (1) The sounds of nature are not noises, but voices expressive of nature's mighty life. (2) The same life that speaks in the sounds of inorganic nature, is expressed in the sounds of her creatures. (3) There is concord between these voices. (4) Wordsworth selects some peculiar tone as the key-note of the scene. (5)

While these sounds are realistically described, they represent a deeper, poetic harmony heard only by the imagination and a heart sympathetic to nature.

Alfred Ainger, "Wordsworth and Charles Lamb" (*Trans.,* No. 6, pp. 57–65). A discussion of Lamb's review of *The Excursion* in *The Quarterly,* with extracts, comment on Gifford's mutilation, and a contrast with Jeffrey. Lamb was the first to point out many things which have since become commonplaces of Wordsworthian criticism.

J. H. Shorthouse, "The Platonism of Wordsworth" (*Trans.,* No. 6, pp. 119–31). Like Plato, Wordsworth reaches the ideal through material and human attributes. Shorthouse suggests that Wordsworth may never have read Plato, but knew him through Coleridge. He believed in the governing principle of good, which unites all things, in all aspects of nature. Also akin to Plato is Wordsworth's mystical conception of good, that in the world of the intellect exists the perfect.

R. H. Hutton, "Wordsworth's Two Styles" (*Trans.,* No. 6, pp. 135–48. The earlier style is marked by a pronounced use of objective fact, elasticity and buoyancy, and a reserved emotion that is suggested rather than expressed. The later style employs less objective fact, with more symbol or bald morality in its place. There is less buoyancy, but the emotion is more freely conveyed and accompanied by a richness of effect quite foreign to the early style.

H. D. Rawnsley, "Reminiscences of Wordsworth among the Peasantry of Westmoreland" (*Trans.,* No. 6, pp. 159–94). A racy piece of reporting from the mouths of the dalesmen who remembered Wordsworth. They seemed to agree that his "potry" was above their heads, that he was a plain, humorless, uncommunicative man, highly respectable but not sociable enough to be loved.

Harry Goodwin, "Wordsworth and Turner" (*Trans.,* No. 7, pp. 21–25). An interesting parallel. Both broke from eighteenth-century tradition and mannerisms in their respective arts, delineating nature and man in their common aspects, but revealing hidden beauty. Both regarded themselves as teachers. Landscape painting received as great an impetus from Turner as poetry received from Wordsworth. Yet Wordsworth's taste in painting was eighteenth-century, as was Turner's in poetry.

John Veitch, "The Theism of Wordsworth" (*Trans.,* No. 8, pp. 24–51). This is a scholarly study, perhaps the cream of the papers. Wordsworth is distinguished by his awareness of both the world of the senses and the infinite world that borders and surrounds the finite. The second stage in his theism, even more important, is his consciousness of a power in the infinite sphere and our consciousness at times of that power or powers. When he felt "Low breathings coming after me," it was not simply fear that overcame him, but awe and reverence.

"A link was formed between the moral world of the finite spirit and the unseen, as if the soul were in the presence of a higher, purer consciousness than its own, unknown until suddenly revealed."[4] Essentially connected with this sense of infinite, is a tendency to rise above details, to seek a relation, connectedness, unity, in the phenomena of sense, to center all in a Unity of Being. What was the nature of this unity? "He holds by a Unity, a transcendent yet manifested Unity, a Unity amid a multiplicity, yet not a blind or unconscious power; a Spirit, Soul, Personality, yet not as the human—not a magnified man. This is the ground, the reason, the living, quickening principle of things—of Nature and Man alike. Of Him we may rise to consciousness, and He may become to us a source of inspiration, imaginative, moral, and spiritual."[5] In a well-ordered argument, Veitch denies that this is pantheism. The spirit is transcendent and in a sense above experience, but it is not an empty abstraction. "It is not even a power dwelling apart, set high up in the heavens, no one knows where or truly what. It lays its touch upon earth, on what we call the outward or material world, and on what we name the soul of man."[6] The soul is not a mere *tabula rasa,* but from our birth we have a certain community with God, although Veitch does not see that Wordsworth gives any theory explaining the touch of the infinite on the finite. The spirit is not anthropomorphic in the sense that it is in the image of man, but it can be perceived by man through his experience.

Alfred Ainger, "Poets Who Helped to Form Wordsworth's Style" (*Trans.,* No. 8, pp. 51–61). Ainger is concerned chiefly with the influence of the Countess of Winchilsea and James Thomson. He argues that Wordsworth was led to write *An Evening Walk* by his recollection of Winchilsea's *Nocturnal Reverie.* Also, in his earlier sonnet *Calm is All Nature,* the figure of the horse "cropping audibly his later meal" seems to have been suggested by a similar description in the *Nocturnal Reverie.* Ainger points out Wordsworth's known admiration of Thomson and finds some possible verbal likenesses.

II

The last quarter of the century saw a great deal of editorial activity and the appearance of at least three important editions of the poetry, which, while far from definitive, remain standard texts in use today. But before discussing these, we must review the major problems that the editor of Wordsworth faced.

Professor Dowden, in his essay, "The Text of Wordsworth's

[4] *Ibid.,* No. 8, p. 28.
[5] *Ibid.,* No. 8, p. 34.
[6] *Ibid.,* No. 8, p. 37.

Poems,"[7] points out that in the case of Wordsworth there is no need to amend a corrupt text, for the poet himself saw many editions through the press, which were carefully proofread by himself and his family. The first problem is to determine what textual reading to use of the texts that were published under Wordsworth's authorization. Wordsworth personally supervised thirty-two editions of his poems, if we can trust Knight's count.[8] Immediately after the publication of *An Evening Walk* and *Descriptive Sketches* in 1793, he began to retouch and continued through the rest of his life the habit of rigorous revision of his published poems. Words and lines were altered, often many times, stanzas canceled and new ones added, and in some cases the last editions would return to the readings of the early ones. The basic text, however, is that of the collected *Poetical Works* of 1849–50, the last to appear in Wordsworth's lifetime. He himself wrote to Dyce in 1830, "You know what importance I attach to following strictly the last Copy of the text of an Author."[9] But several poems were omitted (probably by oversight) from the edition of 1849–50. Moreover, some editors are tempted to print earlier texts of poems which Wordsworth in his late years injured by alterations. At any rate the task of collating the many texts is an extensive one, and the decision must be made regarding the method and extent of printing variant readings.

The second problem is the arrangement of the poems. As is well known, Wordsworth worked out his own intricate and elaborate system based on a psychological classification of the poems. He introduced this method of arrangement in the edition of 1815, shifted poems about from time to time, accepted suggestions from Reed, his American editor, but was unmoved in his insistence on the plan he ultimately settled upon. The classification is confusing and inexact. It is, for instance, difficult to distinguish between poems placed in the class of "Imagination" and those under the head of "Fancy." Wordsworth himself sometimes forgot which was which when referring to these poems in conversation. His family was in disagreement over the arrangement. But Wordsworth regarded a chronological arrangement as ego-

[7] *Contemporary Review,* xxxiii (1878), 734. Reprinted in *Transcripts and Studies,* London, Kegan Paul, Trench and Co., 1888.

[8] *Poetical Works of William Wordsworth,* ed. W. A. Knight, 8 vols., London, Macmillan and Co., 1896, I, xxxii.

[9] *The Letters of William and Dorothy Wordsworth, The Later Years,* ed. E. de Selincourt, 3 vols., Oxford, The Clarendon Press, 1939, I, 473.

tistical, placing the importance of the poet's personal development before the intrinsic value of the poems themselves. Nor is his classification merely a superficial design, but it sets forth what the poet regarded as the organic unity of his entire work. That Wordsworth saw a unity in all his poetry is clear from his statement comparing the poem which was to be called *The Recluse* to the main body of a cathedral, while the minor pieces "when they shall be properly arranged, will be found by the attentive reader to have such connection with the main work as may give them claim to be likened to the little cells, oratories, and sepulchral recesses, ordinarily included in those edifices."[10] Also, as Dowden remarks: "Whether the classification be happy or not, it should be borne in mind, first, that the psychological groups form only part of a larger design, and secondly, that the order of the poems *within each group* is Wordsworth's order, and that it was carefully considered with a view to artistic effect."[11] For these reasons editors have felt hesitant to break up Wordsworth's arrangement. Some, however, have discarded it for the chronological order with its obvious advantages to the studious reader. Only by reading the poems in the order of their composition can we see Wordsworth's development throughout the years, a matter of prime interest to the student whether Wordsworth liked it or not. This is not mere pedantry. The only *natural* order is the order in which the poems were written. It may be pointed out also that they are easier to find when chronologically arranged. Few readers succeed in remembering the poet's classification. But if the chronological arrangement is adopted, the editor is confronted with the problem of undated poems, poems begun at an early date (perhaps only a few lines written) and completed years later, and poems written on the same subject over a period of years, but so closely associated that to separate them would violate their proper relationship.

The third problem is determining the chronology of the poems. The chief sources for the dates of composition are as follows: (1) The dates given by Wordsworth, most of them dictated in notes to Miss Isabella Fenwick in 1843, now called the "I. F." or "Fenwick" notes. Unfortunately they are not always trustworthy. In his old age Wordsworth naturally forgot the

[10] "Advertisement" to *The Prelude, Poetical Works,* Oxford Standard ed., p. 631.

[11] *The Poetical Works of William Wordsworth,* ed. Edward Dowden, 7 vols., London, George Bell and Sons, 1892, I, ix.

exact year he composed many of his poems, and sometimes gave a date some years after the poem was published. (2) Dorothy Wordsworth's *Journals,* chiefly the Alfoxden journal of 1798, and the Grasmere journal, 1800–1803. The poet's sister has thrown a great deal of light on the composition of many of her brother's poems during his prime; her diary is the richest source of information not merely in dating these poems, but in understanding Wordsworth's mood at the time of composition, the external circumstances surrounding their birth, and his method of writing. (3) The large body of letters of the Wordsworth family, which are invaluable in determining dates. (4) Conjecture from internal evidence. However, the chronology of many poems remains vague or questionable.

The fourth problem is the matter of notes. In addition to the comments of the editor we have Wordsworth's notes and the Fenwick notes. Wordsworth himself explained many topographical allusions and references to persons, as well as a variety of other matters. The Fenwick notes serve as a brief introduction to the majority of the poems, giving information relative to the location of objects and places referred to, and to the circumstances of composition. They have their value in heightening the interest of the reader, and for this reason are often placed at the beginning of each poem. They are also of great value in supplying us with many facts about Wordsworth which certainly would otherwise have been lost. But some editors feel that they deserve no such distinction, and print them at the end of the volume lest the incautious reader attach too much importance to them. Nor as has been pointed out, are they always reliable. Not only did Wordsworth confuse dates, but the aged poet sometimes misrepresented the mood and the purpose of the poem.

The nineteenth-century scholars contributed a great deal to the solving of these four large problems of editing. Fortunately they realized that unless the work was done as soon after Wordsworth's death as possible, many sources of information would be closed forever. All readers of Wordsworth owe a debt of gratitude to Knight for his great labors in collecting a mass of information about the poet which would have been difficult or impossible to obtain now. But having paid fitting tribute, we must regret that Knight was not equipped with the power of unswerving accuracy so necessary to the work of an editor and biographer. He and his researches have been wittily called "chaos and old Knight." Happily his editions of the Wordsworth letters and of Dorothy Wordsworth's *Journals* have been superseded by the work of a far abler modern scholar, Professor de Selincourt, but his edition of the poetry still has its use and must be considered here.

Knight's first edition appeared at intervals between the years 1882–89, the first eight volumes containing the poetry and some prose, and the last three a biography. It was sumptuously published in library 8vo size, by William Paterson, Edinburgh. Yet it is not to these volumes, with their many inaccuracies, that the reader should turn, but to Knight's "Eversley" edition, published by Macmillan in eight volumes in 1896. This is a revised and corrected edition, to which, says Knight, "several thousand new notes have been added, many of the old ones entirely recast; the changes of text, introduced by Wordsworth into the successive editions of his Poems, have all been revised; new readings—derived from many MS. sources—have been added: while the chronological order of the Poems has, in several instances, been changed, in the light of fresh evidence."[12]

Knight's basic text is that of 1849–50. The poems, with very few exceptions, are arranged in chronological order. For this reason alone it commends itself to many modern readers over other editions. Changes in text, made by Wordsworth, are given in footnotes, with the dates of the changes. Included also are suggested changes written by the poet in his copy of the stereotyped edition of 1836–37, long kept at Rydal Mount. These collations are far more extensive than are to be found in any other edition, and the full list of variant readings available in no other one place constitutes the chief value of the edition to readers of today. An extensive bibliography of Wordsworthian criticism is included, with an interesting American bibliography compiled by Cynthia St. John. Moreover, a reading of Knight's preface will show that his whole editorial scheme is more ambitious than those of other editors, and the details of his plan are often derived from a sensible editorial policy. But the fact remains that for all his corrections, his chronology is often at fault and his collation inaccurate.

We need mention only briefly Knight's other editorial labors. Continuing in the "Eversley" series, he published *The Prose*

[12] *Op. cit.*, I, vii–viii.

Works of William Wordsworth in two volumes in 1896, one of two editions still in use. Also in the "Eversley" series he published in 1897 his two-volume edition of *The Journals of Dorothy Wordsworth,* the only edition until the appearance of de Selincourt's in 1941. Knight's edition is marred by many deletions and errors. He published in 1907, through Ginn and Company, a three-volume edition of *The Letters of the Wordsworth Family,* the only one until de Selincourt's in 1935–39.

In 1892–93 Dowden published the "Aldine" edition of *The Poetical Works of William Wordsworth* (George Bell and Sons) in seven volumes. In the preface Dowden states the features of his edition, which aims to present the poet's works

> as Wordsworth himself would have approved. It gives:—(1) Wordsworth's latest text; (2) in Wordsworth's own arrangement; (3) all Wordsworth's printed notes; (4) the notes dictated by Wordsworth to Miss Fenwick—here signed "I. F."; notes by the present Editor, dealing with (*a*) the dates of composition and publication of each poem, (*b*) the occasion, where that can be ascertained, (*c*) and recording a large selection from the various readings of editions prior to 1849–50; (5) a chronological table; (6) an Appendix of Poems by Wordsworth not included in his last edition; (7) a reprint of the two poems of 1793, "An Evening Walk" and "Descriptive Sketches" as originally published; (8) a bibliography; (9) a brief memoir.[13]

Dowden's edition is still in use today and is far superior to Knight's in reliability and accurate scholarship. But Knight at least has the advantage of presenting a fuller list of variant readings.

In 1895 appeared Thomas Hutchinson's edition of *The Poetical Works of Wordsworth,* published by the Oxford University Press. This has been reprinted with a few revisions many times and is the standard one-volume edition of Wordsworth in use today. It is based on the 1849–50 edition, and the text is the most reliable we have. Hutchinson's knowledge of the chronology of the poems is also authoritative. He gives an interesting and helpful chronological table of events of Wordsworth's life, including under the dates cross references to other writers of the period. He arranges the poems in Wordsworth's order. The notes are few and variant readings are not given.

In addition to the editions of Knight, Dowden, and Hutchin-

[13] *Op. cit.,* I, v.

son, several others should be mentioned. In 1876 Alexander Grosart published in three volumes *The Prose Works of William Wordsworth* which, together with Knight's, is still in use. In 1888 Macmillan published a one-volume *Complete Poetical Works of William Wordsworth,* edited by John Morley, and known as the "Globe" edition. *The Recluse* appeared for the first time here, the copyright being held by the publishers. The text is that of the 1857 edition, and the poems are given an approximate chronological arrangement. It is accompanied by a bibliography compiled by J. R. Tutin. This edition has been reprinted often. In 1908 appeared Nowell C. Smith's beautiful three-volume edition of *The Poems of William Wordsworth,* published by Methuen. The text is that of 1849–50, and the poems follow Wordsworth's arrangement. Professor Smith has sought and achieved textual accuracy, but as he states in his preface he has aimed at compression, and his notes are written more for the ordinary reader or inexperienced student than for the scholar looking for full critical apparatus.

These texts will undoubtedly be superseded by the magnificent new edition of *The Poetical Works of William Wordsworth,* now in preparation, edited by de Selincourt. The first two volumes have appeared.[14] Wordsworth's arrangement of the poems is retained, and de Selincourt gives the best defense yet made (from the editor's point of view) of this arrangement. The basic text is that of 1849–50, but the poems are edited from the manuscripts with complete *apparatus criticus.* Numerous pieces of juvenilia and fragments hitherto unpublished are included.[15]

The biographies of Wordsworth prior to Legouis' need only brief comment. Many recollections of the poet were printed, and accounts of visits to Rydal Mount, two of the best coming from America. Emerson in *English Traits and Representative Men* has given some vivid touches to the portrait of Wordsworth, and Ellis Yarnall of Philadelphia, in *Wordsworth and the Coleridges* (1899), describes the poet in the last year of his life. Several short biographies were written that are of little value today, such as *Memoirs of William Wordsworth* (1852) by "January Searle," and *William Wordsworth* (1865) by E. P. Hood. However, the

[14] Oxford, The Clarendon Press, 1940 and 1944.

[15] Wordsworthian scholarship has recently suffered a severe loss in the death of Professor de Selincourt. His work on the edition of *The Poetical Works* is being carried forward to completion by Miss Helen Darbishire.

brief biography by F.W.H. Myers for the "English Men of Letters" series remains one of the better condensed accounts of Wordsworth's life, although it is out of date in some respects.

Two biographies, Christopher Wordsworth's and Knight's, however, represent the principal work. Their use today is largely confined to students specializing in Wordsworth's biography, who will find in them basic source material. In 1847 Christopher Wordsworth, the poet's nephew, was entrusted by Wordsworth to compile after his death biographical facts which might be of assistance to posterity in a better understanding of his poetry. The idea of a complete biography was distasteful to Wordsworth, who regarded his "Life" as having been written in his poetry. Christopher Wordsworth, therefore, explains that his work is neither a "Life" nor a critical interpretation. However, his two bulky volumes, published in 1851 as *Memoirs of William Wordsworth,* go far beyond the simple intentions of Wordsworth and the modest disclaimer of the author. Beginning with the poet's own very brief memoranda of his life, dictated to Christopher Wordsworth, the *Memoirs* gather together much information, including some letters, discuss many of the poems, and present a pious and untrustworthy picture of the poet. Important facts are suppressed, and the emphasis is almost wholly upon the later Wordsworth.

Knight's *Life of William Wordsworth,* issued in 1889 as the last three volumes of his edition of the poetry, calls for more respectful attention. It is a better work than the hastily written *Memoirs* of Bishop Wordsworth, and preserves much material that has been of use to later biographers. But Knight, too, fails in interpreting the younger Wordsworth, and his work is not free from errors. Much new light has been shed on Wordsworth since Knight wrote his biography, and it is not recommended for the general reader.

CHAPTER FIVE

BIOGRAPHY AND RELATED MATTERS

I

The twentieth century has seen great activity in the study of Wordsworth. It is not to be expected that the Wordsworthian criticism of our era should be as tempestuous or as vital as that written by the poet's contemporaries, but it has been less prejudiced, more varied, and of far wider range. Victorian criticism can boast of the participation of some distinguished men of letters, but the interpretation of Wordsworth's personality was too strongly influenced by his sober and sedate late years, and the discussion of his philosophic utterances, if learned and sometimes penetrating, inclined towards theological and academic heaviness. Modern criticism has advanced far beyond that of the Victorians. It is more accurate. It is richer in information about the poet. It has constructed from this information a truer interpretation. Modern scholarship and criticism have made Wordsworth more interesting both as a man and as a poet than the Victorians pictured him.

Among the achievements of the present century is a new body of biographical matter, which not only presents more fully and accurately the facts of Wordsworth's life, but which interprets with keen penetration the inner man, his mental and spiritual development to which he often gave expression in his poetry. Also Wordsworth's social and political views, evident both in his personal affairs and in his writings, have been given much clearer emphasis. His philosophy—his teachings in regard to nature, human psychology, religion, and the transcendental experience—while much discussed in the nineteenth century, has continued to be examined and restated, with a fuller comprehension of its varied and rich sources and of its relation to the intellectual movement of the times. There has been a re-examination of his aesthetic experience as the source of his poetic expression. Finnally, much additional work has gone forward on the Wordsworth text.

II

The new biography has been shaped by vigorous research for new facts, and some significant discoveries have been made. But the several important biographies are distinguishable by their different interpretations of the early and late years, rather than by their accumulation of new data alone. This approach involves an extensive discussion of the poet's political and social sympathies and likewise inclusion of something of his philosophy and religion. Therefore some books that throw light on these matters, although not strictly biographical, will be discussed here in so far as they relate to the biography. A fuller discussion of his philosophy as interpreted by twentieth-century critics will follow in the next chapter.

We may summarize briefly the most important sources for the new biography that were not available to the Victorians or were little used. First is the large body of the Wordsworth correspondence of which Christopher Wordsworth made some use, and which Knight collected and used more extensively. But the letters were in a state of confusion when Knight wrote his *Life*. They were not available to other biographers until 1907 when Knight published the collection. Although the edition was inaccurate in text and dates, the letters furnished a wealth of material for biographers. It was not until 1935–39 that a new edition appeared, edited by de Selincourt, correcting Knight's errors and including many newly discovered letters. In 1933 Professor L. N. Broughton of Cornell published the correspondence between Wordsworth and his American editor, Reed. Next in importance to the correspondence are Dorothy Wordsworth's *Journals,* from which Knight published an extensive selection in 1897. This remained the only edition until 1941, when de Selincourt published the *Journals* in as complete a form as possible. An event of great magnitude to the biographer was the publication by de Selincourt in 1926 of the text of *The Prelude* as it represents the poem at its completion in 1805, before the extensive revisions that appear in the final text of 1850. Not only is the early text itself of unique importance, but likewise de Selincourt's notes are a mine of valuable information. In 1869 Thomas Sadler published selections from Crabb Robinson, but the Wordsworth biographer owes much to Robinson's modern editor, Miss Edith

J. Morley, for her copious publications from his manuscripts.[1] It need hardly be pointed out that the active research of many scholars in other figures of the period has been of inestimable worth in writing the new biographies of Wordsworth.

The year 1896 is a milestone in the course of Wordsworthian criticism. In that year appeared Professor Émile Legouis' *La Jeunesse de William Wordsworth—1770–1798—Étude sur le "Prelude,"* the first scholarly biography and critical interpretation. In the following year an English translation was made by J. W. Matthews.[2] The work is monumental in the sense that it set the tone of Wordsworthian criticism until the present. Published fifty years ago, it still remains an extremely valuable book.

The Victorian conception of Wordsworth was based largely on *The Excursion* and Christopher Wordsworth's *Memoirs. The Prelude,* although published in 1850, had not been given the emphasis that it deserved. It was Legouis who saw its supreme value to an understanding of the poet, and his book is a close study of the poem against a background of the events of Wordsworth's life from 1770 to the publication of *Lyrical Ballads* in 1798. The result was surprising and exciting. The "Daddy Wordsworth" of the FitzGerald conception was metamorphosed into a passionate, restless, and unconventional young man, who passed from his peaceful childhood into the turbulence of the Revolution; who, returning to England, suffered a painful and dangerous moral crisis which required the exertion of his utmost strength to meet; but who emerged from the depths with a kindled mind and soul and the fully awakened powers of the poet.

This "early Wordsworth" has proved so attractive that biographers and critics have, until very recently, confined most of their attention to the period of the poet's life before 1815. In 1916 Harper's biography further emphasized these years, treating hurriedly the later period and conveying the impression of a sharp dichotomy between Wordsworth's early and his middle and late years. The notion of the "two Wordsworths" has been accepted by many scholars. In 1933 Miss Edith Batho challenged this view

[1] See especially *Correspondence of Crabb Robinson with the Wordsworth Circle,* 2 vols., Oxford, The Clarendon Press, 1927; and *Blake, Coleridge, Wordsworth, Lamb, etc. . . . from the Remains of Henry Crabb Robinson,* Manchester, The University Press, 1922.

[2] The French edition was issued in "Annales de l'Université de Lyon." The English translation, published by J. M. Dent & Sons Ltd., was reprinted, with Additional Appendix, in 1921 and 1932.

in her book *The Later Wordsworth,* and there has since been a tendency to merge the "two Wordsworths" into one personality, showing a consistent development from the early period into the middle and late years.

Legouis opens with an introduction, which first points out the pessimism and moral disorder of both liberals and conservatives in 1797–98. The French Republic had invaded Switzerland and "showed itself no less the ruthless aggressor than the monarchs who had formed a league for the spoilation of Poland."[3] It was this pessimism that Wordsworth wished to combat when he conceived the idea of his poem *The Recluse.* "The poet's object," writes Legouis, "is precisely that which every one seems ready to abandon as an idle dream; it is the recovery of happiness."[4] He wished to emphasize the true and lasting worth of those possessions which men had cast aside in their search for a dream ideal of man. Since he found in the child and the youth the essential instincts which determine the man, it was necessary first to present the course of his own development before he could give full voice to his optimistic philosophy. Thus came into being his autobiographical poem *The Prelude,* describing the "growth of a poet's mind," the influences that molded his being through calm and stress.

The first five chapters of Legouis' book are devoted to Wordsworth's childhood, youth, and education. He gives a detailed account of the literary background of the period and traces the effect on the young Wordsworth of the poetic style of the eighteenth-century descriptive poets. In concluding this section, Legouis remarks that Wordsworth, until his leaving Cambridge, had drawn from his own consciousness nothing for his poetry except the sensations he had felt in the presence of nature.

> His descriptions are already those of a master; his reflexions still those of a schoolboy. He expresses the thoughts of his generation rather than his own. . . . The shock needful to arouse him was at hand. During his stay in London Wordsworth's transformation began to take shape. It will be continued and extended in the course of the year which he is about to pass in France during the days of the revolution.[5]

Book II, dealing with the Revolution and Wordsworth's

[3] Legouis, *The Early Life of William Wordsworth,* London, J. M. Dent and Sons Ltd., New York, E. P. Dutton and Co., 1932, p. 2.

[4] *Ibid.,* 4.

[5] *Ibid.,* 160.

moral crisis, presented at the time of publication a new view. The account of the French sojourn is given in far greater detail than in earlier biographies. Following closely *The Prelude,* Legouis places the events in their chronological order—so far as possible—and supplements Wordsworth's story with a fuller account of the Revolution and the ferment of ideas to which it gave rise. Of special value is the section tracing the influence on Wordsworth of Beaupuy and the doctrine of the universal love of mankind.[6] He also gives a detailed treatment of the political conditions in England on Wordsworth's return; the conflict between the liberals, who saw in the Revolution the approaching millennium and advocated a republic for England, and the conservatives, who, like Burke and Bishop Watson, were alarmed and sought to suppress republican and revolutionary activity. He describes the plight of the liberals when war was declared between England and France in February, 1793, the wave of panic that drew many lukewarm humanitarians into the conservative camp, and the suppressive acts of Pitt and his government. Legouis emphasizes Wordsworth's republicanism in a full account of the latter's *Letter to Bishop Watson,* and he points to Wordsworth's faith in the Revolution even during the Terror.

Legouis was the first biographer to give a complete study of Wordsworth's moral crisis and recovery, covering the years 1793 to about 1796. His account of the poet's residence in France gave a new emphasis in the delineation of Wordsworth's life and character, but the analysis of the years following the return to England did even more service in exploding the popular Victorian conception of the "Sage of Rydal," serene and placid, whose calm had never been disturbed by perplexity and passion. The intensity of Wordsworth's disturbance during this period, as portrayed by Legouis, explains and gives credence to the "years that bring the philosophic mind." Legouis writes:

> The Revolution . . . convulsed the very depths of his thought, and almost destroyed the groundwork even of his moral being. The eleventh book of *The Prelude* gives a powerful description of the different phases of this profound disturbance. And since in that book Wordsworth has got beneath the exterior of the individual, and has succeeded in reaching the essential feelings which make up the common heart of all mankind, his biography becomes almost an inward history of his

[6] See also Bussière and Legouis, *Le Général Michel Beaupuy,* Paris, 1891.

generation. To learn how, in his case, manhood was developed out of early youth, is to learn how the nineteenth century was born from the eighteenth, so different, yet with so manifest a family likeness.[7]

Wordsworth, who had accepted the current eighteenth-century view of man as good by nature, was easily led to believe in the virtue of the Revolution. There was no struggle until his own country sought by war to suppress the young French Republic. Now he must face the bitter experience of a conflict between his beliefs and his patriotism; "the harmony which prevailed between his revolutionary ideas and his natural feelings became suddenly converted into discord."[8] In the conflict he lost the support of his confidence in France, fell prey to a desiccated rationalism that ran counter to his faith in natural instincts, severed those bonds of joy and love which had bound him to life, and finally gave up moral problems in despair. His recovery was brought about by a removal to a quiet countryside where he renewed his contact with simple and elementary principles of life, by the influence of his sister Dorothy and his friend Coleridge, and by the soundness of his own nature.

In *The Borderers* Legouis finds Wordsworth's repudiation of Godwinism. Embittered, Wordsworth came to mistrust his emotions, his intuitive humanitarianism, and turned to pure reason in the hope of finding stability. His play reflects the darkness of his mood, the questions which he could not answer.

> O wretched Human-kind! Until the mystery
> Of all this world is solved, well may we envy
> The worm, that, underneath a stone whose weight
> Would crush the lion's paw with mortal anguish,
> Doth lodge, and feed, and coil, and sleep, in safety.[9]

But the play expresses likewise Wordsworth's realization that rationalism of the Godwinian stamp makes inhuman monsters of us. It reflects something of Wordsworth's abhorrence of the rationalized killings in France in '93.

While at Racedown, as Wordsworth was recovering his early capacity for admiration and delight in nature, he was also returning to a simple love of humanity as he found it. Legouis

[7] *Op. cit.*, 253.
[8] *Ibid.*, 257.
[9] Quoted by Legouis, *ibid.*, 276.

points out how he learned to distrust hopes of sudden and universal change; how the phantom of the ideal man faded and gave place to interest in man as he is. "It would be an easy matter to follow up this subject, and to show how, by observation of the poor, Wordsworth restores one by one the feelings of which ideal man has been stripped by Godwin."[10] The simple life at Racedown, the realism combined with a sense of joy and beauty which he found in his sister, had gone far to restore him to his true self. "It was Coleridge who provided, or rather assisted him to find, the only thing still needful to make him the poet he finally became, namely, a philosophy."[11] When he removed to Alfoxden he was thrown daily into Coleridge's society. Despondent, and as yet not writing actively, Wordsworth needed the encouragement of Coleridge's admiration for his genius. He also needed something more than Dorothy could give him, the stimulus of Coleridge's teeming mind. When he left Alfoxden in 1798 he was cured of his sickness, and had written his great hymn of thanksgiving to nature, *Tintern Abbey*.

His self-identity, destroyed for a time by a crisis of despair, was restored. The link which was to connect his early years with those of his maturity was happiness; happiness formerly spontaneous, but now the result of conscious reflection; at first mere lightness of heart, but a settled optimism at last. The years of doubt and gloom had fled, leaving behind them merely a fruitful impression, a salutary warning. Those which preceded them, on the other hand, the years of his childhood and early youth, drew near again, until for him they became the present. He recognized that in them, unknown to himself, he had lived the true life; and if for a moment he had gone astray, he would now attempt to ascertain the direction of his first innocent footsteps, in order that he might set his feet once more upon the path which they had followed.[12]

It is thus that Legouis carries Wordsworth through his period of confusion and despair, following his return from France, to the high tableland of *Tintern Abbey* and the beginning of *The Prelude* where he had at last arrived in view of "The consecration, and the Poet's dream." In the remainder of the biography, under the caption "Harmony Restored," Legouis interprets the leading characteristics of the mature Wordsworth: his optimism, his re-

[10] *Ibid.*, 312.
[11] *Ibid.*, 319.
[12] *Ibid.*, 382.

lation to science, his realism, and his doctrine of the imagination and the senses—matters literary more than biographical.[13]

III

The standard biography, *William Wordsworth, His Life, Works and Influence,* appeared in 1916 and is the work of Professor George McLean Harper. The author states in the preface that he has "the deepest admiration" for Legouis' "perfect book," and was encouraged to write the biography on the assurance of Legouis that he himself did not intend to continue the work. And as Harper points out, *The Early Life of Wordsworth,* even for the period it covers, is more a critical essay than a biography. Harper's book has maintained its place as the standard biography because it is the most complete yet published, utilizing a mass of letters and journals not available earlier; because of the rich scholarship with which the author has reconstructed the period, indicating the social and cultural trends from which the poet's writings were derived, and introducing many people who either were associated with him or indirectly affected him; and finally because Harper has brought to his subject a devotion to Wordsworth which dates from "the sunny mornings of a happy childhood when my mother trained me to memorize Wordsworth's poems, and instilled into my heart a love for his name."[14] The interpretations have not all been acceptable to critics—there are some very fundamental points on which other scholars have differed—but Harper's picture of Wordsworth, at least the Wordsworth before 1815, is unsurpassed in warmth of portrayal and in essential truthfulness to the subject.

The first volume extends through the year 1801. It will be noted at once the emphasis Harper has given to the early Wordsworth. He states unequivocally that in his early and best period Wordsworth was the fine flower of the culture of the Enlighten-

[13] Two studies, following Legouis' at the turn of the century, are of interest. Mention has been made of Leslie Stephen's "Wordsworth's Youth," evoked by Legouis' book. Stephen is inclined to lessen somewhat the radicalism of Wordsworth's sympathies with the French Revolution, and to indicate that there was no change in his principles when he broke with France. He renounced the Revolution and radical theories because they came to represent not humanitarianism but the system of the economists of the new industrial era. Likewise, in 1898, appeared William Hale White's book, *An Examination of the Charge of Apostasy against Wordsworth,* London, Longmans, Green and Co. White maintained that to the very last Wordsworth was true to his principles—an early statement of Batho's view.

[14] *William Wordsworth, His Life, Works, and Influence,* 2 vols., London, John Murray, New York, Charles Scribner's Sons, 1916, I, ix.

ment, but as the nineteenth century moved forward into Romanticism, he developed a mystical and irrational philosophy which was somewhat out of line with his early devotion to nature and reason. Referring to the fundamental cultures, Harper says:

of two eternally opposed and equally unconquerable kinds of thought, one, represented by Locke and Hume and Godwin, enjoyed, towards the close of the eighteenth century, a degree of general acceptance which until lately it has not enjoyed since; while the other kind, eloquently preached by Burke and Carlyle, and always more openly, more officially, more popularly held, has been for a much longer time dominant.[15]

Wordsworth was a product of the Age of Reason and a prophet of the new age of science, rather than a Romanticist.

Originally and characteristically he was nothing of the sort [a Romanticist]. When he was most himself, he found sufficient inspiration in the natural world. Romanticism looked to the past, to the supernatural, to the extraordinary. Wordsworth, the true Wordsworth, dwelt in the present, felt that nature was herself divine, and strove, with the zeal of a controversialist, and at considerable risk, to show that the ordinary is as wonderful and instructive as the exceptional.

It is in this sense that he was peculiarly the prophet of an age of science. What biologists and chemists have done to reveal the wonders of the physical world, he did, in a measure, for the relations between man's mind and the objects upon which the mind plays. . . . Nothing, he thought, was unworthy of regard. . . . This state of mind in Wordsworth was a result of his conversion to the equalitarian creed of the French Revolution.[16]

Harper, unlike Legouis, gives little emphasis to Wordsworth's moral crisis following his return from France. Nor does he regard Wordsworth's active political interest in the Revolution as visionary. Beaupuy, he says, "turned the young man's vague idealism into firm principle."[17] Even more than Legouis, Harper writes sympathetically of the English radicals, Paine, Thelwall, Fawcett, Price, and Priestley, giving an account not only of the liberal movement in England, but also of the Revolutionary clubs at Blois which Wordsworth attended. The influence of Godwin on Wordsworth has generally been regarded as the height of his moral crisis. Legouis depicts Godwinian influence as something

[15] *Ibid.*, I, 254.
[16] *Ibid.*, I, 12–13.
[17] *Ibid.*, I, 162.

of a disease. Harper is the first critic of Wordsworth to attempt to do justice to the inspiration which Godwin exerted, not only on Wordsworth, but on all the young liberal thinkers of the day. His defense of *Political Justice* is one of the most notable things in his book.[18] He writes:

I am acquainted with no account of Wordsworth's life that does justice to the strength and attractiveness of the philosophy upon which he disciplined his powerful reasoning faculties, and to which he gave a brave and stubborn allegiance from his twenty-third to his twenty-ninth year. When one considers how, in the lives of nearly all poets, the third decade stands pre-eminent as a formative and productive period, it seems impossible to exaggerate the value of Godwin's ideas to Wordsworth. And Wordsworth is admitted to be a great philosophical poet. Yet all his biographers have termed Godwin's system "preposterous." Wordsworth, even when he renounced it, fully appreciated its compulsive appeal. And for at least three or four years it claimed both his intellectual assent and his active support.[19]

Some of the effects of Godwin's philosophy on Wordsworth are thus stated:

Wordsworth, one of the first, as he was the greatest of its converts, adhered to the Godwinian system for six years. He met the passion of the hour with his own deep inward passion. He conquered love of country with love of mankind. He rebuked with a reasoned hatred of war the elemental instincts of a people in arms. For six years his tenacious and inwardly energetic nature held fast its own religion. . . . He was unable or unwilling, before Coleridge furnished him with a more supple dialectic than his own, to take advantage of the obvious defects of Godwinism, its inattention to human history, its blindness to the natural world, its indifference to the many irrational cravings of mankind. It is significant that both Goethe and Wordsworth, the greatest poets who crossed the threshold of the nineteenth century, were for a time votaries in the temple of rationalism, a temple nobly bare and generously open whether for entrance or egress, and that neither of them could compel himself to remain.[20]

It was when Wordsworth was forced into the mold of the nineteenth century that he changed. Politically, it was the undis-

[18] The poet's latest biographer, George W. Meyer, likewise defends Godwin and points to some beneficial influences of the philosopher upon Wordsworth (*Wordsworth's Formative Years,* "University of Michigan Publications Language and Literature," XX, Ann Arbor, University of Michigan Press, 1943. See pp. 174 ff.). He also feels that Wordsworth's "moral crisis" has been much exaggerated.

[19] Harper, *op. cit.,* I, 253.

[20] *Ibid.,* I, 260.

guised tyranny of Napoleon and his threat to destroy the independent existence of England that impelled him to accord with the war with France.

We shall see that then the conflict of opposed sympathies in Wordsworth's mind was stilled; his duty stood out plain. A great epoch of his life came to an end. Although he continued to be a poet of political ideas, a poet of national and large social interests, the impulse of his thought was to flow henceforth from a different direction. For him the early nineteenth century, with its reactions, its panics, its distrust in rationalism, its backward-looking to the Middle Ages, its checking of the high-hearted Renaissance, began during the ominous pause that followed the treaty of Amiens, when *"ce siècle avait deux ans."* It was in a sense the negative side he went over to, the timid Tory side. Perhaps that was a more satisfactory choice than if he had thrown himself into the current of what was then deemed the progressive movement, the middle-class industrial movement, in which the clear and unimpaired strain of Revolutionary philosophy was scarcely to be recognized.[21]

In philosophy, the change is apparent in the last three books of *The Prelude*. The triumph recorded there of the Imagination, hailed by the poet (and his biographers, including Legouis, Garrod, and Herford) as the recovery from his moral crisis, is regarded by Harper as the beginning of the loss of his boldness and vitality, dimmed by the protecting mists of Romantic transcendentalism.

He insists on the superiority of the "living mind" to all external things, and glorifies Imagination as a power which can work with nature and even constrain her. By thus exalting the mind of man above "the frame of things" as having an existence independent of nature, he places himself among the Transcendental philosophers.[22]

This change becomes more evident in succeeding poems.

Wordsworth was travelling with Coleridge, with German philosophy, with his age. He was reacting against the great positive, naturalistic movement of the preceding century. He was breaking with his own past, abandoning his own faith.[23]

The consequences of his rejection of the naturalism of the Enlightment for the nineteenth-century mysticism of Coleridge and, in a measure, of Carlyle are thus stated:

[21] *Ibid.*, II, 10.
[22] *Ibid.*, II, 147–48.
[23] *Ibid.*, II, 148.

> Whether or not we regret that he left vacant the priesthood which had once been his, and which Shelley was to accept later, we must acknowledge that there was more loss than gain for poetry. "The Prelude" relates only the beginning of the change. One is left to infer, on finishing its perusal, that the poet, having lost joy, the vital principle of poetic creation, has at length recovered it, and thus passed safely through the only danger to which his genius was liable. But the recovery of joy was followed by complacency, and this by self-consciousness, and this again by timidity.[24]

To recapitulate Harper's account of the first thirty-five years of the poet's life: he gives a full study of the French Revolution and the liberal movement in England, influences which he regards as the most powerful that affected Wordsworth; he sees Wordsworth's dominant vision to be one of passionate joy in the proclamation of the divinity in nature, a philosophy arising from the Age of Enlightenment rather than from the transcendental tendency of the Romantic Movement; and he discovers as early as 1805 an inclination to substitute nineteenth-century Romanticism for realism and a rational outlook, an attitude that grew with the century (nor was it confined to Wordsworth) and later became a frantic reaction from the inevitable growth of science and social philosophy.

This central interpretation has been denied by some critics or regarded as overstated. It at least presents one very large aspect of Wordsworth. But whether this interpretation is fully accepted or not, the essential value of Harper's book remains. It is primarily a biography, and Harper has presented a full, accurate, and sympathetic narrative. Likewise, his interpretations of many of Wordsworth's poems are judicious, and show the discriminating criticism of a long and intimate study of the poet.

Before leaving the subject of Harper's biography, brief mention should be made of his account of Wordsworth's liaison with Annette Vallon, a matter which had long been suppressed. The young man met the French woman while at Orléans and Blois, fell in love with her, and intended to bring her to England as his wife. She gave birth to their daughter Caroline before he left France at the end of 1792. War was declared in February, 1793, and this, together with Wordsworth's unsettled circumstances, prevented the marriage. Although it appears that he

[24] *Ibid.*, II, 149.

attempted a journey to France in the autumn of 1793, there is no certain evidence that he saw Annette again until his brief visit to Calais during the Peace of Amiens in 1802. By this time any notion of marriage seems to have been mutually abandoned, and Wordsworth married Mary Hutchinson the same year. Some correspondence took place between William and Dorothy, and Annette in 1793, when Dorothy expected to welcome her new sister to England; and after 1802 the Wordsworths paid one or two visits to Annette and Caroline when they were on the Continent, and a friendly relationship continued to exist until Wordsworth's death. The affair explains some of Wordsworth's misery in 1793–95, throws possible light on some of his poems, and above all puts beyond doubt the reality of his attachment to France. Much more has been made of it, as we shall see, by some of his later biographers.[25]

IV

Another view of Wordsworth's political beliefs is set forth in A. V. Dicey's *The Statesmanship of Wordsworth,* which was published in 1917. While not a biography, it deals directly with the subject that is pivotal in interpreting the stages of Wordsworth's life. Appearing one year after Harper's work, it is in a measure a challenge to Harper's stand. It is the fullest explanation yet written of Wordsworth's nationalism and views on government from 1802 to 1815, the period of the great political sonnets and *The Convention of Cintra,* when he was under the influence more of Burke than of Godwin and the Revolutionary liberals. While recognizing something of the radicalism of the early years, Dicey believes that Wordsworth at heart remained the same through life. There is no reason, he asserts, to believe that his sympathies with the Girondists ever died. He possessed a natural republicanism, heightened by his Girondist sympathies in France; but the unsound political philosophy of the Revolution, which he for a time had accepted, was soon tempered by Burke so that he came to distrust abstract liberalism. But Wordsworth remained to the end a "revolutionist," even under his apparent conservatism.

But the burden of Dicey's book is the period before Words-

[25] For an account of the discovery of this episode in Wordsworth's life and for fuller details than Harper gives in his biography, see his little book, *Wordsworth's French Daughter,* Princeton, N. J., Princeton University Press, 1921; and Émile Legouis, *William Wordsworth and Annette Vallon,* London, J. M. Dent & Sons Ltd., 1922.

worth's conservative opinions became strongly evident. With great clarity and penetration he analyzes the doctrine of *The Convention of Cintra,* and supplements with apt quotations from the *Sonnets Dedicated to National Independence and Liberty.*

Wordsworth's political doctrine was one of nationalism.

> He was a nationalist who anticipated the nationalism of the Victorian era; he was assured that, on the one hand, the independence of England could be maintained only by asserting the national independence of other European States, and that, on the other hand, the independence of every other European country . . . would never be safe until England had succeeded in maintaining her own independence by the destruction of Bonaparte's Empire.[26]

Wordsworth, Dicey remarks, anticipated by more than twenty years the nationalism of Mazzini. His dogma, at the beginning of the nineteenth century, was novel and startling.

The principles of his nationalism are summed up as follows: (1) national independence is the necessary condition to freedom and progress; (2) it is to the interest of every independent nation to maintain the national independence of every other country; (3) no state ought to possess such irresistible military power that it will become a menace to the independence of other countries; (4) the French under Napoleon possess such dangerous power, which must be broken for the safety of all; (5) it is desirable to create a new balance of power to guarantee the independence of each separate state, and to remodel Europe on the basis of linguistic boundaries.

It will be noted that Wordsworth's nationalism was by no means the same as his early republicanism. He was not interested in establishing a popular government in the states of Europe; the end of his policy was simply to restrain conquests. He believed that every state, if not molested by foreign tyrants, could best set up its own form of government and in the long run be free of domestic oppression. Wordsworth's poetic powers were in full vigor at the time he wrote the political *Sonnets* and *The Convention of Cintra,* and Dicey's explanation of his politics is an essential study in rounding out this period. As the *Letter to Bishop Watson* and *The Prelude* are the most complete expressions of Wordsworth's republicanism, so *The Convention of*

[26] A. V. Dicey, *The Statesmanship of Wordsworth,* Oxford, The Clarendon Press, 1917, p. 76.

Cintra and the political *Sonnets* set forth his settled views of nationalism. This change in emphasis cannot be overlooked by the biographer. Dicey's study points ahead to the emphasis placed by Professor Garrod, not on Wordsworth's Revolutionary crisis, but on the strength of his reaction to its failure; to Professor Herford's opinion that his greatest political utterances were written between 1802 and 1807; and especially to Miss Batho's important re-examination of the later Wordsworth.

In 1923 appeared H. W. Garrod's *Wordsworth,* an important critical study containing material that throws light on the interpretation of the biography. Garrod remarks that Harper has done service in killing a false conception of Wordsworth, but the book goes too far in assuming that only the republican Wordsworth matters.

> We have been too long and too much in the habit of regarding Wordsworth as belonging wholly and essentially to the order of sabbatical men, too prone to 'fancy that the mighty deep was even the gentlest of all gentle things.' We have associated him too exclusively with that 'harmony' and that 'deep power of joy' which belongs to his supreme period. It is salutary to be reminded that this sabbatical calm was not a talent, but a conquest. Behind it is conflict.[27]

But at this point Garrod differs from Harper. "The real man," he says, "is seen, not in the conflict, but in the issue of the conflict."[28] The triumph was in the glorious period from 1798 to 1807.

Like Legouis, Garrod regards Wordsworth's adherence to the French Revolution and to Godwinism as a preparation for his golden decade of composition. The great writing did not come until he had rubbed off the sharp edges of both these influences.

Garrod's chief contribution to the biography is first his endeavor to set the date of Wordsworth's Godwinian period: from the spring of 1793 to the summer of 1795, an epoch of semi-Godwinism; and from July, 1795, to the composition of *Lyrical Ballads* sometime in 1797, a period of fuller Godwinian influence. Second, Garrod has presented valuable evidence and speculation toward a reconstruction of the confused chronology of the events in Wordsworth's life in 1793.

In 1930 appeared C. H. Herford's *Wordsworth,* the best of

[27] Second ed., Oxford, The Clarendon Press, 1927, p. 22.
[28] *Ibid.,* 23.

the short biographies for the general reader. Aside from its discriminating comments and interpretations of Wordsworth's poems, it presents nothing new. Herford accepts the "commonplace of criticism" that little of interest can be said of Wordsworth after the appearance of *The Excursion,* and that the poems written after 1810 are "almost wholly unread and a full third of them generally unknown by name."[29] He therefore devotes only a few closing pages to the later years. Even if this period is less interesting, such scant treatment detracts from the value of the book as a complete biography. Briefly stated, Herford finds in Wordsworth when he is at his greatest "the mystic sense of absolute unity" in all things; and it is "the disintegration of this hold both upon the inner unity and upon the imaginative apprehension of the parts, which marks, on the psychological side, Wordsworth's poetic decline."[30]

In 1930 appeared another biographical study, the series of brilliant lectures delivered at Trinity College, Cambridge, by Professor Herbert Read.[31] This book and Hugh I'A. Fausset's *The Lost Leader* (1933) represent the most extreme view yet taken of Wordsworth's decline, or "fall," after about 1807. Both writers go much farther than Harper or Garrod or Herford in viewing the later Wordsworth as a self-defeated man. Read's thesis is thus clearly stated:

> There are two Wordsworths. There were two Wordsworths even during his life—a real Wordsworth and a legendary Wordsworth. It is the legendary Wordsworth that has persisted in the imagination of the public. In the obvious sense there was the Wordsworth of the poems published in 1807; there was the Wordsworth who lived for another forty-three years, forty-three long years devoid of poetic vitality, but filled with another activity which is that of the mind seeking compensations for its defunct emotions.[32]

Read draws the picture of the young Wordsworth, even before his residence in France, as a freethinker and a republican, but as yet without that passionate feeling for nature which in *The Prelude* he ascribes to his early years. The feeling for nature came as an aftermath of his bitter disappointment in the French Revolution. The portrait of the child and youth, as presented in

[29] London, G. Routledge and Sons Ltd., 1930, p. 190.
[30] *Ibid.,* 192.
[31] *Wordsworth,* London, Jonathan Cape, 1930.
[32] *Ibid.,* 15–16.

The Prelude, Read regards as pure idealization. But the key to Read's interpretation of Wordsworth is the poet's liaison with Annette Vallon. "Much else happened to him, as we shall see when we come to deal with the development of his opinions during this period. But nothing happened comparable in importance with his love affair."[33] A heavy burden of remorse descended upon him from the time of his forced separation from Annette in 1793, and he suffered deep mental stress until they agreed to part in 1802. Read regards *Guilt and Sorrow, The Borderers,* and *Margaret* as "projections of his confused state of mind—efforts, unconscious perhaps, to cast off the burden, to resolve the crisis in the objectivity of a work of art."[34] With the loss of his love for Annette came the breaking of his ties with France and the cooling of his zeal for republicanism. He buried his emotional loss under cover of his antagonism for France and what France had symbolized to him.

> Wordsworth was recovering his stability, finding his ideal self or personality, his philosophy of nature and his poetic genius; he was losing Annette, his faith in youth and change, his fundamental honesty.[35]

Read's series of lectures has fearlessly approached the problem of why Wordsworth's poetic powers came to so sudden a decline; and in his discussion of inhibitions and repressions he has introduced an interesting and possibly clarifying method from the science of modern psychology. But he assumes the major premise, with no certain evidence in support. It is far from certain that Wordsworth suppressed his emotions in the matter of Annette, or that he made any great effort to hide the affair until years later. Indeed, the evidence is to the contrary. Other critics, on very good grounds, have denied that the liaison was the most important thing that happened to him in his youth.

Fausset's book is also an analysis of the moral and spiritual causes of Wordsworth's breakdown as a poet by 1807. He states as follows the thesis of his biographical interpretation:

> Wordsworth, in short, was a potential mystic who failed to complete himself at a crucial point, failed to pass from the state of childhood and boyhood when the spiritual is inevitably a condition of the natural to a creative maturity when the natural should be as inevitably a condi-

[33] *Ibid.,* 96.
[34] *Ibid.,* 118.
[35] *Ibid.,* 134–35.

tion of the spiritual. Hence, when his natural forces began to decline, he not only ceased to grow imaginatively, but he began to die.[36]

The dilemma of Wordsworth, his failure to adjust the natural to the spiritual, Fausset regards as the failure of the nineteenth century, one which we today have inherited. Hence the importance in trying to understand Wordsworth's failure.

Fausset, with full biographical detail, carries the life of Wordsworth to the time of the publication of *The Excursion,* and like Read, concludes with a discussion of *Laodamia.* With profuse quotation from *The Prelude,* Fausset builds up a picture of Wordsworth as a "primitive" in "the state of nature." He was not yet conscious of *self,* and the "purely instinctive harmony of his being" was not yet disturbed. The "auxiliar light" referred to in *The Prelude* was a creative force, as instinctive as the singing of the birds, and marked the harmony of his being. With the "dawn of self," during his Cambridge years, he began to seek "the same active intimacy with the human universe as he had enjoyed and continued to enjoy with the natural."[37] His early association with shepherds and vagrants had begun this interest, but it was not until later, until he was fully conscious of *self,* that he began to enter deeply into the pain and struggle of humanity.

Wordsworth's residence in France, of course, brought these tendencies rapidly to full growth. But the French experience was to prove fatal. After the love affair with Annette Vallon, to which Fausset attributes as much importance as does Read, Wordsworth could never again trust his instincts. He fell into a "state of sin." For in France he had lost his integrity "and entered the path of compromise." But it is not his fall that Fausset deplores. It is his failure to achieve a new harmony between *selflessness* and *self,* and between nature and the spirit. Instead of completely humbling himself he developed his strong individualism into a deep-seated pride, which took the form (in the phrase of Keats) of the "egotistical sublime" in his poetry, and which eventually hardened into the arrogant and provincial morality of his later years.

Read's interpretation of Wordsworth's life is a psychological one. Fausset, using a great deal more of the factual apparatus

[36] *The Lost Leader,* London, Jonathan Cape, New York, Harcourt Brace and Co., 1933, p. 8.
[37] *Ibid.,* 70.

of the biographer, has given an almost completely spiritual cast to his subject. Both are special pleaders, bringing to their task a mode of thought which they deem fits their subject. In justice, it must be remembered that their interest is not to write a general biography, but to explain the cause of Wordsworth's "disease" and decline. The one finds the answer in Wordsworth's psychological frustration due to restraints and inhibitions. The other finds the poet's defeat in his failure to purify himself, and to rise to the plane of the true mystic.

V

A new turn in Wordsworthian criticism came in 1933 with the publication of *The Later Wordsworth* by Edith C. Batho. The book takes sharp issue with previous biographies, especially Harper's for imputing to Wordsworth a retreat from a bold and liberal outlook to obscurantism and political timidity.[38] The work is a biography only in the sense that it re-examines the data pertaining to Wordsworth's later years. A new evaluation of the last thirty-five years of Wordsworth's life is certainly of prime importance, and the credit goes to Miss Batho for launching the first considerable defense of this despised period.

The first chapter, by citing the testimony of many witnesses, discredits the opinion that Wordsworth in late life was a man whose mind was closed, who was arrogant towards the new generation of writers, and who, surrounded by picturesque scenery and domestic worship, refused to entertain progressive or disturbing ideas.

> When all this is considered, it would appear . . . that he was a man of strong passions and feelings, strong and vigorous intellect, clear and independent thought and judgment in life, letters and politics, in the last as in the first half of his life. He mellowed, as good men of strong character do . . . but he did not weaken, nor did he become rigid in mind and thought.[39]

The second chapter gives a thorough examination of Wordsworth's political views. Wordsworth, Miss Batho points out, did not lose his faith in humanity, but he felt that the people should be trained for freedom.

[38] Even stronger is Miss Batho's brief but devastating attack on the "amateur psycho-analysts" who recently have written on him.

[39] *The Later Wordsworth,* Cambridge, Cambridge University Press, New York, The Macmillan Co., 1933, p. 117.

He refused to subscribe to the sentimental creed which takes no account of the actual state of humanity; he refused to believe against all his experience that "the people," as long as they remained untrained and unthinking, were fit to rule themselves; but he was convinced that they were capable of being trained; and his fears were, not that anarchy or tyranny would ultimately triumph, but that impatience on the part of the lovers of freedom would delay the triumph of freedom longer than need be.[40]

Thus it may be said that "Wordsworth's views on political conditions in England itself were those of an idealist with a strong sense of reality and of history."[41] He acted on two principles from which he did not deviate: (1) all political reforms must avoid the danger of anarchy, reaction, and the repetition of the struggle for liberty; (2) and even more fundamental, unity within the country must be maintained.

In his zeal for national unity he hated class conflicts, and, "apart from names, he was upholding the ideals of his youth, Liberty and Fraternity, and even Equality, since that is endangered by class warfare more than by any other foe."[42] From his love of national unity stems one of the most important of his political beliefs—his staunch advocacy of the Established Church and his hostility to any movement that might weaken it. He believed a close alliance between the State and religion was necessary to social unity, and he argued that "to be effective, this alliance could exist between only one form of religion and the State."[43] Anything, therefore, that weakened the temporal power of the Church of England, or any substitution of other spiritual authorities "was an attack upon the whole life of the country, upon the unity which it should be the part of every Englishman to maintain. Hence his opposition to Catholic Emancipation on the one hand, and to concessions to the Nonconformists on the other. Both kinds of relief tended to introduce a confusion of authorities and interests, both in Parliament and in the nation at large."[44] National unity, Wordsworth believed, was likewise fostered by the aristocracy. The manufacturing interests, which constituted so large a part of the Whig following, were destroying the constitution of England and its ancient ideals. The landed gentry, the

[40] *Ibid.*, 148–49.
[41] *Ibid.*, 153.
[42] *Ibid.*, 211.
[43] *Ibid.*, 161.
[44] *Ibid.*, 161.

enemies to greedy industrialists, must preserve the lower classes from unwittingly becoming victims of the changes that were undermining the character of Great Britain. Thus Wordsworth's objections to the so-called enlightened reforms were rooted in his desire to preserve humanity from the rapidly increasing evils of a commercial civilization. This in no way indicates a change of principles from his early years.

The strongest evidence that Miss Batho presents of Wordsworth's continued liberal political views is the *Postscript* of 1835, "Of Legislation for the Poor, the Working Classes, and the Clergy." In this essay Wordsworth advocates state support for those unable to obtain work or sufficient wages. He argues that man, even as a member of a social order, does not forfeit his fundamental right of self-preservation, and if denied the means of subsistence, he can *take* what he requires providing he can do so without injuring others. Although Wordsworth deplores trade unions, he advocates joint-stock companies so that workers might invest their savings in the industries in which they are employed, and thereby enjoy some of the benefits of capital.

Miss Batho concludes that Wordsworth in his later years retained his enthusiasm for liberty and humanity, kept an open mind on political affairs, and while his distrust of the Whigs drove him closer to the Tories than he otherwise would have gone, was never a party advocate. He might be called a "Revolutionary Tory."

Too much stress has usually been laid on his Toryism, except in his early days, when it is overlooked, and too little on the revolutionary elements in that Toryism. Moreover, few of his critics have realized the close connection between certain kinds of Toryism and more than one kind of Radicalism, particularly in the later years of Wordsworth's life.[45]

Passing from the subject of Wordsworth's politics to his religion, Miss Batho points out that his early training was in the tradition of the High Church. To Wordsworth,

the Bible was more familiar than any other book, and next to it came the Prayer Book and the works of the great Anglican divines. . . . He was brought up on the Church Catechism. . . . And there is something Wordsworthian in its very beginning, with its revelation of the mysteries that lie hidden in the apparently ordinary.[46]

[45] *Ibid.*, 226.
[46] *Ibid.*, 242.

Reared under this churchly influence from boyhood, Wordsworth did not surrender to orthodoxy in the composition of the *Ecclesiastical Sonnets* or in his later reliance on the Established Church. His orthodoxy was a late expression of characteristics indigenous to his nature. Miss Batho attempts to demonstrate that his theology expressed in *Tintern Abbey* might be in the Anglican tradition, and shows the influence of Jeremy Taylor as much as that of Spinoza. American critics, she asserts, have not understood Wordsworth because they have not been brought up in the Anglican faith. Anglican orthodoxy is not the narrow, intolerant thing that orthodoxy is in America. The orthodoxy of Wordsworth's late years was a natural outgrowth of the orthodoxy of his youth, and neither was confined to narrow, theological prescriptions. Wordsworth's mysticism, it is pointed out, deepened as he learned the lessons of self-discipline.

Finally, Miss Batho explains that Wordsworth's later poetry lessened in volume not because of failing or solidifying mental and emotional powers, but because of his serious eye disease to which she has given considerable study. She agrees that his great period begins about 1797 and extends to about 1815. Between 1789 and 1797, the period in which he might have been influenced by the French Revolution and his love for Annette Vallon, he wrote only bad poetry that is rarely read for its own sake. She likewise makes a defense of his poetry written after 1815. It "contains much that is good, some that is magnificent, and little that is positively bad."[47]

To conclude, Miss Batho reasserts that Wordsworth was neither a Whig nor an orthodox Liberal. He maintained an "unconquerable mind" to the end of his life, showing power and insight as a political thinker. He attached himself to the church of his baptism for combined political and religious reasons, but without bigotry and intolerance. He wrote less poetry in his later years, not because of a moral or spiritual decline, but because of a physical affliction. This picture may appear less interesting than that of the "Lost Leader," but Miss Batho believes it to be the truer one.

By necessity her book contains much special pleading. The case of the contrast between the Wordsworth of the *Letter to Bishop Watson,* or of *Tintern Abbey,* or of many prevailing passages in *The Prelude,* and the writer of *Ecclesiastical Sonnets,* or of

[47] *Ibid.,* 315.

the *Sonnets on Capital Punishment,* or of many reactionary political utterances of the later letters, cannot be easily dismissed. But the book emphasizes aspects of the later Wordsworth which have been neglected. It places the demand on Wordsworth's biographers to consider much contradictory evidence concerning these later years, and to present and explain a more intricate psychological problem than the easy theory of the "two Wordsworths" recognized.

VI

Dean Willard L. Sperry's book, *Wordsworth's Anti-Climax* (1935), is a critical interpretation rather than a biography, but it should be noted here that, as the title indicates, he does not fully accept Miss Batho's views. "Attempts have been made," he writes, "to rehabilitate 'the later Wordsworth,' but they tax the ingenuity of their authors and the credulity of their public."[48] It is the opinion of Sperry that we can praise the work of the poet's last thirty or forty years only at the expense of the eight or ten years after 1797, and since we cannot have it both ways we had best trust the instinct which prefers the earlier work. But Sperry is in agreement with Miss Batho both in minimizing the inspiration of the French Revolution and the love of Annette as sources of Wordsworth's poetry, and in maintaining that Wordsworth changed not his political principles, but his political program. His decline was purely in poetic power, and came not from his severance from France and liberalism, nor from self-inhibition because he refused to face the moral crisis that developed from his liaison with Annette, nor indeed, as Garrod believes, because of his separation from Coleridge. The anticlimax in his poetry resulted from his restricted theory of art, from his limited subject matter which allowed no epic or dramatic themes, and from his habit of looking backward towards his past to the exclusion of present joys.

> I am persuaded, therefore, that Wordsworth's decline was a foredoomed conclusion to his life as a poet, given his technical premises and the restricted subjects which were his patrimony from the earlier years of simple sensations and ideas. . . . His capital was sunk in a concern which by its own articles of incorporation was destined to go bankrupt.[49]

[48] Cambridge, Mass., Harvard University Press, 1935, p. v.
[49] *Ibid.,* 142.

A recent biography, *William Wordsworth of Rydal Mount*[50] by Miss Frederika Beatty, is in a measure an expanded version of the first chapter of Miss Batho's *The Later Wordsworth,* except that Miss Beatty does not exclude the less flattering among her "Two or Three Witnesses." The book is a storehouse of citations and quotations from many sources which give the picture of Wordsworth and his varied circle of friends during the last ten years of his life. Many of the quotations are familiar ones, but the book draws together into one picture the variety and multitude of Wordsworth's friends, acquaintances, and admirers in the later years of his life.

In 1942 appeared a specialized study by Miss Mary Burton, significantly entitled *The One Wordsworth.*[51] It is an examination of Wordsworth's revisions of *The Prelude,* and arrives at different conclusions from those of de Selincourt in his variorum edition. Miss Burton finds that Wordsworth's emendations after 1805 show an advance in artistic power rather than a decline; give evidence that he grew more modest and humble rather than more egotistical; demonstrate that he made no vital changes in his religious philosophy, but rather related his pantheistic philosophy to his Christian beliefs; and reveal that he did not recant his political principles or seek to conceal his feelings about the French Revolution, but that he showed a better understanding of public affairs than in his early years and even strengthened his expressions of his love of liberty. Therefore, Miss Burton concludes: "Our examination of the changes the later Wordsworth made in *The Prelude* should serve to turn the tide of criticism farther in the direction indicated by Miss Batho, in 1933."[52]

These conclusions, in as far as they relate to the improvement of the style of the poem, are acceptable. De Selincourt has himself remarked that "Wordsworth retained his critical acumen far longer than his creative energy," although a portion of the revisions can be pointed out as examples of a deterioration in style. Miss Burton's conclusions regarding Wordsworth's way of thinking may appear more dubious. Her interpretation of some of the revisions does not wholly absolve Wordsworth from the charge of altering the tone of his earlier attitude, although he may not deliberately have substituted orthodoxy for heresy. But Miss

[50] London, J. M. Dent and Sons Ltd., 1939.
[51] Chapel Hill, University of North Carolina Press, 1942.
[52] *Ibid.*, 223.

Burton's examination throws doubt on de Selincourt's statement, regarding especially the last book, that it "leaves a totally different impression from that created by the earlier text." In all these studies of the revisions it must be borne in mind that what Wordsworth retained from the earlier text is no criterion of what he may have believed at the time of the revisions. It is not a case of apostasy. Even though his views might have altered as he grew older, he had the artistic honesty not to change fundamentally what he had, in the period covered by the poem, believed.

The most recent critical biography is by George W. Meyer, *Wordsworth's Formative Years,* published in 1943. This study offers some new and interesting interpretations. It seems to be built on the theory that Wordsworth from his earliest years experienced bitter injustice; that the period before 1798 represented no mere doctrinaire attitude toward social evil, but a very personal feeling toward wrong; and finally, that the poet achieved a synthesis of naturalism and moral philosophy represented by his poems of 1798. Meyer recounts the story of the severe injustice that the Wordsworth family received at the hands of the Earl of Lonsdale, who withheld payment of the considerable sum borrowed from the elder Wordsworth, thereby thwarting and pinching the lives of the children. He points also to Wordsworth's long frustrated desire for home and family. Thus, in Meyer's opinion, the poet in *The Prelude* idealized his youth. His environment was more complicated and worldly than the poem would indicate. All of these things are reflected in his early poetry—*An Evening Walk, Descriptive Sketches, Guilt and Sorrow*—and in his *Letter to Bishop Watson.* In *The Borderers* Meyer sees not a play of pessimism nor a disillusioned reaction from Godwinism. Rather, he states, its theme is the conflict between pride and benevolence, with the triumph of the latter. Meyer takes pains to show that Oswald is no true picture of Godwin's malicious doctrine. Indeed, in Godwin and Hartley, Wordsworth found the ideas of benevolence, goodness, and the higher virtues, which, combined with his naturalism, gave him his mature philosophy of 1798.

Thus, in Meyer's book, we have a return to the emphasis on the rebellious, unorthodox youth of the poet.

In reviewing the biographical studies since the time of Legouis, we see that, after the neglect by Bishop Wordsworth and

Knight of the unorthodox side of Wordsworth's life, the new biography gave such prominence to Wordsworth's youth and his daring that the record of his sober middle and late years seemed almost that of a different man. It was to be expected that a second reaction would occur, returning to an emphasis on the later years, but examining them more judiciously than Christopher Wordsworth and Knight had done, with an attempt to discover in the later Wordsworth a development consistent with his youth. These most recent investigations have not yet been fully established, and a new, revitalized life of the whole Wordsworth remains to be written.

CHAPTER SIX

WORDSWORTH'S PHILOSOPHY

I

How is Wordsworth's poetry interpreted by the modern scholar? In answer, there is available a wealth—one might almost say a wilderness—of studies; and it is the purpose of this chapter to extract those most typical of the leading trends.

There can be no doubt that an understanding of Wordsworth's philosophy is necessary to experience fully his poetry, Matthew Arnold to the contrary.[1] We need not claim for him a system of philosophy, but he is a philosophical poet, as Coleridge declared. He is not a poet of pure sensation; neither does his worth rest on simple observations regarding the physical and moral worlds; nor can he be understood in an exclusively spiritual light. But sensation is the beginning of his poetry, and it often ends in pronouncements regarding nature and morals and transcendental values. But these perceptions become distorted or meaningless if we disregard the interlinking chain of thought and emotion that completes the poetic expression of his philosophy.

Wordsworth values the senses because they supply the mind with the forms and objects of the world about us. Accurate observation through the senses is essential to the truthfulness of our perceptions. Coleridge called attention to Wordsworth's matter-of-factness, and while it sometimes betrayed him into prolixity, it was (at least in his earlier verse) a cardinal point in his theory of poetry. Wordsworth, writes Professor Havens, was "not a sentimentalist but a hard-headed, keen-eyed, matter-of-fact man, impatient of inaccuracy in observation or expression."[2] These accurate sense perceptions are not an end in themselves alone. They provoke our feelings, our pleasure or pain, our love or hate or fear. Finally, these primary perceptions and the emotions that cluster around them are transmuted into thought. Thought may

[1] For a recent discussion of this ancient feud, see J. Dover Wilson, *Leslie Stephen and Matthew Arnold as Critics of Wordsworth,* Cambridge, Cambridge University Press, 1939. Wilson defends Stephen's *Ethics of Wordsworth,* and is in opposition to Arnold's attempt to discredit the importance of Wordsworth as a philosopher.

[2] *The Mind of a Poet,* Baltimore, The Johns Hopkins Press, 1941, p. 6.

be long removed by time from the primary sense perceptions and emotions, and it may be (and in its most exalted form is) a complete re-creation, since the active principle in the mind modifies, combines, and transforms the impressions that it receives.

No one who has read the first two books of *The Prelude* can deny that sensation is of primary importance. Also, the well-known lines from *Tintern Abbey* state emphatically the poet's reliance on the functioning of the senses.

> Therefore am I still
> A lover of the meadows and the woods,
> And mountains; and of all that we behold
> From this green earth; of all the mighty world
> Of eye, and ear,—both what they half create,
> And what perceive; well pleased to recognise
> In nature and the language of the sense
> The anchor of my purest thoughts, the nurse,
> The guide, the guardian of my heart, and soul
> Of all my moral being.

In interpreting these lines, Harper remarks: "If we know nothing except what was originally revealed to us through our senses, then, he [Wordsworth] assumed, we have no use for a supernaturally revealed religion."[3] *To My Sister, Expostulation and Reply,* and *The Tables Turned,* for all the misunderstanding to which they have given rise, are simple assertions that we must respond to the sense impressions derived from the external world or all our reasoning may be false and artificial. These sense impressions are our direct contact with external reality, and when they are pleasant they convey to us the feeling of rightness, which in turn is a guiding light to our reasoning.

> Love, now a universal birth,
> From heart to heart is stealing,
> From earth to man, from man to earth;
> —It is the hour of feeling.

* * * *

> The eye—it cannot choose but see;
> We cannot bid the ear be still;
> Our bodies feel, where'er they be,
> Against or with our will.

[3] *Poems by William Wordsworth,* ed. G. M. Harper, New York, Charles Scribner's Sons, 1923, p. xviii.

Nor less I deem that there are Powers
Which of themselves our minds impress;
That we can feed this mind of ours
In a wise passiveness.

And in a moment of revulsion from pure intellectualism, and perhaps an overdose of Coleridge and Spinoza, he writes:

One impulse from a vernal wood
May teach you more of man,
Of moral evil and of good,
Than all the sages can.

Introducing these and similar utterances, Garrod says:

Wordsworth's poetry is essentially mystical. But whereas the mysticism of other men consists commonly in their effort to escape from the senses, the mysticism of Wordsworth is grounded and rooted, actually, *in* the senses. The natural world speaks, not to the intellect, but to that in us which is most 'natural,' viz. our senses.[4]

And Legouis remarks:

Every one of man's fundamental errors arises from the fact that he no longer simply *feels* nature, that he neither *sees* nor *hears* her, but that a rapid and almost irresistible act of his intelligence causes him immediately to reason upon what he feels, hears, and sees. Wordsworth believes himself to be a poet, because he, for his part, beholds the earth with the eyes of the first human being, as if he 'were her first-born birth, and none had lived before him.' He is a poet-philosopher because he has the 'inevitable' eye and ear. The senses are the only great metaphysicians; they alone, at certain moments, can grasp the central life of the world, the essence of truth.[5]

[4] *Wordsworth,* Oxford, The Clarendon Press, 1927, p. 105.

[5] *The Early Life of William Wordsworth, 1770–1798,* London, J. M. Dent and Sons Ltd., 1897, p. 451. A long controversy has arisen over these and related poems from *Lyrical Ballads.* In 1888 John Morley wrote: "When he tells us 'one impulse from a vernal wood [etc.]' such a proposition cannot be taken as more than a half-playful sally for the benefit of some too bookish friend. No impulse from a vernal wood can teach us anything at all of moral evil and of good." (Introduction, *The Complete Poetical Works of William Wordsworth,* London, Macmillan and Co., 1888.) This statement is challenged by Walter Raleigh, who accepts the seriousness of these poems (*Wordsworth,* London, Edward Arnold and Co., 1903, pp. 130–33). Lane Cooper implies that Wordsworth, in *Expostulation and Reply,* and in *The Tables Turned,* was speaking of transient moods, was "half-playful," and was speaking "in two imaginatively assumed voices" ("A Glance at Wordsworth's Reading," *MLN,* xxii [1907], 84). In like manner O. J. Campbell argues that these poems are not seriously philosophic, but are a dramatized bit of waggishness with the mad-cap Matthew ("Wordsworth Bandies Jests with Matthew," *MLN,* xxxvi [1921], 408–14). The interpretations of this paper are challenged by H. S. Pancoast ("Did Wordsworth Jest with Matthew?" *MLN,* xxxvii [1922], 279–83). For good comments on the poems, see Herford, *Wordsworth,* London, G. Routledge and Sons Ltd., 1930, pp. 103–6; Gingerich, *Essays in the Romantic Poets,* New York, Macmillan and Co., 1924, pp. 110–14; and Beach, *The Concept of Nature in Nineteenth-Century English Poetry,* New York, Macmillan and Co., 1936, pp. 135–40.

"Pure organic pleasure," the purely sensory, is closely associated with feeling or emotion, as these poems testify. "It is the hour of feeling," says Wordsworth. Under the influence of the mild early spring day a genial love permeates and unites man and earth. Our emotions can also have a profounder influence. In *Tintern Abbey* he says that our "affections" (by which he means our feelings of pleasure or pain) gently lead us on until we forget the body and finite matter and "see into the life of things." Other feelings, equally salutary, may also be aroused. Everyone remembers the boat-stealing episode in Book I of *The Prelude,* and how deep was the effect of fear upon the boy. It took intense terror to unsettle the base nature of Peter Bell.[6] The sheer delight of intense feeling is described in *Tintern Abbey* in the period characterized by the "aching joys" and "dizzy raptures" derived from the forms, colors, and sounds of nature:

> An appetite; a feeling and a love,
> That had no need of a remoter charm,
> By thought supplied, nor any interest
> Unborrowed from the eye.

In the words of Havens, "he attached great importance to the emotions, regarding them as our chief dynamic, our guide, as well as the source of much of our joy, and recognizing that they profoundly affect our thinking."[7] Likewise, "Thus passion is the link which connects the sensible world with the imagination and makes possible their action upon each other."[8]

Thus, from pure sensory experience man moves through the affections to his highest achievement, the immeasurable reaches of the imagination and the consciousness of the unity of man, of nature, and of the spiritual world. Garrod explains this process:

> The imaginative faculty is that faculty which, by binding the things of sense to the moral affections, transmutes them, makes them a part of poetry—whether the poetry of books or of life—and, in so doing, links us with the things in the world which are permanent, and assures us of immortality. The vision of the senses melts and dissolves, but it melts into the revelation of permanent supersensual realities. The fashion of the world passes away; but it fades before a mind conscious of an order of things fashioned immortally.[9]

[6] For a discussion of the function of fear, see Havens, *op. cit.,* Chap. III, "The Ministry of Fear."

[7] *Ibid.,* 31.

[8] *Ibid.,* 34.

[9] Garrod, *op. cit.,* 129–30.

Wordsworth says (*The Prelude,* XIV, 190–92) the imagination

> Is but another name for absolute power
> And clearest insight, amplitude of mind,
> And Reason in her most exalted mood.

Whether the imagination be identified with the mystical experience, or whether it be the complete and final accord of all man's faculties of perception, it is a great deal more than simple sense experience, or mere feeling, or pure rationalism. Havens remarks that Wordsworth's "anti-rationalism" is apparent from his reliance on fear, loneliness, solitude, and other states provocative of feeling. His deepest interest was transcendental. He sought to reach the *Binnenleben* (as explained by William James), "these stores of power and wisdom hidden in the depths of the subconscious."[10]

> This two-fold truth, the one interior life that lives in all things and the hiding-places of power, is, ultimately, the subject of the greater part of Wordsworth's more thoughtful poetry. Nature, the immediate subject of much of his verse, is connected with the more fundamental topic through nature's being a chief means of entering into communion with the One and of discovering and drawing upon the sources of power. It is not itself primarily a source of power but a means of reaching such a source. So with the imagination, which is the subject of *The Prelude*: it is important not merely because it is the life of poetry but because through it we commune with the One and become conscious of all nature as permeated by the One, because spiritual love cannot exist without it, and because through it alone we enter into the hiding-places of power.[11]

This framework of being, which we have seen in brief review, Wordsworth had fully accepted at a date not later than 1798. He retained it when he wrote *The Prelude,* which is indeed an elaborate explanation of this process of life, leading towards man's goal of joy and love. Later, in *The Excursion,* the same pattern is visible, but with a much stronger emphasis on ethical and religious objectives, some of which were not present in the earlier statements of the philosophy.

II

Recent scholarship has exhibited a basic disagreement in the interpretation of Wordsworth's philosophy. There are those who

[10] Havens, *op. cit.,* 3.
[11] *Ibid.,* 4.

see Wordsworth as essentially a rational thinker, one whose chief tenets rest on a naturalistic interpretation of phenomena. No one maintains that his rational philosophy is pure intellectualism or that he is a materialist. But they find in him a great preponderance of the philosophy of the eighteenth-century Enlightenment, and little identification between his spiritual tenets and the transcendentalism of the Romantic period. On the other hand, there are critics who feel strongly the mystical element in Wordsworth, who regard his suprasensuous philosophy as predominant over his naturalism, and who recognize in him some of the tendencies of Spinoza and Kant. These two views need not be mutually exclusive. In fact Wordsworth in some of his poetry emphasizes naturalism, although at the same time he unhesitatingly recognizes spiritual reality. At other times, he seeks to unite naturalism with transcendentalism, and the latter receives the greater emphasis. The extreme complexity of Wordsworth arises from these causes: (1) in his earlier period he was more boldly naturalistic, but his attitude shifted and he became more markedly spiritual; (2) he attempted to unite the naturalistic with the transcendental; and (3) he embodied elements of both the eighteenth-century sensational school of philosophy, and the mystical and suprasensuous thought of the Neoplatonists and of the German transcendentalists.

The strongest advocate of the rational basis of Wordsworth's thought is Professor Arthur Beatty. He is the first critic to give a full and scholarly explanation of Wordsworth's "three ages"—sensation, feeling, and thought—and to investigate the relationship between his philosophical poetry and the sensational philosophy of David Hartley, and to a lesser degree of Locke and other seventeenth- and eighteenth-century philosophers. His book, *William Wordsworth. His Doctrine and Art in Their Historical Relations,*[12] which appeared first in 1922, is a painstaking piece of research, long demanded for a scholarly understanding of Wordsworth, and outmeasures any other study of the philosophic backgrounds of Wordsworth's poetry. Beatty's interpretations have perhaps been pushed too far and have been challenged by other critics, but the book remains in the first rank of Wordsworthian criticism because it points out with clarity and fullness many of

[12] "University of Wisconsin Studies in Language and Literature," No. 17, Madison, University of Wisconsin Press, 1922; 2nd ed. revised, No. 24, 1927.

the essentials of Wordsworth's philosophy, and presents the intellectual soil from which his ideas grew.

Beatty believes that the theory of the three ages of man is fundamental in Wordsworth's philosophy and art, and he points out its presence in *Tintern Abbey, The Prelude, Ode on Intimations of Immortality, The Excursion, The Convention of Cintra, Letter to "Mathetes,"* and elsewhere.[13] He makes the following claim for the importance of the doctrine.

> Thus we see that from 1797–8 to 1820 Wordsworth made habitual use of the doctrine of the three ages of man in dealing with all the important problems of his life and art. We have specially noted with regard to this doctrine of the three ages that it is a real doctrine and not a mere external manner of classifying his experiences, for it is to be marked, (1) that each of the ages is regarded as being distinct the one from the other . . . (2) that the ages are causally related the one to the other; and (3) that they represent the manner in which every normal mind develops.[14]

This scheme of being is first set forth in *Tintern Abbey*. Childhood is the age of sensation; youth is the age of feeling; and the after years, or maturity, are the age of thought.

> Thus each age has its own integrity and at the same time the earlier is essential to the development of the later. In the light of this philosophy the poet found comfort for the loss of the immediate joy of boyhood and youth; for, in accordance with his theory, it is the general law of life that the vividness of sensation and feeling should die away with the coming of maturity, and it is equally the law of life that thought, intellect, the philosophic mind, which are the compensations of maturity, should be attained only in the last stage of development.[15]

All of this is based on the system of David Hartley (*Observations on Man,* 1749), which Wordsworth embraced in his reaction from Godwin.[16] Beatty denies that Wordsworth was a slave to Hartley's system, or that it explains the whole of his poetry. But he found in Hartley's philosophy a completeness of method, a common-sense foundation, and a deep spiritual enthusiasm.

[13] See *Ibid.,* 75, n. 14 for a list of the specific places where Wordsworth mentions this doctrine.

[14] *Ibid.,* 96.

[15] *Ibid.,* 74.

[16] G. W. Meyer believes that "Godwin sent Wordsworth to the original Hartley, and that Hartley, with his quasi-scientific grounds for optimism, sent Wordsworth enthusiastically back to Godwin's arguments for disinterested benevolence." (*Wordsworth's Formative Years,* "University of Michigan Publications Language and Literature," XX, Ann Arbor, University of Michigan Press, 1943, 239n.)

Thus a rational basis was offered him for all his fondest hopes; and a method was furnished him by which he could satisfactorily account for many facts in his own experience which were inexplicable by the systems of thought to which he had hitherto given his allegiance.[17]

The extensiveness of the Hartleian influence is indicated by the following summary:

. . . Wordsworth accepted Hartley's theory as regards (1) the operation of association, (2) the origin of all knowledge in experience, (3) the secondary and derivative nature of emotion, (4) optimism, (5) necessitarianism, (6) individualism, (7) the nature of virtue, (8) the end of man as happiness, and (9) the three stages by which the mind develops.[18]

The theory of associationism, basic to most of the principles named above, had the strongest effect upon Wordsworth. This system, which Hartley founded on the philosophy of Locke, banishes all innate ideas, and affirms that all mental states are ultimately derived from sensation. Some of the principles of Hartley's theory are thus summarized by Beatty:

Thus we have a hierarchy of mental complexes:

(1) Sensations, which arise from impressions from external objects.

(2) Simple ideas of sensation; or 'sensible' ideas; that is, ideas surviving sensations after the objects which caused them have been removed. This is the mind's first step in the 'purer' forms of thought, but such ideas are closely allied to sensations, and are hardly distinguishable from them. It is to be noted that from them arise all the other ideas—'the elements out of which they are compounded.'

(3) Complex ideas; that is, intellectual ideas, compounded from the simpler ideas under the power of association.

But Hartley does not look upon man as a mere machine for registering the impressions of external nature. There is from the very earliest and simplest sensation an activity or motion of the human soul, or spirit, which transmutes these experiences into their appropriate personal values, which are classified under the heads of *pleasure* and *pain*.[19]

There follows the classification, ranging from pure sensation to benevolence, theopathy, and the moral sense.

It will be seen at a glance that this schema resembles Wordsworth's principle of the three ages: the age of "pure organic

[17] Beatty, *op. cit.*, 109.
[18] *Ibid.*, 124.
[19] *Ibid.*, 110.

pleasure" and the prime importance of sensation direct from nature; the age of feeling, the ecstasy of pleasure and pain derived from contact with the objects that have peopled the mind with their images; the attainment of the intellectual plane, "the years that bring the philosophic mind," when all is transmuted from flesh and sensation into the highest reaches of man's mind and spirit. This chain of being appears again and again in Wordsworth's poetry.

In Beatty's chapter on Wordsworth's doctrine of nature he gives little of the religion of nature, little of the spiritual. He sees in this aspect of the poet's thought a purely rational philosophy based on Hartley. Nature is explained as it is connected with the problem of the development of the mind, in terms of the three ages. Beatty concludes:

> Thus the function of Nature is to furnish us with the materials of true knowledge, and the education of man is to adjust his relations to her so that she becomes the helper, and not the usurper, of a power and place which she should not possess. But she is the necessary aid to the attainment of Imagination and right reason; and the function of Imagination and right reason, when they are attained, is to view her in due proportion to the whole of life and knowledge.[20]

Beatty likewise finds Hartley the source of Wordsworth's statement of the active principle that is present in the mind and in the universe. Locke states that, there being no innate ideas, knowledge must be won by the active employment of our faculties. Hartley affirms that all real knowledge is achieved by the activity of the mind in accordance with the principle of association, "for the mind has the power to create ideas and judgments by its own inherent power."[21]

> Wordsworth seizes upon this activity of the mind, which resolves all things to itself. . . . Mind is the ultimate and primary fact of the world, and determines man's relations to the rest of the sum of things . . . and the particular aspect of mind to which he devotes special attention is its activity, accepting all the notions of Locke and the associationists concerning this aspect of the mind and carrying his analysis deeper and his deductions farther than they dreamed of doing.[22]

Another characteristic of the mind which Wordsworth stresses is the essential unity of consciousness. Beatty explains

[20] *Ibid.*, 149.
[21] *Ibid.*, 153.
[22] *Ibid.*, 153–54.

that in this matter Wordsworth adopts the system of associationism, which transmutes sensations into higher knowledge, emotions (which, like Hartley, Wordsworth regards as extrinsic) into the intrinsic forms of mentality, and conflicting experiences into the ultimate unity of life. Like Hartley, Wordsworth believes that the fluidity of the mind is an instrument of good, which absorbs all particles of experience into unity, and which sublimates extrinsic experience into the completely intrinsic life of the mind. This is the ultimate stage of the imagination, when man reaches his truest realization.

> This is the foundation of the genuine structure of the Imagination, as the poet demonstrates all through *The Prelude.* This factual and realistic attitude to Imagination is very important for an understanding of Wordsworth's whole attitude towards his art; for it is most essential to perceive that he regards this power of Imagination as having its origins, not in some far and mystic experience, but in the intimate and almost daily experiences which all of us, even the least poetical, may know.[23]

Thus the central doctrine of Beatty's book is the interpretation of Wordsworth as a philosophical poet whose guiding light was the sensational philosophy of the school of Locke and the principles of associationism elaborated by Hartley. Any serious reader of Wordsworth's poetry and prose will follow through with interest Beatty's application of this philosophy to Wordsworth's theory of the origin of poety, and his detailed analyses of the shorter poems, *The Prelude,* and *The Excursion.* No other critic has so overwhelmingly confounded Arnold's attempt to overlook the philosophy of Wordsworth; none has presented with equal learning the philosophic background of the poet's writings.

Beatty's study provides for an almost complete interpretation of Wordsworth in terms of eighteenth-century Enlightenment. Even with the most liberal interpretation of the sensational school of Locke and Hartley, even with the changes of emphasis and the entirely new combinations and conclusions which Beatty shows that Wordsworth reached, the poet appears chiefly as a psychologist explaining the intellectual and spiritual stuff of the mind as a growth of sense perceptions germinating by associationism and the inherent power of the mind. As a guide to this interpretation, one need scarcely look beyond the writings of David Hartley.

[23] *Ibid.,* 163.

It is inevitable that such a view should be challenged. First, while most critics agree that there is much of associationism in Wordsworth, to rely so heavily on Hartley oversimplifies the explanation. Second, a host of critics, while acknowledging Wordsworth's explanation of the growth of the mind, put much greater emphasis upon his spiritualization of man and nature.

Professor Melvin Rader has written the most systematic refutation of Beatty's book. He thus states his conclusions:

> This rapid survey of the evidence reveals: (1) that direct proof of Wordsworth's adherence to Hartley has not been advanced; (2) that Coleridge's enormous influence upon Wordsworth was early directed against associationism; (3) that Coleridge, a supreme authority, regarded *The Prelude* and the *Ode on Intimations of Immortality* as non-Hartleian, and expected that Wordsworth's anti-associationism would find a clear enunciation in *The Excursion*; and (4) that Wordsworth unambiguously expressed transcendental doctrines, quite opposed to Hartleianism. We are forced to conclude that Mr. Beatty has greatly overestimated the influence of associationism upon the Lake poet.[24]

One of the most interesting points in Rader's investigation is his comments on Wordsworth's theory of the three ages of man. Rousseau, he says, had popularized the belief that the mind develops in three stages; but without the need of suggestions from either Rousseau or Hartley, Wordsworth's theory is deep-rooted in his own biographical experience. Moreover, Rader points out in *Tintern Abbey* a fourth stage, overlooked by Beatty, "a mystical experience," arising from the influence of the "beauteous forms" of nature. This fourth stage, one of mysticism, is likewise dwelt on in the *Ode on Intimations of Immortality,* and is here attributed not to the influence of nature, but to the presence of innate ideas surviving from childhood.

The third section of Rader's paper consists of a series of quotations from Wordsworth and Coleridge the import of which makes it impossible to assume that Wordsworth's whole theory rests on the assumption "that thought originates in experience, and that out of the product of sensation, or experience, ideas and the more complex forms of mentality are developed." Rader believes further that "Wordsworth's deepest allegiance was to a mystical philosophy."

[24] "The Transcendentalism of William Wordsworth," *MP,* xxvi (1928), 169–90.

These points and others are more extensively treated in Rader's monograph, "Presiding Ideas in Wordsworth's Poetry."[25] In stating the "presiding ideas" the book neatly links the mechanistic basis of Wordsworth's philosophy with his idealism or transcendentalism, although the sensational phase of the development of the mind is given a somewhat sparing treatment.

Rader states that Wordsworth passed through two stages, pantheistic and theistic. We can attribute the change from one to the other to Coleridge, who "overthrew necessitarianism, revised associationism, adopted a transcendental solution of the problem of knowledge, and changed from pantheism to an immanent theism. And Wordsworth attained, with Coleridge's assistance, to substantially the same philosophy."[26]

A closer view of the history of his development reveals five special stages, or "ages" (cf. Beatty's three ages): (1) sensation; (2) emotion; (3) fancy; (4) reason; and (5) imagination. These are the dominant forces, but they are not exclusive to each period.

> What I have called the stage of sensation is very idealistic; the stage of emotion is thoughtful and creative; imagination almost dominates the stage of fancy; the period of analytical reason brings an interval of intense hunger and passion; the stage of imagination and the 'grand' reason is often merely fanciful, and frequently logical in the narrow sense. . . .
>
> By this approach I have sought to make one fact clear: Wordsworth's mind was not a mechanical structure in which one function excluded another; it was a vital evolution in which the early processes of growth were incorporated into the completed economy.[27]

Wordsworth's account of the associational process, says Rader, is more modern than that of Hartley, in that it admits a kind of mental evolution. Wordsworth "by no means minimizes the report of the senses." But what the senses accumulate, the mind, the "divine and mysterious underpresence," creates into something new.[28] To summarize:

> The base of the world is God, from 'whence our dignity originates.' The highest faculties, when pricked on by the senses, arise inwardly from this base. These powers or faculties not only give being to man, but also maintain an 'ennobling interchange' with the outer

[25] *University of Washington Publications in Language and Literature,* VIII, No. 2, Seattle, University of Washington Press, 1931, 121–216.

[26] *Ibid.,* 129.

[27] *Ibid.,* 145.

[28] *Ibid.,* 170.

world, which rests upon the same foundation and which calls them into play. . . . The mightiest life is to be achieved by combining the empirical and transcendental factors into a most potent unity.[29]

III

Both Beatty and Rader, each with a different emphasis, have helped to clarify Wordsworth's doctrine of the mind and the stages of his development. Rader's studies are a bridge between the sensational and psychological aspect of the poet's philosophy and his higher metaphysics, his spiritualism and his possible mysticism. But these last aspects, often pointed out by earlier critics, cannot be fully understood without a recognition of the claims made by Beatty for the essentially rational nature of much of Wordsworth's thought.

Much emphasis has been given recently to the suprasensuous aspects of Wordsworth's doctrine. First, it is clear that he shows kinship with other philosophers of a different stamp from Hartley. The claim for Platonism in Wordsworth is strong, and there is evidence likewise of a relationship with Spinoza and possibly Kant. What, then, can we say of Wordsworth and Plato?

The inquirer would do well to turn first to J. A. Stewart's paper, "Platonism in English Poetry."[30] Stewart distinguishes between "traditional" and "personal" Platonism. Spenser and the seventeenth-century Platonists are examples of the former; Wordsworth is the most complete exemplification in English of the latter. Having made this differentiation, Stewart states categorically that *The Prelude* is "the classic authority on Platonism in poetry."

Platonism is love of the unseen and eternal cherished by one who rejoices in the seen and the temporal. This is the platonism of Plato himself, and, what concerns us especially now, it is the platonism which is vital in great poetry.[31]

There follows the application of this explanation of "personal" Platonism to *The Prelude*. Stewart draws this conclusion:

The essential nature and the necessary conditions of the platonist mood, as experienced by one who is a poet, are set forth by Wordsworth, in the *Prelude,* with so much first-hand knowledge, and with such subtlety of analysis and completeness of circumstance that . . . the

[29] *Ibid.,* 158–59.
[30] In *English Literature and the Classics,* Oxford, The Clarendon Press, 1912.
[31] *Ibid.,* 30.

study of this poem ought to precede the study of platonism in other English poets, especially when the platonism is much influenced by tradition.[32]

But if Wordsworth fits this large conception, it is also evident that he knew Plato and directly, or indirectly, was influenced in some of his utterances.[33] There is a strong tinge of Platonism or Neoplatonism in the *Ode on Intimations of Immortality.* John D. Rea argues that the *Ode* seems to have been begun under the influence of Coleridge's melancholy recognition of his loss of the buoyancy and insight of his earlier years, as voiced in his *Dejection: An Ode,* written in the spring of 1802, the same time when it now seems certain that Wordsworth composed at least the first four stanzas of his *Ode.*[34] To Wordsworth's questions as to the cause of this change, Coleridge had suggested a philosophical explanation might be found in the Neoplatonic philosophy of Proclus. The two had discussed this philosophy, and Wordsworth embodied it in stanzas V–VII, which present the conception of the child bringing into the world visions of an earlier ideal existence which become dimmed by the experiences of earth.[35] Herbert Hartman gives further evidence for establishing a connection with Coleridge's reading of Proclus, and adds the Neoplatonism of Fénelon as likewise contributing to Wordsworth's *Ode.*[36] Frederick Pierce, accepting the conventional later date (1804–6) for the composition of stanzas V and following, suggests that since Coleridge was then in Malta, Wordsworth may have found these ideas in Thomas Taylor's *Works of Plato,* published in 1804. He

[32] *Ibid.,* 35.

[33] J. H. Shorthouse ("The Platonism of Wordsworth," *Transactions of the Wordsworth Society,* No. 6, pp. 119–31) states that there is no direct evidence that Wordsworth read Plato, and his acquaintance may have been only through Coleridge. More recent critics have also pointed out Platonism as infiltrated through Coleridge. But there is reason to believe that Wordsworth had read Plato. See E. A. White, "Wordsworth's Knowledge of Plato," *MLN,* xxxiii (1918), 246–48; Lane Cooper, "Wordsworth's Knowledge of Plato," *MLN,* xxxiii (1918), 497–99; and H. E. Cookson, "Wordsworth and Plato," *TLS,* Nov. 25, 1926, p. 868.

[34] "Coleridge's Intimations of Immortality from Proclus," *MP,* xxvi (1928), 201–13. See also Rea, " 'Intimations of Immortality' Again," *PQ,* xi (1932), 396–400. Beatty had earlier pointed out a connection between the two odes (*op. cit.,* 81–87).

[35] In the Fenwick Note Wordsworth says two years elapsed between the composition of stanzas IV and V, but Rea givs plausible reasons for dating the first 129 lines in 1802. Fred M. Smith accepts Rea's dating, but contends that Coleridge followed Wordsworth. *Dejection,* he believes, is an answer to Wordsworth's *Ode,* in which Coleridge contrasts his hopeless loss of joy and his shaping spirit of imagination with Wordsworth's sense of loss but recovery of spirits ("The Relation of Coleridge's 'Ode on Dejection' to Wordsworth's 'Ode on Intimations of Immortality,' " *PMLA,* l, [1935], 224–34).

[36] "The 'Intimations' of Wordsworth's 'Ode,' " *RES,* vi (1930), 129–48.

detects parallels between Taylor's editorial comments and lines in the *Ode*.[37]

These discussions are confined to one poem of Wordsworth's, and largely to one utterance, the theory of prenatal existence which he later repudiated as a serious doctrine, although his emphasis throughout the *Ode* on a suprasensuous experience is not thereby invalidated. Other studies of the *Ode* have dwelt on its mysticism and transcendental values. E. C. Baldwin has seen in it traces of the Hermetical books, and its similarity to Vaughan's *Retreat* has been the subject of comment; other affinities have been found between Wordsworth and the seventeenth-century Neoplatonists and "metaphysical school."[38] All these studies point to Wordsworth's interest in a philosophy quite opposed to the sensationalism of Hartley. Although Beatty attempts to fit the *Ode* into the Hartleian pattern, it is difficult to see in this poem anything but almost a repudiation of Hartley. This is the view of Professor Beach, who describes the *Ode* as "virtually a recantation of the earlier doctrine of nature." He comments in the following passage:

> Coleridge certainly hailed it in *The Friend* as the manifesto of a very different philosophy, and cited it in support of a purely idealistic metaphysics . . . . Altogether, the 'Intimations' ode registers an almost complete abandonment of the Hartleian psychology. Our spiritual life is no longer regarded as the end-product of the process starting with simple sensations, but as the starting point of that process.[39]

Professor N. P. Stallknecht's interpretation likewise seems at a remote distance from pure naturalism and Hartleian psychology. In comparing Coleridge's *Dejection* with Wordsworth's *Ode* and passages from *The Prelude,* he says: "They believed that creative and appreciative imagination engenders a love of man, and they did not hesitate to affirm that this love is a profoundly religious

[37] "Wordsworth and Thomas Taylor," *PQ,* vii (1928), 60–64.

[38] Baldwin, "Wordsworth and Hermes Trismegistus," *PMLA,* xxxiii (1918), 235–43; L. R. Merrill, "Vaughan's Influence upon Wordsworth's Poetry," *MLN,* xxxvii (1922), 91–96; Muriel Morris, "A Note on Wordsworth and Vaughan," *MLN,* xxxix (1924), 187–88; Helen McMaster, "Wordsworth's Copy of Vaughan," *TLS,* April 12, 1934, p. 262; Helen McMaster, "Vaughan and Wordsworth," *RES,* xi (1935), 313–25 denies that Wordsworth knew Vaughan). G. C. Moore Smith, "Wordsworth and George Herbert," *N&Q,* Jan. 13, 1923, p. 30. Abbie F. Potts, "The Spenserian and Miltonic Influence in Wordsworth's *Ode* and *Rainbow,*" *SP,* xxix (1932), 607–16; G. Bullaugh, "The Origin of the Soul in English Poetry before Wordsworth," *N&Q,* April 23, 1932, pp. 290–94, and April 30, 1932, pp. 308–11.

[39] Beach, *op. cit.,* 155–56.

experience which owes its power to the mystical communion with a cosmic spirit."[40]

It is clear that by 1802 Wordsworth had moved on from the absorption in naturalism and sensational psychology of 1798 and *Tintern Abbey,* and of the early books of *The Prelude.* Indeed, the last three books of *The Prelude* show an increased emphasis on the suprasensuous experience. But it is a mistake to suppose that there is a sharp division; that Wordsworth was a believer in pure naturalism until 1802, and a mystic thereafter. He at all times believed a transcendental experience to be a high peak in the mind's apprehension of truth, even when he entertained complete confidence in naturalism and the experience of the senses as the gateways to the mind. *Tintern Abbey* and the early books of *The Prelude* bear testimony that the "third age" is something more than the final category of an associational psychology.

The infiltration of German mysticism into Wordsworth's thought has been well explained by Stallknecht.[41] The poet's mysticism has two phases: Spinozistic in *The Prelude* and the poems written before 1805; Kantian in the *Ode to Duty* and *The Excursion.* Thereafter his philosophy changed little.

Stallknecht thus describes the general development of Wordsworth's thought. In his early contacts he had an intuitive love of nature, a mystical awareness of a vast spirit that was the reality of nature, "divinely aloof from all turbulence and change, that underneath all passion lives a steadfast life. In this vast soul he saw all the things of Nature embedded." But this intuitive apprehension was later weakened by his absorption in man (the French Revolution), his consciousness of man's evil and failure, and his groping to find an intellectual proof in all things. At this juncture he lent a ready ear to Coleridge's enthusiasm for Spinozistic mysticism. The mysticism that Wordsworth attained involves two aspects: one, a sense of dynamic life striving towards an end; and two, a "luminous, calm self-sufficience that embraces all change in immutability." In general it grew out of his aesthetic enjoyment of nature. "Thus for him mystical insight was closely bound with the apprehension of beauty."

Stallknecht points out the pertinent aspects of Spinoza's

[40] "The Doctrine of Coleridge's 'Dejection' and its Relation to Wordsworth's Philosophy," *PMLA,* xlix (1934), 196–207.

[41] "Wordsworth and Philosophy," *PMLA,* xliv (1929), 1116–43.

philosophy. We may know objects in three ways: (1) mere experience, whereby we may know an object but have no conception of its nature; (2) reason, which teaches us the properties and laws of objects, giving us not the object, but the abstract rationale; (3) intuition, which combines the other two; the perception of the object and the rationale, inseparably united, perceived simultaneously, hence "intuitive." Intuition is closely related to the intellectual love of God.

All thought, Spinoza maintained, is organized in an infinite intellect, the intellect of God, who knows all things, through the third mode of knowledge. Now, when it grasps an object intuitively, the human mind is absolutely identical, in so far as that act of knowing is concerned, with the intellect of God. . . . Of our identification with the divine mind we become conscious . . . when performing the act of intuition. We know then that we exist in God who is the sustaining cause of all our activities. Thus when we rejoice in the intuition we rejoice in God, who is the cause thereof.[42]

What is similar in this to Wordsworth's philosophy? "The relation of intuition to the awareness of God, and the belief that we not only know but feel our immortality are the great points of similarity." But Wordsworth interprets the third mode of knowledge "as a description of esthetic imagination." He attained the doctrine of the intellectual love through the apprehension of the imagination. This explains his early optimism in man and nature.

In the first place, he found in the life of the imagination a *summum bonum* by which to judge the value of human actions. Thus he was no longer baffled in his search for a criterion of good and evil. He could call all actions good that tend to promote the life of imagination, understanding, and freedom. The problem of obligation was also solved. For coupled with understanding, the desires of the religious man are to be trusted. . . . Considered in this light, moral problems center about the question, 'Do I really want to act thus?' rather than about, 'Should I act thus?'[43]

Turning to the Kantian aspect of the *Ode to Duty* and *The Excursion,* Stallknecht points out a shift of emphasis from Spinozistic intuitive knowledge or imagination, to the categorical imperative. According to this Kantian doctrine our actions should be tested by their rationality and their universality. The purpose

[42] *Ibid.,* 1128–29.
[43] *Ibid.,* 1134.

of nature seems to be the production of the rational life; the purpose of human activity should be the preservation of rationality. There are two kinds of will: a sovereign will, which of its own desire seeks good; and a will not absolutely good, but actuated by duty and moral necessity. Thus in the *Ode to Duty* Spinozistic intuition is replaced by moral obligation, or the second type of will.[44] Although the poet, in *The Excursion,* still expresses a belief in his mystical communion with nature, these experiences seem more wayward and uncertain, and like Kant he finds aid in faith and moral duty.[45]

These affinities in Wordsworth to German thought establish claims for a broader philosophic interpretation than Hartleian influence alone would admit. By inclination and early intellectual environment Wordsworth was disposed towards a philosophy of naturalism and elements of the school of Locke and Hartley provided him with the rationale for such a doctrine; but he felt also a hunger for a spiritual insight deeper than even the most exalted naturalism could provide, and he sought satisfaction in an increasingly transcendental outlook. The studies of Beatty and Stallknecht furnish us with the backgrounds of both these phases of the poet's thought.

The religious element in Wordsworth has long been of interest. Of course it is implicit in any discussion of his philosophy, but many studies have been made that have given it special consideration. John Veitch's "The Theism of Wordsworth" (*Transactions of the Wordsworth Society,* No. 8, pp. 24–81), and

[44] See also Stallknecht, "Wordsworth's 'Ode to Duty' and the Schöne Seele," *PMLA,* lii (1937), 230–37.

[45] Stallknecht's later paper, "Nature and Imagination in Wordsworth's 'Meditation upon Mt. Snowdon,'" (*PMLA,* lii [1937], 835–47) is another important contribution showing how much farther Wordsworth's philosophy goes than sensationalism and associationism, and it likewise points out Spinozistic influence. The article we have cited, however, is built on a broader foundation. For further discussion of Wordsworth and German thought, see the following: R. A. J. Meusch, "Goethe and Wordsworth," *Publications of the English Goethe Society,* VII (Old Series, 1893), 85–107; Otto Heller, "Goethe and Wordsworth," *MLN,* xiv (1899), 131–33; Margaret Cooke, "Schiller's 'Robbers' in England," *MLR,* xi (1916), 156–75; M. J. Herzberg, "William Wordsworth and German Literature," *PMLA,* xl (1925), 302–45; A. C. Bradley, "English Poetry and German Philosophy in the Age of Wordsworth," *A Miscellany,* London, Macmillan, 1929 (the essay was originally published by the University Press, Manchester, 1909); C. H. Herford, "Goethe and Wordsworth," *Publications of the English Goethe Society,* VII (New Series, 1930), 8–31; Margaret Sherwood, *Undercurrents of Influence in English Romantic Poetry,* Cambridge, Harvard University Press, 1934; Barker Fairley, "Goethe and Wordsworth," *Publications of the English Goethe Society,* X (New Series, 1934), 23–42; L. A. Willoughby, "Wordsworth and Germany," *German Studies Presented to Professor H. G. Fiedler,* Oxford, Clarendon Press, 1938.

Stopford Brooke's *Theology in the English Poets* and "Wordsworth, the Poet of Nature" (*Naturalism in English Poetry,* pp. 141–63) have been mentioned in earlier chapters. A. C. Bradley, in the last section of his lecture on Wordsworth (*Oxford Lectures on Poetry,* London, Macmillan and Co., 1909, pp. 125–45), points out the visionary power of Wordsworth. There is a strong tinge of religion in Miss Margaret Sherwood's discussion of Wordsworth (*Undercurrents of Influence in English Romantic Poetry,* pp. 148–202). She traces the philosophic backgrounds, chiefly in the seventeenth and eighteenth centuries, of the nineteenth-century concept of the oneness of man and nature. She sees in Wordsworth a mystic, but one whose "Imaginative Will" insists upon individual consciousness and creative effort rather than absorption of the individual identity in the infinite. Sperry (*Wordsworth's Anti-Climax,* pp. 185–202) denies the possibility of identifying Wordsworth's religion with any particular belief or sect because he "manifests the elemental genius of all religions." Havens (*The Mind of a Poet,* pp. 179–200) also concludes that Wordsworth's religious beliefs cannot be formulated, that orthodoxy affected him little, and that his response to religion was in his experience of joy, mystery, solitude, and nature. Miss Katherine Peek has made interesting investigations concerning Wordsworth's relations to the Catholic Revival and the Broad Church movement (*Wordsworth in England,* Bryn Mawr, Pa., 1943, pp. 101–61).

Perhaps Professor S. F. Gingerich gives in relatively brief space the most comprehensive as well as penetrating study of the religious aspect of Wordsworth.[46] He gives due attention to Wordsworth's naturalism, drawing on many poems written from 1798 to 1802. He sees clear evidence, in this period, of Wordsworth's religion in the utterances concerning the immanence of the spirit in nature and man. By 1802, however, the poet was fully aware of the transcendence above matter of both the spirit and the mind of man. Gingerich believes the poems of this period are the richest and deepest. The broad basis of his interpretation is evident when he says:

Immanence and transcendence are not used here as representing sharply fixed philosophical concepts, but as indicating tendencies in Wordsworth's spiritual growth. Wordsworth cannot be put into any

[46] Gingerich, *op. cit.,* 91-191.

one formula, and the truth about him has been beclouded by the efforts of critics to do so, to make him, for instance, a Pantheist (Elton), or an Associationist (Beatty), or a Philosophic Sensationalist (Garrod),—to cite but a few examples of recent critics. The growth of Wordsworth's mind, instead of being simple, as is usually supposed, is extraordinarily complex. One of the chief causes of this complexity is that Wordsworth was loath at any time to relinquish what he had once gained. . . . Wordsworth . . . attempted to conserve and carry forward the best parts of his former conceptions, to adapt them by modification to the truth of his wider experience.[47]

The various tendencies which we have examined in sections II and III of this chapter are well assimulated in the pages that Beach devotes to Wordsworth in his scholarly book, *The Concept of Nature in Nineteenth-Century English Poetry*. His treatment is marked by balance and sanity, taking the middle ground between the extreme materialistic interpretation and the position of those critics who emphasize the religion and pure mysticism of Wordsworth. Beach's discussion of the aspects of Wordsworth's conception of nature and his relation to other thinkers is thus admirably summarized:

Prominent in Wordsworth is the idea of a universal nature, a 'spirit of nature' or 'soul of all the worlds'—an active principle sufficient to account for the animated and purposive behavior of things and so avoid the stigma of a purely mechanistic philosophy. I find it most likely that this concept of Wordsworth is grounded mainly in English natural theology of the seventeenth and eighteenth centuries, strongly supported as that was by the scientific theories of Newton, and given a decidedly 'platonic' cast by writers like Cudworth, Henry More, Shaftesbury and Berkeley. Among other possible influences in shaping this concept were the pantheism of Spinoza, the materialism of writers like Priestley, and the world-soul theories of foreign writers like Schelling relayed to Wordsworth through Coleridge. The imaginative association of this universal nature, or spirit of nature, with country life and the beauties of natural scenery had been made by Shaftesbury and established as a tradition by certain of the eighteenth-century poets.

[47] *Ibid.*, 138–39. The following is a fuller list of references on the religious aspects of Wordsworth's thought: A. D. Martin, *The Religion of Wordsworth*, London, George Allen and Unwin Ltd., 1936; L. D. Weatherhead, "The Idea of Immortality in Wordsworth," *London Quarterly Review*, cxlii (1924), 185–97; W. A. Claydon, "The Numinous in the Poetry of Wordsworth," *Hibbert Journal*, xxviii (1930), 601–15; Basil Willey, "Wordsworth's Beliefs," *Criterion*, xiii (1934), 232–51; J. P. Lilley, "Wordsworth's Interpretation of Nature," *Hibbert Journal*, xix (1921), 532–50; G. Wilson Knight, "Wordsworth's Vision of Immortality," *University of Toronto Quarterly*, i (1932), 216–35; J. S. Collis, "Wordsworthian Pantheism," *Aryan Path*, v (1934), 716–20.

Wordsworth took for granted the purposiveness, harmony, benevolence of nature; and here he was in agreement with nearly all schools of eighteenth-century thought, atheist, deist and Christian. . . . In his earlier poetry there was, I believe, a more strongly naturalistic trend than was to be found in writers on natural theology; and this may possibly be referred to the influence of writers like d'Holbach and Godwin, and almost certainly to that of Hartley. . . . His tendency was, in this period, to lay his emphasis more on nature than on God, and to assume that man's spiritual faculties were developed (if not actually originated) by natural means during a man's lifetime. The problem of the origin of man's mind (or spirit), however, was too difficult of solution by reference merely to nature: a growing dualism shows itself in Wordsworth's emphasis on imagination as a spiritual faculty necessary to the reading of nature, and he ended by virtually giving up nature and deriving man's spirit directly 'from God, who is our home.'[48]

Thus, in Beach's interpretation, Wordsworth is a poet of the main stream of seventeenth- and eighteenth-century thought. He cannot be identified exclusively with one system; and in his shift from naturalism to spiritualism there is an accompanying change in the type of thinkers who may have influenced him, or with whom he shows kinship.

IV

Before concluding this chapter, special mention should be given to the most complete study that has been made of Wordsworth's mind, Havens' *The Mind of a Poet.* The two books on the subject are unquestionably Beatty's and Havens'. Beatty presents a learned and invaluable analysis in the light of a peculiar system of thought. Havens gives the broader view, the leading attributes of Wordsworth's thought, largely as they appear in *The Prelude.* He is not concerned with the sources of Wordsworth's ideas, but he gives a full account of the peculiarities of the poet's mind. He chooses to stress the transcendental, which is completely the opposite emphasis from that of Beatty. He writes:

Accordingly the following pages will stress rather than minimize the transcendental in Wordsworth and will try to show that the unusual aspects of his mind are not isolated and did not seem to him fanciful or merely personal, but so many paths, difficult, hard to find and harder to follow, leading to the great central truth which is the goal

[48] Beach, *op. cit.*, 12–13.

of all man's loftier strivings. This truth has two aspects, the divine and the human: God and 'the hiding-places of man's power.'[49]

After discussing the realism, or "matter-of-factness" of Wordsworth, and the importance the poet attached to feeling or passion, Havens devotes chapters to those interesting aspects of Wordsworth's poetry which have never before been given their due attention: "The Ministry of Fear," "Solitude, Silence, Loneliness," and "Animism." There follows the chapter on "Nature," which reveals some new and interesting points. Fundamentally, Wordsworth valued nature "for what she does rather than for what she is, and is valued the more in proportion as she is felt rather than seen, as esthetic appeal is subordinated to imaginative and spiritual ministry."[50] In his youth Wordsworth did not theorize about nature; he was content to enjoy his sensuous response to her and accept the spiritual harmony that accompanied this. Later, after his return from France, and partly under the influence of Coleridge, he attempted to discover a philosophy that would explain the benefits that he had derived from nature. "Much of the philosophical part of Wordsworth's poetry is an attempt to find a rational justification for the importance which his feelings and his experience told him that nature held for man."[51] Havens, therefore, makes a distinction between what nature did for Wordsworth and what he theorizes that it does for man. "Wordsworth's assertions as to what nature is and his theories as to her fostering meekness, democracy, orderly thinking, and the love of man are of value only for the light they throw on his mind; but when he speaks of what she has done for him the case is entirely different. Here he is on solid ground."[52] Havens makes a point of denying that nature has anything to do with man's social and moral benefits as Wordsworth supposed. But the poet himself did receive ministrations from nature.

Persons who have themselves felt only relaxation and mild pleasure in the woods and fields are inclined to regard as sentimental nonsense the belief that sunsets, moonlight, and moving waters may bring deep joy, calm, consolation, uplift, scorn of little aims that end in self, and the integration of personality. The answer to such critics is to be found in the experience of those—and they are neither few nor, as a

[49] Havens, *op. cit.,* 2.
[50] *Ibid.,* 101.
[51] *Ibid.,* 89.
[52] *Ibid.,* 118.

rule, intellectually contemptible—who have found in nature a great aid to noble living and high thinking. To Wordsworth she was clearly the greatest of such aids; the mighty world of eye and ear was the main gateway to the world of the spirit, the center of his emotional and religious life, the soul of his moral being, the chief means of communion with his higher self and with the Infinite.[53]

Reference has already been made to Havens' comments on Wordsworth's antirationalism and his religion.[54] Writing on the mystic experience, Havens amply illustrates the "trance-like state of consciousness" to which Wordsworth was early accustomed. "Anyone who is familiar with the literature of mysticism will recognize them as examples of those brief periods of ecstasy, insight, and oblivion to be met with in all races and all periods of history which are known as mystic experiences."[55] In these experiences he "tapped a spiritual reservoir and strength flowed into him."[56] However, Havens points out, Wordsworth never thought of these experiences as being mystical. He confused them with the experience induced by the imagination, "the faculty by which we see things as they are not seen by the senses and give them a significance which they do not in themselves possess. . . . He did not make the distinction. He did not see that in his greatest moments, when the light of sense went out, imagination had no part."[57] Moreover, these mystic experiences contain little that indicates communion with God. They seem mostly to have arisen from contemplation of nature, passing into something ineffable. The later poems record none of these experiences, says Havens. They seem to have ceased about 1805.[58]

In order to understand Havens' distinction between the mystic experience and the imagination, we must turn to his final chapter on that function of the mind, which he regards as the most essential attribute of a poet. All other subjects in the book, Havens remarks, lead up to the discussion of the imagination.

He believes that Wordsworth's views on the subject were essentially his own, although he and Coleridge had much in

[53] *Ibid.*, 118.

[54] *Vide*, p. 125.

[55] Havens, *op. cit.*, 159–60.

[56] *Ibid.*, 164.

[57] *Ibid.*, 169.

[58] It should be noted that Havens designates by the term "mystical" a more specialized experience than does Stallknecht or Rader, who use the word to describe the larger visionary powers of Wordsworth.

common. Coleridge distinguishes between the primary and the secondary imagination. The first is a unifying and interpreting power possessed by all persons. The secondary, possessed by the few, is identified with the primary, but it not merely unifies but also "dissolves, diffuses, dissipates, in order to re-create."[59] Wordsworth does not observe this distinction very clearly. "Indeed, the unifying capacity of the imagination would seem to be not separate from the conferring, abstracting, and modifying but to be carried on by means of them."[60] Another function of the imagination (illustrated by the vision on Mount Snowdon) is its power to transfer or shift attributes. "That is, nature always works as with an imaginative power for we perceive plants, trees, and stones, not as each is in itself or would appear in a laboratory, but as it is modified by surrounding objects."[61] In this way we achieve a unity of perception.

Wordsworth associated emotion with imagination; only natures of deep feeling are capable of imaginative activity. Thus reason cannot do the work of imagination. Coleridge thought of imagination chiefly as relating to poetry and as a conscious activity of the mind, but Wordsworth "usually conceived of it as the transformation wrought within the mind rather than any expression of such a transformation in a work of art."[62] Wordsworth felt it was independent of the will; Coleridge did not. Wordsworth regarded youth as the period of the greatest activity and vigor of the imagination.

The most distinctive point that Havens makes in his explanation is the fact that imagination is not a faculty of insight nor an instrument for the discovery of truth. The reason, not the imagination, may be an instrument of knowledge. The imagination is valuable, not for acquiring, but for using knowledge.

> There can be no question as to Wordsworth's belief that the imagination teaches truth, just as the senses do, by furnishing, through its unifying and transforming power and through its embodying abstractions, some of the materials from which reason derives truth. But this is not to say that the imagination or the senses are organs of insight.[63]

Nor should imagination be confused with the mystic experience.

[59] Havens, *op. cit.*, 208.
[60] *Ibid.*, 210.
[61] *Ibid.*, 212.
[62] *Ibid.*, 220.
[63] *Ibid.*, 232.

Then the light of sense goes out, "whereas it is by the light of sense or the recollection of it that the imagination works."[64] Havens, however, modifies this position by admitting that perhaps in "a general way" the imagination might include the mystic experience, but should not be limited to it.

Although the imagination furnishes "types and symbols of Eternity," Havens emphasizes Wordsworth's association of the imagination with the real, not the strange and improbable.

> Although Wordsworth associated the imagination with the higher love, with the invisible world, with spiritual things, yet when he thought of it in relation to his fellowmen and to everyday life he conceived of it not so much as an idealizing agent as one through which the mind perceives the beauty and nobility of the actual.[65]

Concluding, Havens states that his study has dealt with those forces that fed Wordsworth's imagination, "the central, the one essential quality of the poetic mind."[66] His valuable book, marked by taste, learning, and judicious judgment, is essential reading to any student of the poet. However, it would seem that it is not the final synthesis, since in stressing the transcendental it fails to take fully into account the inescapably important aspect of Wordsworth's "mind" presented by Beatty. Havens has given us the "Romantic" Wordsworth, but the Wordsworth who was the child of the seventeenth and eighteenth centuries does not emerge so clearly.

[64] *Ibid.*, 233.
[65] *Ibid.*, 246.
[66] *Ibid.*, 255. The second section of Havens' book is a copious line-by-line commentary on *The Prelude*.

CHAPTER SEVEN

SOME LITERARY TENDENCIES

I

The social and political views of Wordsworth and his philosophy of man, nature, and the spirit, are all inseparably a part of his art as a poet. To examine his philosophy and thought, and his poetic art, independently, is to lose something of the signification of the whole. In treating the various aspects of the poet's mind, Havens has recognized the difficulty of separation. Anyone who has taught Wordsworth to a class of students is familiar with the vexing question of where to begin. The essence of Wordsworth is unity and synthesis. However, there are many studies of a more purely literary nature than those discussed in the last chapter; it is these that we shall now examine, bearing in mind that the two types of studies often overlap and always have a common axis.

The many discussions of separate poems are too numerous to include here. For such discussions, and likewise for general estimates and over-all criticisms of Wordsworth's verse, the reader will find very helpful G. M. Harper's *William Wordsworth*; Walter Raleigh's *Wordsworth* (London, Edward Arnold and Co., 1903); Oliver Elton's *Wordsworth* (London, Edward Arnold and Co., 1924); C. H. Herford's *Wordsworth*; and A. C. Bradley's "Wordsworth," in *Oxford Lectures on Poetry.* In surveying the articles and monographs, it is interesting to note that the most attention has been given to *Guilt and Sorrow* and *The Borderers,* to the *Lucy Poems,* and to the *Ode on Intimations of Immortality. The Prelude,* of course, has been extensively used to explain Wordsworth's development and his social and philosophic thought; rich and detailed commentaries have been provided for it by de Selincourt and Havens, and it is basic to such studies as that of Garrod.

In this chapter we shall note some of the studies that have been made of Wordsworth's Prefaces and theory of poetry, and then examine the specialized discussions of his literary tendencies and aesthetic development.

II

Wordsworth's theory of poetry, the subject of such animated controversy in his day, is discussed in all the general studies of the poet. Special attention, however, should be called to Legouis' excellent chapter on Wordsworth's early poems.[1] In a detailed study of *An Evening Walk* and *Descriptive Sketches* he traces the effect on the young Wordsworth of the poetic style of the descriptive poets of the eighteenth century. Acquaintance with this chapter, immediately before reading the Preface of the 1800 edition of *Lyrical Ballads,* would go far to prevent a misunderstanding of the spirit and aims of that notable manifesto. Besides pointing out the artificial language and style of *An Evening Walk* and *Descriptive Sketches,* Legouis calls attention to the tone of melancholy especially in *Descriptive Sketches,* a mode that he attributes largely to the well-established convention among the eighteenth-century imitators of Milton.

A thorough discussion is provided by Miss Marjorie Latta Barstow in her book, *Wordsworth's Theory of Poetic Diction.*[2] She regards some acquaintance with eighteenth-century criticism as necessary to an understanding of Wordsworth's Prefaces, and after giving an adequate survey, she concludes:

> The theory of a special diction for poetry was the result of the emphasis placed by Dryden and Pope upon the selective power of the poet, and upon the value of imitation. The poet must employ the current speech, but he must also avoid anything vulgar or unintelligibly specific. Moreover, he was permitted, even advised, to incorporate into his verse the happiest inspirations of his predecessors. The result was the development of the notion that there is a special language of poetry—a treasure of fine phrases descending from bard to bard, and especially consecrated to the uses of the imagination.[3]

The section on *An Evening Walk* and *Descriptive Sketches* supplements Legouis, and disagrees on some points. Miss Barstow admits the influence of eighteenth-century landscape poets on Wordsworth's Hawkshead verse, but denies this influence on *An Evening Walk* and *Descriptive Sketches.* Instead, she sees the strong influence of Milton, and a desire on the part of the young poet to use the less restricted order of Latin verse. She remarks

[1] *The Early Life of William Wordsworth, 1770–1798,* London, J. M. Dent and Sons Ltd., 1897, pp. 120–60.

[2] "Yale Studies in English," LVII, New Haven, Yale University Press, 1917.

[3] *Ibid.,* 57.

that in these poems he was more original in syntax than in vocabulary. In his figurative language he shows accurate observation and special susceptibility to color and sound, qualities that indicate not so much imitation of an old style as the promise of a new. Whatever may have been the date of the revisions of these poems (she believes them to have been made early), Miss Barstow observes that,

> as early as 1796, Wordsworth had attained to an austere and imaginative simplicity of style. A slight awkwardness of language was still visible, but the extraneous and exaggerated ornaments were gone. As far as can be determined, this improvement was solely on the basis of reading confined, in the field of English literature, to the poets of the eighteenth century and the three great elder bards—Milton, Spenser, and Shakespeare. Apart from these he had been especially interested in Italian and Latin poetry.[4]

Noteworthy is the chapter "Coleridge and his Circle," which throws light on the background of the Preface of 1800. Miss Barstow points out an article, which appeared in 1796 in *The Monthly Magazine,* entitled "Is Verse Essential to Poetry?" The substance parallels closely the Preface. She believes that the article might have been written by Coleridge.[5] She also calls attention to the discussions of Lamb, Southey, and Coleridge on simplicity in poetic style. In discussing the Preface itself, she affirms that by the term *language* Wordsworth meant not so much words and syntax, but figures of speech. Thus the ordinary man, in a state of emotion, uses figures drawn from living reality, speaking of one thing in terms of another equally vital and real. This is in contrast to conventional figures, staled by repetition and imitation, which have no immediate link with reality.[6] She points out that the vocabulary of *Lyrical Ballads* consists of words, the heavy majority of which occur in Skeat's glossary to Chaucer. They are certainly of the permanent body of English words. She also presents analyses of the devices of syntax and the narrative style of *Lyrical Ballads.*

Another study of diction is that of Srikumar Banerjee, *Critical Theories and Poetic Practice in the 'Lyrical Ballads.'*[7] He finds

[4] *Ibid.,* 111–12.

[5] Garrod doubts that Coleridge had a hand in this essay (*Wordsworth,* Oxford, The Clarendon Press, 1923, p. 155n.).

[6] Barstow, *op. cit.,* 134–39. This interpretation is drawn not from the Preface alone, but in part from the Appendix on Poetic Diction.

[7] London, Williams and Norgate Ltd., 1931.

in the Prefaces a good deal of contradiction and lack of clarity. His study is largely an attempt to determine whether Wordsworth, in associating the language of prose with that of poetry, meant and intended to use not only the vocabulary of prose but likewise its order and arrangement. The conclusion that he reaches, as he admits, is none too definite.

The final upshot of all of this is that Wordsworth succeeds in demonstrating, not that identity under all circumstances between the language of poetry and prose which he fondly expected to do, but only an experimental truth that the simple words in everyday use, generally arranged according to prose order, are sometimes capable of attaining to the highest effects in poetry.[8]

But for all the shortcomings that Banerjee discovers in Wordsworth's theories and practice, the critic concludes that Wordsworth more than any other poet has shown the kinship between the essential spirit of prose and fine lyric verse. Banerjee's book throws no new light on the subject.

A very sane survey of Wordsworth's theories, which is not made top heavy by fine-spun analyses, is the paper by Alexander Brede, "Theories of Poetic Diction in Wordsworth and Others and in Contemporary Poetry."[9] Avoiding cavil over the obvious ambiguities and at times inconsistencies of which Wordsworth was guilty, Brede sets forth clearly the poet's primary critical objectives. He interprets Wordsworth's loose phrase, "selection of language really used by men," to mean "a selection of his own ordinary language, the language spoken under pressure of the emotions."[10]

Garrod (his chapter, "The Preface to 'Lyrical Ballads,'" is especially recommended) interprets this phrase not to mean that poets should write no better than the commonplace speech of commonplace men. "The poet," he says, "who composes in a selection 'from the real language of men' escapes 'the language of any other man of common sense' in the exact degree in which he is a poet."[11] Lest we lose sight of the central driving force of the Preface, Garrod says:

Throughout life Wordsworth held with passionate insistency to the belief which he here forces upon the attention of the reader of the

[8] *Ibid.*, 6.

[9] *Papers of the Michigan Academy of Science, Arts, and Letters*, XIV (1930), Ann Arbor, University of Michigan Press, 1931, 537–65.

[10] *Ibid.*, 545.

[11] Garrod, *op. cit.*, 163–64.

Preface—that a true style can be founded upon no other base than a true observation of Nature (or of human character and manners).[12]

Miss Marian Mead has gathered together in her book, *Four Studies in Wordsworth,*[13] a plenitude of evidence of Wordsworth's keen visual ability, details concerning his sense of color, and his ideas on landscape and architecture. To the student of Wordsworth's language, her collection of color words, which are compared to those of Keats, is of interest. In Miss Burton's study of the revisions of *The Prelude,* she examines his use of words and lines of verse.[14] A good summary may be found in her essay, "How Wordsworth Changed the Diction of 'The Prelude,' "[15] in which she draws the conclusion that the changes represent an orderly set of principles by which the poet in his later years revised to advantage. Edwin B. Burgum has advanced the theory that "literary language actually reflects group interests . . . and that Wordsworth's diction represents the attainment of bourgeois supremacy at the opening of the nineteenth century."[16]

One of the most refreshing and fruitful studies of Wordsworth's language is that of Miss Josephine Miles, *Wordsworth and the Vocabulary of Emotion.*[17] The book, avoiding the old lines of controversy, investigates the words that Wordsworth uses denoting emotion, and the results open extensive avenues of critical thought. Accurate word-counting is involved, but the book is far from limited to statistical findings.

The basic problem is the named emotions in Wordsworth's poetry. It involves four major steps:

(1) Establishment of the words to be included in the limits of 'vocabulary of emotion,' the names of emotion and standard signs of emotion.

(2) Counting of the number of names (also called statements, limited to single words) in every poem, group, and in the complete poetical works of Wordsworth, in terms of occurrence of such names by number of lines.

(3) Observation and classification of main kinds of immediate context: that is to say, with respect to those things with which the

[12] *Ibid.,* 170.

[13] Menasha, Wis., George Banta, 1929.

[14] *The One Wordsworth,* Chapel Hill, University of North Carolina Press, 1942, Chapters IX–XII.

[15] *College English,* iii (1941–42), 12–24.

[16] "Wordsworth's Reform in Poetic Diction," *College English,* ii (1940–41), 207–16.

[17] "University of California Publications in English," XII, No. 1, Berkeley, University of California Press, 1942.

named emotions are most closely connected in phrases in which they appear.

(4) Relation of the body of this vocabulary and context (a) to the author's poetry as a whole, (b) to his critical thinking and philosophical view, particularly as expressed in his prose, and (c) to the same vocabulary as used by other poets in the same and other periods.[18]

Something of the import of this procedure is evident from the following observations:

Consider what traditional problems could be moved a little toward solution by the sort of knowledge a great many detailed studies of poetic vocabulary could provide. What words by stress-emphasis of elaboration and repetition and abundance in many poets—have been most important to poetry? Have their references and their contexts altered widely? By the words that poetry chooses, is it possible to know as important the things, qualities, actions that poets and their times have considered important? How do new words enter the realm of poetic publicity and grow in favor and become prime? What, in other words, are some of the relations of the language of poetry to language in general, not only in respect to *ordonnance,* as Coleridge would have it, but in respect to simple presence of terms?[19]

The method, as applied in Miss Miles' particular study, raises "and perhaps answers" traditional questions such as the following:

Was stated emotion characteristic of romantic as opposed to or in agreement with neoclassic poetry? What place did it have in Wordsworth's criticism of his predecessors, in his revolutionary moves in poetry, in his philosophy of "real" language? Did his theory and his practice agree in regard to it, and was his audience pleased by the result in its terms? What did these words have to say that the worlds of Johnson and of Arnold were equally ready to hear?[20]

Miss Miles observes that for Wordsworth poetry "links to its objects the names of the feelings," and that "the terms of emotion had an especial poetic weight in practice and in a conscious theory of value."[21] He uses the "object-to-response-and-back-again" pattern. That is, he names the emotion specifically, less frequently permitting the object to represent the emotion (the theory and practice of much modern poetry). To him the names constitute a direct and immense poetic signification.

The groundwork of Miss Miles' study involves a threefold

[18] *Ibid.,* 5–6.
[19] *Ibid.,* 6–7.
[20] *Ibid.,* 7.
[21] *Ibid.,* 29.

classification: (1) the words; (2) the variety of contexts in which they are used; and (3) the number and percentages of the words by the total number of lines. First, she includes only words that in Wordsworth's day signified emotions: general terms, like *passion* and *affection*; the more specific, such as *love, hate, fear*; and "signs," such as *tears, laughter.* "They ranged in Wordsworth's day a middle way from sensations to concepts, leading from the simpler to the more complex, from lower to higher . . . ."[22] Many of the words had derived a certain amount of specialized signification in the eighteenth century through their use in philosophical systems and other modes of thought. The passions were entities for the eighteenth century, as well as for Wordsworth and his contemporaries, and words represented them. Second, the context. Half of Wordsworth's words of emotion are used singly, without modification. But when they are modified, there are five means of characterization: (1) "general" (abstract), or modified by other words, viz., "Vital feelings of delight"; (2) "physical" (concrete), or locating the seat of the emotions, viz., "Felt in the blood, and felt along the heart . . ."; (3) "bestowal," or transferring to the outer world the emotion experienced by the observer (cf. the "pathetic fallacy"), viz., "every flower Enjoys the air it breathes"; (4) personification; (5) "objectification," "whereby the emotion by metaphor receives some of the characteristics or relationships of the outer objects," viz. "food of pride," "links of love."

Wordsworth, then, enlarges, amplifies, specifies his stated emotion in the ways in which he thinks of it: as abstract force, as physically felt force, as shared with nature, as having human forms and objects' qualities. The proportions of these tend to be, in the *Lyrical Ballads,* and also in his work as a whole, the general, one third; the physical, one third; and the other three together, one third, with personification the weakest and bestowal the strongest of these last.[23]

Of special note are the interesting tables which show various percentages in the works of Wordsworth and other major poets. In the total of 53,000 lines of verse written by Wordsworth, 9,000 lines contain named emotions, or about one-sixth of the total.

This is the basic material with which Miss Miles works. She develops it extensively along critical and historical lines, carrying it back into the eighteenth century, investigating it in relation

[22] *Ibid.,* 16.
[23] *Ibid.,* 21–22.

to the theories of Wordsworth and his contemporaries, and making a thorough examination of Wordsworth's own practice. The vocabulary of emotion makes up the substance of much of Wordsworth's verse and prose, and it was to him and his contemporaries poetic language.

Miss Miles concludes that an atmosphere of terms had grown and developed into the social fabric, and that the terms of emotion held an important place.

> In Wordsworth's own part of this atmosphere the place was as great. His young fondness for his poetic predecessors, his strong humanitarian leanings and disturbances, his physical sensitivity which eighteenth-century philosophy accounted for and enforced ethically, his growing comfort in the general as the particular seemed less and less immediate—all these ideas and feelings were significant in their universal truth and their simple names. The names, then, had the prime nature and the vitality of meaning which made for poetry. In naming the heart they named what was then the heart's interest. The poetry was rich with the plain accumulated significance of these terms.[24]

In concluding this section on Wordsworth's critical theories and practice, attention should be called to the discussion of Wordsworth's Prefaces by Professor O. J. Campbell and Professor Paul Mueschke in the second section of their essay, "Wordsworth's Aesthetic Development, 1795–1802."[25] The authors observe that too much modern criticism has confined itself to the old points of controversy on diction, and has overlooked the more permanent and original contributions of the Prefaces. They disagree with Garrod's statement that the chief value of the Prefaces is that they cleared the way of false eighteenth-century practices, but that they are aesthetically and metaphysically inchoate. It is in the positive metaphysical and aesthetic contributions of the Prefaces that Campbell and Mueschke find original and sound affirmations. They point out at length the influence of the "school of taste" on the Prefaces, an influence not confined to Hartley, but also deriving much from Sir Joshua Reynolds. Perhaps most

[24] *Ibid.*, 162–63. See also Miles, "Wordsworth and 'Glitter,' " *SP*, xl (1943), 552–59; F. B. Snyder, "Wordsworth's Favorite Words," *JEGP*, xxii (1923), 253–56; and Lane Cooper, "Some Wordsworthian Similes," *JEGP*, vi (1906–7), 179–89, who remarks concerning Wordsworth's figures that they hold a deep underlying truth "to their author and to the constitution of things as he saw it."

[25] *University of Michigan Publications Language and Literature*, X, Ann Arbor, 1933, 1–57.

important was Reynolds' idea "that the basic principles of criticism as well as those of creativity are traceable to the interaction of mind and external nature," an idea acceptable to modern psychologists.[26]

> The poet was right in thus realizing that every aesthetic experience must be embedded in its larger natural habitat, and that objects which appeal to our sense of the beautiful are not isolated in our consciousness from all other. They are centers of innumerable relationships which can establish their lines of communication only through the medium of brooding, omnipresent Nature.[27]

Wordsworth's second great affirmation, in the opinion of Campbell and Mueschke, is comparing the poet with the man of science. "Wordsworth, because he is able thus to reintegrate science and art in a new psychological monism, proceeds in his Preface to celebrate the harmonious interplay of the scientific and poetic impulses . . ."[28] Finally, Wordsworth's third permanent contribution to aesthetic theory is his insistence that poetical genius is essentially normal, an idea underlying the entire Preface and forming its principal unity.

III

Leaving now the Prefaces, we come to some of the broader aesthetic approaches to Wordsworth. No writer has insisted more strongly on the transcendental interpretation of Wordsworth than Professor Bennett Weaver, but his approach is aesthetic rather than purely philosophic. Wordsworth's metaphysics Weaver regards as the unfortunate prose aspect of what Wordsworth tried to make into poetry.

> It would have been better for Wordsworth had he known that rhyming stuff of the meddling intellect, or giving pentameter flow to religious or moral speculation, is not to achieve in poetry. That there are times when he did know it is manifest. My purpose for the moment is to point out that the critic who fixes great significance to philosophic matter embedded cold within a poet's lines is doomed to illusion and error by the same token that the poet was who left the matter there.[29]

[26] *Ibid.*, 49.
[27] *Ibid.*, 52.
[28] *Ibid.*, 55.
[29] "Wordsworth: The Growth of a Poet's Mind," *Papers of the Michigan Academy of Science, Arts, and Letters*, XXIV (1938), Pt. IV, Ann Arbor, University of Michigan Press, 1939, 109–22.

Weaver does not deny that philosophic systems influenced Wordsworth, but he asserts that when Wordsworth spoke as a poet what he said was not derivative. The poet himself made the mistake of trying to explain in the dry terms of a psychology the sources of his poetic insight. He struggled to fit a system of sensational psychology onto his mystical experiences. The true source of his poetic power is his transcendental union with the eternal and Divine. This became clearer to him after 1802 and reached full realization by 1805. The growing light may be found in the difference between Books I and II of *The Prelude* and those that follow after an interval of three or four years. The first two books show the struggle to fit a psychology "fundamentally foreign to his poetic genius" into an explanation of the source of his poetic insight and inspiration. The effort is subordinated in the later books, and Wordsworth "changes toward a higher quality of thought."

Weaver begins by warning the reader not to attempt to find exact biographical statements in *The Prelude,* and then to interpret the poem from them.[30] Wordsworth was drawing from the wells of memory, trying to fix the "wavering balance" of his mind. He was reaching for that "obscure sense of possible sublimity" (II, 317–18) which he retained in his memory as a part of the soul of his youth, but, he said, "Remembering how she felt, but what she felt Remembering not" (II, 316–17). Weaver remarks: "We are here twice removed from factual accuracies, if indeed we are not on another plane entirely." Moreover, Wordsworth himself admitted to the difficulty of making himself clear. He was dealing with what passed within himself, which "in the main lies far hidden from the reach of words" (III, 138–39). Thus it is, Weaver points out, that Wordsworth "is really involved in the master paradox of his majestically paradoxical mind: he is communicating the 'incommunicable.' "

Next, Weaver explains that *The Prelude* involves "the *poetic* function of memory."[31] Wordsworth's memory of the past was more than factual. It was creative, like the power of imagination in his poetry. The past, the present, the clusters of feelings and associations merged into something more than recollection.

[30] "Wordsworth's 'Prelude': An Intimation of Certain Problems in Criticism," *SP,* xxxi (1934), 534–40.

[31] "Wordsworth's 'Prelude': The Poetic Function of Memory," *SP,* xxxiv (1937), 552–63.

The poet, then, would give up his integrity and the proper understanding of himself if he dealt with the past as fixed or dead actuality. He must treat the past after his true nature, letting his living mind proceed creatively into the past. . . . In other words, through the nature of poetic memory, the vitality of the mind assimilates all into the mind; and the poetry which results is of another truth than the truth of tabulation. . . . This is not to impugn the soundness of certain data in the poem, but rather to keep from confusing whatever of mere biography there is in it with whatever there is of pure poetry.[32]

With these approaches in mind, we can apprehend Wordsworth's growing spiritual conception of himself in the successive books of *The Prelude*. The "shaping spirit" of that poem is the imagination.[33] As he composed, "the mind of the poet" developed, and Wordsworth saw mystical truth more clearly at the end than at the beginning. The shaping spirit, the true Wordsworth, forced him to forget his alien philosophy of sensism.

The poet makes his own world, a living world, living to him and to the God who knows the life of it; for the life in the work of the worker is the life of the Creator himself. . . . Within my mind [says the poet] I recognize that visionary power which rather makes than finds what it beholds. I have come up now to an eminence, and my mind is now possessed of the shaping spirit of imagination.[34]

Wordsworth first reacted in a physical way to the forms and images of nature, but later he was spiritually affected by the "eternal Beauty," the source of these things.[35] His heart was ennobled by the "mountain's outline" because his mind had bestowed upon it "a pure grandeur." Moreover, it was in "forms that Wordsworth finds a substantial power not only arresting him from wild vagaries, but also releasing him to noble creation." But as he escaped the dominance of outward forms, the imagination became eventually the "lord and master." As Wordsworth cast off sensism, as "the senses are remanded to their due place and the system falls off like a dry shell," Wordsworth reached a pure aesthetic consciousness.[36] Finally, when the aesthetic fulfilled itself in the spiritual, the poet was in the presence of Divinity.

It is in the light of this mystical aesthetics that Weaver interprets *The Prelude*. His criticism acts as a healthy corrective to

[32] *Ibid.*, 556–57.
[33] "Wordsworth's 'Prelude': The Shaping Spirit," *SP*, xxxvii (1940), 75–87.
[34] *Ibid.*, pp. 81–82.
[35] "Wordsworth: Forms and Images," *SP*, xxxv (1938), 433–45.
[36] "Wordsworth: The Aesthetic Intimation," *PQ*, xix (1940), 20–28.

the tendency of some who might regard *The Prelude* as an exact factual autobiography, and have been troubled by some of the inconsistencies between the poet's narrative and other biographical data. Memory we know is an operative force in Wordsworth's conception of poetry; it is not merely a storehouse of past experience. However, it must be remembered that *The Prelude* describes and explains the formative forces that affected the poet during a definite period of years. Therefore some caution is desirable in agreeing with Weaver's strong emphasis on the spiritual and mystical elements (which he truly remarks Wordsworth did not fully attain until 1805) and with his inclination to belittle the significance of the earlier stages of sensism, which are just as certainly a part of the record of Wordsworth's growth as are the mystical experiences. Many critics will no doubt disagree with Weaver's statement that the first two books show a struggle to fit a psychology "fundamentally foreign to his poetic genius" into an explanation of the source of his poetic experience. The record of the first two books contains little, if any, "philosophic matter embedded cold within the poet's lines." The experience delineated in these books is a vital one, causally related to the poet's later stage of development. However, few critics have shown more clearly than has Weaver that *The Prelude* is not pure biography, or a system of philosophy out of the schools, but that it is essentially an expression of poetic experience.

Professor Richard Rice has explained Wordsworth's mind in its relationship to Romanticism.[37] Wordsworth's energy, like that of Coleridge, Shelley, and Byron, sprang "from an emotional egotism that seeks its *milieu* of sympathy and expression in surrounding nature, . . . discovering there symbols for a readjustment in the relationship of man with nature and of man with society."[38] This Rice regards as the essence of Romanticism. In his discussion of *The Prelude,* Rice shows that its purpose "is to record the growth of the poetic consciousness; to show how emotional egotism becomes a form of poetic energy that seeks its *milieu,* its means of expansion and expression, in surrounding nature; to show how objects become for the poet images of thought and symbols of the great relationship of nature with man and of man with his fellow beings."[39] Thus Rice gives an inter-

[37] *Wordsworth's Mind,* "Indiana University Studies," I (XI), No. 7, Bloomington, University of Indiana Press, 1913.

[38] *Ibid.,* 23.

[39] *Ibid.,* 30.

pretation of *The Prelude* that is not primarily autobiographical in the ordinary sense of the word, but he reads it as an aesthetic portrayal of "poetic energy." James Smith, in an ably written article, has likewise pointed out that Wordsworth's aesthetic impulse was to find himself, the external world, and their relationships.[40] Wordsworth, he says, "creates . . . a kind of being in which both the external world and himself can share. It combines the characters of both," internally active like himself, but outwardly immobile like the world.

One of the most thorough studies of Wordsworth's aesthetic development is furnished by O. J. Campbell and Paul Mueschke in a series of essays. The first step is laid by Campbell in his paper "Sentimental Morality in Wordsworth's Narrative Poetry."[41] He argues that the tragic aspects of many of Wordsworth's short narrative poems were not aimed at rational social reform, but were written upon the principle of eighteenth-century sentimental morality, i.e. virtue in distress evokes tears and painful emotions in the reader, which process stimulates moral sensibility.[42] Campbell presents a series of eighteenth-century precedents. In Wordsworth's practice of this genre he was repudiating Godwin's scorn for pity and sympathy, and was in line with Hartley's ascending scale of motives: sympathy, theopathy, and moral sense. Painful emotions aroused by undeserved suffering are one of the connecting links leading to joy and the higher morality. Campbell denies that Wordsworth was taught this by Hartley, since he had before him ample eighteenth-century precedent, but this represents another point in Hartley's philosophy that he recognized. The regenerative effect of tears shed in pity of undeserved suffering, Campbell finds as the aesthetic motive of many of Wordsworth's poems written between 1796 and 1804, and of some of the later verse, such as the stories told in *The Excursion*.

The theory broadens out in two later papers written jointly by Campbell and Mueschke: " 'Guilt and Sorrow': A Study in the Genesis of Wordsworth's Aesthetic," and " 'The Borderers' as a Document in the History of Wordsworth's Aesthetic Development."[43] These studies, the authors say, seek "to rescue the poet

[40] "Wordsworth: A Preliminary Survey," *Scrutiny*, vii (1938), 33–55.

[41] *University of Wisconsin Studies in Language and Literature*, No. 11, Madison, University of Wisconsin Press, 1920, pp. 21–57.

[42] It will be remembered that Mr. G. W. Meyer *(Wordsworth's Formative Years)* takes issue here and insists on Wordsworth's social indignation which animates these poems. *Vide*, p. 105.

[43] *MP*, xxiii (1926), 293–306; 465–82.

from the philosophers," and "to replace at the center of Wordsworth's poetical activity, his art." They recognize the influence of Godwinism in *Guilt and Sorrow,* as pointed out especially by Garrod, but they believe that interpreting the poem purely in terms of Godwinism disregards Wordsworth's aesthetic conception. The story of the "Female Vagrant," the conception of which they date as early as 1791–92, reflects the aesthetic intention of sentimental morality. But to this now familiar artistic motive is added another. It is Burke's theory that terror is the source of the sublime in art, that wonder and astonishment produce the sublime, and pity is associated with terror. To this theory are to be added the devices of the Gothic romances. Directed by these influences, Wordsworth wrote the introduction with its terrifying picture of the heath and the solitary hut, the violent action in the narrative of the sailor, and the episode of the boy beaten by his father. The complete poem, the authors believe, is weak because "it is a piece of aesthetic patchwork, the product of two distinct and inharmonious artistic modes." Campbell and Mueschke add that the unexpected confession of the soldier's wife that she has her "inner self abused" is a reflection of Wordsworth's remorse for his treatment of Annette, since this confession seems causeless, and also because Wordsworth was always unable to dramatize anything but himself. We shall see that the authors make more of this "dramatic ventriloquism" (the phrase is from Coleridge) in their later papers.[44]

In their paper on *The Borderers* the authors continue tracing the road of Wordsworth's aesthetic development. They see the same contradictory forces at work in the play that appeared in *Guilt and Sorrow,* but in different relationships. The play throws light on the transformation which took place in Wordsworth's aesthetic principles during the years 1793–97. "It carried him from the philosophy of William Godwin, and its artistic expression through the modes of terror and sentimental morality, to his own original conception of 1798." They do not believe in the "spasmodic development" which other critics (Garrod, for example) have maintained. Their position is made clear thus:

We believe that this drama offers clear evidence that its initial aesthetic impulse was the remorse that his abandonment of Annette had

[44] R. D. Havens takes issue with the statement that the poem is an aesthetic patchwork, and with the attempt to connect the woman's confession with Wordsworth's personal distress ("Wordsworth's 'Guilt and Sorrow,'" *RES,* iii [1927], 71–73).

aroused in him. We believe that he endeavored to cleanse his mind from that paralyzing emotion by adopting the rational doctrines of Godwin, in the hope that they would emancipate his will from the control of his feelings. These theories failed him completely. The remorse persisted. He began to see, therefore, that the natural ties and fundamental relations from which he had attempted to escape were more fundamental than the Godwinian rationalism to which he fled. They, therefore, became the facts upon which his new aesthetic was built. In other words, we shall show that Wordsworth's mature artistic practice, in most of its details, is the result of a clash between Godwin's philosophy and his own bitter and searching personal experience.[45]

In the character of Oswald, who is not a thoroughgoing Godwinian, Campbell and Mueschke see reflected a balancing in Wordsworth's mind of a not yet dead rationalism and a natural feeling as yet not matured into intuitive insight. More significant is the case of Marmaduke, whose remorse for his crime cannot be cured by necessitarianism and Godwinian release from natural ties. This is a reflection of Wordsworth's remorse, and is the genesis of the play. The authors note especially how the drama involves the desecration of the natural love between father and daughter, which indicates something of Wordsworth's feeling of guilt toward his daughter Caroline.

The authors draw the discussion to focus on the inclusion in the play of the two popular contemporary aesthetics of tragedy—sentimental morality and horror. The emotional essence of the play is an appeal to our pity. "According to this aesthetic, then, grief which comes to the witness of undeserved suffering produces a peace deep and stable as infinity. In that peace lies the essence of the aesthetic experience, as Wordsworth always conceived it."[46] Also Wordsworth introduced horror, using properties borrowed from the Gothic romances, but blending the two aesthetics, which he was unable to do in *Guilt and Sorrow*. From this he developed a new point in his aesthetic experience.

The significant implication, however, to be discovered in Wordsworth's use of these two aesthetics in *The Borderers* is that, through an interpretation of his own life, he has come to realize that in the aesthetic experience, memory is a central fact. Both horror and suffering, he believes, are transformed through the serene operation of this faculty

[45] Campbell and Mueschke, *op. cit.*, 466.
[46] *Ibid.*, 480.

into the peace which is the essential quality of the aesthetic experience.[47]

Finally, the play reveals Wordsworth's realization of the importance of the feelings based on natural relationships.

Wordsworth, the artist, therefore, saw that they must serve as the bases upon which to build any vital aesthetic experience. The poet became in his eyes pre-eminently the 'upholder and preserver of these natural feelings carrying with him everywhere relationship and love.' In other words, Wordsworth discovered the truths later enunciated in the Preface to *The Lyrical Ballads*.[48]

Campbell and Mueschke give the final development of their criticism in the paper, "Wordsworth's Aesthetic Development, 1795–1802,"[49] tracing the growth of Wordsworth's aesthetic from the composition of *The Borderers* to the time when his experiment with the ballad form reached its full success. In their extensive discussion of *The Convict, The Ruined Cottage,* and *Peter Bell,* the authors find the same artistic impulse that they have shown animated *Guilt and Sorrow* and *The Borderers:* that is, Wordsworth's emotional conflict of remorse for his treatment of Annette, and the aesthetics of terror and sentimental morality. The following statements regarding *The Ruined Cottage* reveal the nature of Wordsworth's aesthetic advance as the authors see it:

The Ruined Cottage reveals but a glimpse of these new aesthetic forces. In the main it is closely akin to a conventional tale designed to preach sentimental morality. Yet, by infusing it with feelings of remorse not associated with the conventions of the genre, Wordsworth makes it a vehicle of profound emotional experience. In this case the poet attains some artistic maturity, not by revolting against the sentimental tale, but by deepening its emotional content. Moreover, in this work Wordsworth discovered how to give, in a conversational narrative poem, psychic distance to personal experience. This fact evidently strongly commended to him a quasi-dramatic poetic form and led him to experiment with the ballad as a type of conversational narrative at once simple, objective, and dramatic, and to compose *Peter Bell*.[50]

These points in Wordsworth's developing aesthetic—sentimental morality, and Wordsworth's remorse to which he gives "psychic

[47] *Ibid.*, 481.
[48] *Ibid.*, 482.
[49] *University of Michigan Publications Language and Literature,* X, Ann Arbor, University of Michigan Press (1933), 1–57.
[50] *Ibid.*, 16.

distance" in dramatic and narrative forms of composition—are carried forward in *Peter Bell,* which involves also the moral renovation of pity and terror.

When they come to *Lyrical Ballads,* the authors point out that the properties of the Gothic romances seldom appear, having given place to forms of folk superstition. The sentimental morality theme continues, and in many of the poems we find Wordsworth's personal distress over Annette given "psychic distance" by means of the ballad narrative. But the poet had discovered other uses of the ballad form, its possibilities in the simple depiction of the fundamental and typical human passions which have now become a part of his aesthetic creed. Therefore, he used the form in many poems that have no connection with his remorse. The chief stimulus for these poems "must be sought in his unreserved belief in the direct expression of feeling, an aesthetic affirmation to which he had come by courses which we have described."[51] Hence the significance of the title *"Lyrical* Ballads." Campbell and Mueschke find a place in the scheme of development for *Tintern Abbey,* a poem which shows none of the characteristics that we have observed in the ballad or narrative type. The poem shows that Wordsworth had found a rationale in Hartley's system of psychology, but they disagree with Beatty, who sees in the poem little else than an expression of the growth of the mind. They write: "It is rather a revelation to the poet of the aesthetic illumination which lies in the realization of the mind's place in the unitary life of Nature that leads him to ecstasy."[52]

Thus, sentimental morality, the tale of terror, and the ballad and conversational narrative forms, are steps in Wordsworth's aesthetic development. They served to give objective expression to his most personal emotional experience, and to convey the fundamental passions which had replaced rationalism in the poet's philosophy.

Soon after, Hartley's psychological theories gave a philosophical basis to all his cherished artistic practices and reduced them to a coherent system. Then there came, in a kind of mystical vision induced by Nature, a flash of insight which fused all these disjunctive elements into one brilliantly illuminated experience. In the light of that he was able for a decade to compose great original poetry.[53]

[51] *Ibid.,* 27.
[52] *Ibid.,* 32.
[53] *Ibid.,* 39.

Campbell has added to his already impressive body of criticism a paper entitled "Wordsworth's Conception of the Esthetic Experience,"[54] in which he points out the poet's final aesthetic development in *The White Doe of Rylstone, The River Duddon Sonnets,* and *The Ecclesiastical Sonnets.* Life's experiences of change and mutability wrecked Wordsworth's faith in a naturalistic basis for his philosophy and aesthetics, and with the crumbling of this foundation went his belief in the functional unity of nature and the mind of man. In these three compositions Campbell sees symbols of Wordsworth's second philosophic and aesthetic view. The poet "seeks . . . a principle of thought and feeling independent of sensation, anterior to it—a law of the Universe in whose will he can find peace."[55] In *The White Doe* is voiced the "transcendence of the mind over the objects brought into it by sensation."[56] The *Duddon* series is even better adapted to this purpose, in that the river is a more fitting symbol than the doe. In *The Ecclesiastical Sonnets* Wordsworth pictured the life of the Church as a holy river which "flows through Time without being defiled by its decay."[57]

These studies, perhaps more than any others, show a logical development in Wordsworth's early poetry, not of a philosophic nature but along purely literary lines. The authors have so plausibly linked the numerous separate poems of the period that the notion of "spasmodic development" seems very doubtful. How thoroughly the student of Wordsworth will agree with Campbell and Mueschke depends upon how far he is willing to go in accepting the sentimental morality convention as a prime force in the genesis of the poet's art; and to what extent he accepts Wordsworth's remorse over his French liaison as apparent in many of these poems. On both these matters the opinions of critics differ. Wordsworth's use of the Gothic properties is less controversial; and the authors make an excellent case for the poet's transference into the objective ballad material, regardless of whether the earlier, more personalized poetry reflects remorse or is derived principally from other causes of despair which are recognized as a part of this period.

[54] *Wordsworth and Coleridge,* ed. E. L. Griggs, Princeton, Princeton University Press, 1939, pp. 26–46.

[55] *Ibid.,* 37.

[56] *Ibid.,* 39.

[57] *Ibid.,* 44.

IV

Nearly one hundred fifty years have passed since Wordsworth published the Preface to the 1800 edition of *Lyrical Ballads*—a step that plunged him into the bitterness of twenty years or more of ridicule and disparagement—and some of the points of that Preface are still a matter of controversy. His theory of the subjects and diction of poetry is yet a basis for argument, and there is disagreement over exactly what he meant. But it is generally admitted, in principle, that Wordsworth introduced what we know today as "realistic" poetry. It may likewise be said that other matters of the Preface—Wordsworth's theory of poetry and of the poet—have in the course of years been recognized as of equal or of more interest than his theory of diction. Moreover, Wordsworth's poetry has long ceased to be judged strictly by the reader's opinion of the Preface.

Of Wordsworth's life, little remains to be told except for the facts concerning one or two obscure periods in the years before 1798. The interpretation, however, of his early and late years remains a matter of controversy. But there can be no return to the false notion of the "Daddy Wordsworth" stamp. That he was a man of force, sometimes almost violent in his nature; that he espoused humanitarian and political causes with passion, integrity, and generally with wisdom; that he reflected in his poetry a mode of life vigorous and intense; that he achieved the final peace and deep serenity of his philosophy by means of doubt and conflict, not by the undisturbed seclusion of the recluse—all of these things have gradually become established as essential aspects of the life and character of Wordsworth.

His philosophy of man and nature is intricate, and as long as his poetry arouses the emotions and stimulates the minds of his readers there will be a variety of emphases and interpretations. But we see more clearly today the formative forces at work in his thought, the variety of ideas that converged in his mind and were transmuted into his poetic philosophy. He drew from experience his belief in the beneficent effect on the mind of the senses in contact with nature; but he was not alone since something of his creed, as we can now see, was shared by thinkers and philosophers who may have played a part in clarifying for the poet the epistemology of naturalism. Wordsworth's deep spiritual insight, which strangely permeates his naturalism, was derived from a need within him which demanded expression, but this aspect of his thought likewise reflects contact with other great minds. Part of his attitude toward nature and some of the qualities he attributes to her have been challenged by a more scientific age, but we can understand better today than could Wordsworth's contemporaries his great preoccupation with the mind of man and its relation to all that is outside it:

> How exquisitely the individual Mind
> . . . to the external world
> Is fitted:– and how exquisitely, too—
> Theme this but little heard of among men—
> The external World is fitted to the Mind.

That Wordsworth was no "prematurely cow-like son of Cumberland" is not only demonstrated by Professor Douglas Bush's delightfully written paper "Wordsworth and the Classics,"[58] but likewise by the great host of writers whose work has revealed innumerable facets of interest in the poet and his poetry. The horizons of Wordsworth's art are constantly being broadened by the many studies that throw light on his methods, his purposes, and his relationship to other writers and thinkers. Jeffrey—with his sneers and easy condemnation, with his "This will never do" and his "the natural drawl of the Lakers,"—might well be confounded could he be aware of the great interest in Wordsworth manifested in the last hundred years, and the ever widening influence which his poetry has exerted. Antagonism and misunderstanding of what he said haunted the poet through life, and hostility and misstatements of his meaning and purpose have by no means died out in the present day. Wordsworth will never command the ready ear of acceptance that we give to Chaucer, to Shakespeare, to Milton. But his readers have grown in numbers with the years, and he has commanded the interest and sometimes the devotion of many great minds of the past century and of the present. It has proved true that extensive investigation of Wordsworth's thought and the forces contributing to his poetry has not obscured his light or revealed an essential meagerness of genius, as it might if he were a lesser man. Rather, the more we know of Wordsworth, the better we understand him and the more impressive becomes his stature. The intensive study by scholars of his thought and philosophy and the many voices

[58] *University of Toronto Quarterly*, ii (1933), 359-79.

proclaiming the various aspects of his art, all unite in enriching our understanding of Wordsworth the poet—who, "being possessed of more than usual organic sensibility," has "also thought long and deeply," and "who rejoices more than other men in the spirit of life that is in him."

PART II: BIBLIOGRAPHY

I. NOTE ON ITEMS PRIOR TO 1850

Inasmuch as the bibliography begins with the period after Wordsworth's death, there is inserted here for quick reference a brief list of standard criticism by Wordsworth's contemporaries. Fuller information will be found in Part I, Chapters One and Two.

BYRON, LORD

Rev. of *Poems in Two Volumes, Monthly Literary Recreations,* July, 1807 (see Elsie Smith, *An Estimate of William Wordsworth by his Contemporaries, 1793–1822,* Oxford, Basil Blackwood, 1932, pp. 70–72).

English Bards and Scotch Reviewers (1809).

COLERIDGE, S. T.

Biographia Literaria (1817). See especially Chapters IV, XIV, XVII–XXII.

DE QUINCEY, THOMAS

"Literary and Lake Reminiscences," *Tait's Magazine,* Jan., Feb., April, 1839.

"On Wordsworth's Poetry," *Tait's Magazine,* Sept., 1845.

(See David Masson, ed., *Collected Writings of Thomas De Quincey,* 14 vols., Edinburgh, A. and C. Black, 1889–90.)

HAZLITT, WILLIAM

Rev. of *The Excursion, Examiner,* Aug. 21, 28, Oct. 2, 1814.

Lectures on the English Poets (1818).

My First Acquaintance with Poets (1823).

Spirit of the Age (1825).

(See A. R. Waller and Arnold Glover, eds., *Collected Works of William Hazlitt,* 12 vols. and Index, London, J. M. Dent and Co., 1902–4.)

HUNT, LEIGH

Feast of the Poets (1811).

JEFFREY, FRANCIS

Rev. of *Poems in Two Volumes, Edinburgh Rev.,* xi (Oct., 1807), 214.

Rev. of *The Excursion, Edinburgh Rev.,* xxiv (Nov., 1814), 1.

D. N. Smith, ed., *Jeffrey's Literary Criticism,* London, Henry Frowde, 1910.

KEATS, JOHN

M. B. Forman, ed., *The Letters of John Keats,* 2 vols., Humphrey Milford, Oxford University Press, 1931.

LAMB, CHARLES

Rev. of *The Excursion, Quarterly Rev.,* xii (Oct., 1814), 100 (see Elsie Smith, *op. cit.,* 169–75).

E. V. Lucas, ed., *Letters of Charles and Mary Lamb,* 3 vols., New Haven, Yale University Press, 1935.

LANDOR, W. S.

"Southey and Porson," *London Magazine,* July, 1823, and *Blackwood's Magazine,* Dec., 1842. Included in *Imaginary Conversations* (see T. E. Welby, ed., *Complete Works of Walter Savage Landor,* 16 vols., London, Chapman and Hall Ltd., 1927–36, V, 139–213).

ROBINSON, HENRY CRABB

Edith J. Morley, ed., *Blake, Coleridge, Wordsworth, Lamb, etc. Being Selections from the Remains of Henry Crabb Robinson,* Manchester, The University Press, 1922.

WILSON, JOHN

"Wordsworth" (see Ferrier, ed., *Works of Professor Wilson,* 12 vols., Edinburgh, W. Blackwood and Sons, 1865–67, V, 387–408).

II. BIBLIOGRAPHY OF SELECTED EDITIONS

1849–1850

1. *The Poetical Works of William Wordsworth,* 6 vols., London, Edward Moxon, 1849–50.

This is the standard text, the last edition published during Wordsworth's life, with his final revisions. *The Prelude, The Recluse,* and some twenty-three minor poems that appeared in previous editions are not included.

1876

2. GROSART, A. B., ed. *Prose Works of William Wordsworth,* 3 vols., London, Edward Moxon, 1876.

This edition and Knight's (1896) are still standard. In addition to Wordsworth's formal prose, it includes his notes to his poetry, some of his letters, and a section on "Conversations and Personal Reminiscences of Wordsworth."

1879

3. ARNOLD, MATTHEW, ed. *Poems of Wordsworth,* London, Macmillan and Co., 1879.

This volume of selections was the most influential in establishing Wordsworth's reputation in the Victorian period. The famous Introduction (which also appeared in *Macmillan's Magazine,* xl [1879], 193) was reprinted in *Essays in Criticism,* Second Series, London, Macmillan and Co., 1888. Both in his selection of poems and in the Introduction, Arnold seeks to discard much of the "dead" Wordsworth and to emphasize the vital poet. He opposes the "Wordsworthians" (referring especially to Leslie Stephen's essay "Wordsworth's Ethics") who maintained that Wordsworth expresses a system of philosophy. To do the poet justice, says Arnold, "we must dismiss his formal philosophy." See 50.

1888

4. MORLEY, JOHN, ed. *The Complete Poetical Works of William Wordsworth,* London, Macmillan and Co., 1888.

The introductory essay was influential in molding the late Victorian opinion of Wordsworth. Like Arnold, Morley believes that Wordsworth's ethics and philosophy have little to do with the power his poetry exerts over us. Morley comments on Wordsworth's moral quality, his tendency (acquired from the Revolutionary era) to simplify life. The final impression that remains from this essay is that the chief contribution of Wordsworth's poetry is "to assuage, to reconcile, to fortify." The text is from the 1857 Moxon edition, and includes *The Recluse,* published for the first time. Poems arranged in chronological order; the text has often been reprinted.

1892

5. DOWDEN, EDWARD, ed. *The Poetical Works of William Wordsworth,* 7 vols., London, George Bell and Sons, 1892.

One of the standard editions, with valuable introduction and notes. The variant readings supplied are more accurate than Knight's, but not so full. Poems arranged according to Wordsworth's order.

1895

6. HUTCHINSON, THOMAS, ed. *The Poetical Works of William Wordsworth,* London, Oxford University Press, 1895.

This, perhaps the best one-volume edition, has been reprinted many times. Hutchinson's text and dates are the most reliable of any editor. Notes are scanty. Poems according to Wordsworth's arrangement.

1896

7. KNIGHT, W. A., ed. *The Poetical Works of William Wordsworth,* 8 vols., London, Macmillan and Co., 1896.

Based on Knight's edition of 1882–86. This text is somewhat revised and contains fuller notes. The record of variant readings is more complete than in Dowden, but there are numerous errors in both the textual notes and the dates of the poems. Poems arranged in chronological order.

8. ———. *Prose Works of William Wordsworth,* 2 vols., London, Macmillan and Co., 1896.

This and the 1876 edition by Grosart are still standard.

1897

9. HUTCHINSON, THOMAS, ed. *Poems in Two Volumes,* 2 vols., London, David Nutt, 1897.

The text is reprinted from the original edition of 1807. A valuable note on the Wordsworthian sonnet is included.

1898

10. HUTCHINSON, THOMAS, ed. *Lyrical Ballads,* London, Duckworth and Co., 1898.

A reprint of the 1798 edition, including other poems of the same date, with an introduction and notes.

1903

11. SAMPSON, GEORGE, ed. *The Lyrical Ballads, 1798–1805,* London, Methuen and Co., 1903.

A well-edited edition of the complete *Lyrical Ballads.*

1904

12. GEORGE, A. J., ed. *The Complete Poetical Works of William Wordsworth,* Boston, Houghton Mifflin Co., 1904.

This, the "Cambridge Edition of the Poets" series, is the standard American edition, in one volume. It includes Wordsworth's notes, Fenwick notes, and a few by the editor. Poems arranged in chronological order.

1905

13. SMITH, N. C., ed. *Wordsworth's Literary Criticism,* London, Henry Frowde, 1905.

A convenient collection of the Prefaces, essays, and comments in letters.

1907

14. KNIGHT, W. A., ed. *Letters of the Wordsworth Family from 1787 to 1855,* 3 vols., Boston and London, Ginn and Co., 1907.

Long standard, this is now superseded by de Selincourt's edition. See *28, 31, 32.*

1908

15. SMITH, N. C., ed. *The Poems of William Wordsworth,* 3 vols., London, Methuen and Co., 1908.

Contains a very good introduction, and somewhat brief but scholarly notes. Poems arranged according to Wordsworth's order.

1914

16. DARBISHIRE, HELEN, ed. *Wordsworth's Poems in Two Volumes, 1807,* Oxford, The Clarendon Press, 1914.

A reprint of the Bodleian copy, with introduction and textual and critical notes. The introduction presents a penetrating interpretation of Wordsworth's art, distinguishing between the artistic purpose and achievement of *Lyrical Ballads* and the new poems included in the 1807 collection. The notes contain a valuable commentary on Wordsworth's sonnets, and Appendix II gives a table of metrical forms.

1915

17. DICEY, A. V., ed. *Wordsworth's Tract on the Convention of Cintra,* London, Humphrey Milford, 1915.

The best edition of this important pamphlet on Wordsworth's political views in 1809.

1920

18. SAMPSON, GEORGE, ed. *Coleridge. Biographia Literaria, Chapters I–IV, XIV–XXII. Wordsworth. Prefaces and Essays on Poetry, 1800–1815,* Cambridge, The University Press, 1920.

A convenient grouping of the Prefaces and relevant portions of the *Biographia Literaria,* with notes and an introduction by Sir Arthur Quiller-Couch. See *124*.

1922

19. POTTS, ABBIE F., ed. *The Ecclesiastical Sonnets of William Wordsworth. A Critical Edition,* New Haven, Conn., Yale University Press, 1922.

Includes a discussion of the manuscripts and of the dates of composition, and an analysis of the structure of the series. Copious notes.

Rev. Bright, *MLN,* xxxviii (1923), 380.

1924

20. LITTLEDALE, H., ed. *Wordsworth and Coleridge. Lyrical Ballads. 1798,* London, Oxford University Press, 1924.

A reprint of the original edition.

1926

21. DE SELINCOURT, ERNEST, ed. *The Prelude,* Oxford, The Clarendon Press, 1926.

The variorum edition. This is the first publication of the 1805 text, with copious textual and critical notes. A book of first importance.

Rev. *TLS,* Apr. 29, 1926, p. 309. Saintsbury, *Nation-Athen.,* xxxix

(June 26, 1926), 356. Harper, *SRL,* Oct. 2, 1926, p. 154. G. C. M. Smith, *MLR,* xxi (1926), 443–46. *Library* (4th Series), vii (1926), 332–34. Havens, *MLN,* xlii (1927), 256–58. Broughton, *JEGP,* xxvi (1927), 427–32. Reed, *YR,* Oct., 1927, pp. 182–85. Doughty, *RES,* iii (1927), 473–79. Brandl, *Archiv,* Sept., 1927, 130–31.

22. ———. *Wordsworth's Guide to the Lakes,* London, Humphrey Milford, 1926.

In "The Oxford Miscellany." This text is from the fifth edition (1835), and is well supplied with textual and illustrative notes. It is the best edition of the *Guide,* Wordsworth's significant book on scenery and matters of taste.

23. *The Noel Douglas Replicas. Lyrical Ballads, 1798,* London, Noel Douglas, 1926.

A reproduction of the British Museum copy with the rare Bristol imprint.

1932

24. Reynolds, E. E., ed. *The Prelude,* London, Macmillan and Co., 1932.

In the introduction and notes the editor has kept his material abreast of recent research. "The present editor keeps closely to the 1850 text except when Professor de Selincourt's examination of the manuscripts has revealed obvious errors."

1933

25. Broughton, L. N., ed. *Wordsworth and Reed. The Poet's Correspondence with his American Editor: 1836–1850,* Ithaca, N. Y., Cornell University Press, 1933.

These letters are not included in de Selincourt's edition of *The Letters of William and Dorothy Wordsworth.*

Rev. *TLS,* Sept. 14, 1933, p. 606. Crawford, *PQ,* xiii (1934), 409–10. E. J. Morley, *RES,* x (1934), 486–88. Beatty, *MLN,* li (1936), 182–84.

26. De Selincourt, Ernest, ed. *The Prelude,* London, Oxford University Press, 1933.

A convenient and inexpensive edition of the 1805 text, with introduction and textual notes. The volume is an abbreviation of de Selincourt's important variorum edition, with some revisions. See *21.*

27. HUTCHINSON, THOMAS, ed. *The Poetical Works of Wordsworth,* New York, Oxford University Press, 1933.

The "Oxford Standard Edition," the same as No. *6,* except that it includes an introduction by Harper.

1935

28. DE SELINCOURT, ERNEST, ed. *Early Letters of William and Dorothy Wordsworth (1787–1805),* Oxford, The Clarendon Press, 1935.

The first volume of de Selincourt's definitive edition of the Wordsworth letters. See *31, 32, 25, 36.*

Rev. *TLS,* Aug. 25, 1935, p. 528. Sackville-West, *Spect.,* Oct. 4, 1935, p. 514. *New Sts.,* Sept. 7, 1935, p. 314. Harper, *SRL,* Nov. 2, 1935, pp. 22–23. Van Doren, *Nation,* Oct. 23, 1935, p. 484. *N&Q,* Aug. 31, 1935, p. 161. Blunden, *Merc.,* xxxii (1935), 481–82. E. J. Morley, *RES,* xii (1936), 362–64. Havens, *MLN,* li (1936), 389–93. *Archiv,* clxx (1936), 117–18. De Vane, *YR,* Autumn 1937, pp. 188–90. Maclean, *MLR,* xxxii (1937), 104–7. *N&Q,* Mar. 27, 1937, pp. 233–34. Burra, *Crit.,* xvi (1937), 741–44.

29. REYNOLDS, E. E., ed. *The Excursion, Preceded by Book I of The Recluse,* London, Macmillan and Co., 1935.

This and Reynold's edition of *The Prelude* bear the stamp of up-to-date research.

1936

30. DE SELINCOURT, ERNEST, ed., *George and Sarah Green, A Narrative,* Oxford, The Clarendon Press, 1936.

This narrative, written by Dorothy Wordsworth, tells the story of the violent deaths in a snow storm of a local farmer and his wife, and the pathetic plight of the orphaned children.

1937

31. DE SELINCOURT, ERNEST, ed. *The Letters of William and Dorothy Wordsworth, 1806–1820,* 2 vols., Oxford, The Clarendon Press, 1937.

These, the second and third volumes of de Selincourt's definitive edition, include the letters of the "Middle Years." See *28, 32, 25, 36.*

Rev. *TLS,* March 13, 1937, p. 184. *N&Q,* March 27, 1937, pp. 233–34. Garnett, *New Sts.,* Apr. 3, 1937, p. 556. Blunden, *Merc.* xxv (1937), 631–32. Sackville-West, *Spect.,* Apr. 16, 1937, p. 729. Lovett, *NR,* Aug. 11, 1937, pp. 23–24. De Vane, *YR,* Autumn 1937, pp.

188–90. Harper, *SRL,* July 3, 1937, p. 20. Van Doren, *Nation,* Apr. 24, 1937, pp. 481–82. Havens, *MLN,* liii (1938), 395–96.

1939

32. DE SELINCOURT, ERNEST, ed. *The Letters of William and Dorothy Wordsworth, 1821–1850,* 3 vols., Oxford, The Clarendon Press, 1939.

These three volumes complete de Selincourt's edition of the letters. See *28, 31, 25, 36.*

Rev. *TLS,* Feb. 18, 1939, pp. 104–6. *N&Q,* clxxvi (1939), 125–26. De Vane, *YR,* xxviii (1939), 829–31. Harper, *SRL,* Apr. 8, 1939, p. 18. Sackville-West, *Spect.,* Apr. 7, 1939, p. 604. Graham, *ELH,* vii (1940), pp. 15–16.

1940

33. COMPARETTI, ALICE P., ed., *The White Doe of Rylstone,* "Cornell Studies in English," XXIX, Ithaca, N. Y., Cornell University Press, 1940.

The text of 1850, with variant readings. The introduction includes an account of the composition and publication, the sources, and interpretations and criticisms. There are notes and a compendium of critical estimates.

Rev. Jones, *JEGP,* xl (1941), 303–4. Wellek, *PQ,* xx (1941), 92–93.

34. DE SELINCOURT, ERNEST, ed. *The Poetical Works of William Wordsworth. Poems Written in Youth. Poems Referring to the Period of Childhood.* Oxford, The Clarendon Press, 1940.

This is the first volume of what is expected to be the definitive edition of Wordsworth's poetry. The text and dates are based on sound modern research. A full *apparatus criticus* is supplied. An appendix includes some juvenilia not in other editions, portions of which are printed for the first time. Poems are arranged according to Wordsworth's order. See *38.*

Rev. Read, *Spect.,* Nov. 22, 1940, p. 534. E. J. Morley, *RES,* xvii (1941), 242–45. *TLS,* Jan. 25, 1941, p. 39. Batho, *MLR,* xxxvii (1942), 219–21. Havens, *MLN,* lviii (1943), 563–64.

1941

35. DE SELINCOURT, ERNEST, ed. *Journals of Dorothy Wordsworth,* 2 vols., London, Macmillan and Co., 1941.

This edition replaces that of Knight (London, Macmillan and Co., 1897). The *Journals* are for the first time published in their entirety. All, except the Alfoxden *Journal,* are printed from the manuscripts. The text of the Alfoxden *Journal* is given from Knight, since the manuscript is lost.

Rev. *TLS,* June 27, 1942, p. 318. Christopher Morley, *SRL,* June 13, 1942, p. 7. Batho, *RES,* xix (1943), 100–2. Nowell Smith, *English,* iv (1943), 84–85.

1942

36. BROUGHTON, L. N., ed. *Some Letters of the Wordsworth Family, Now First Published, with a Few Unpublished Letters of Coleridge and Southey and Others,* "Cornell Studies in English," XXXII, Ithaca, N. Y., Cornell University Press, 1942.

Contains a group of letters to George Huntly Gordon, which hitherto have been published only in fragments or not at all. Also some letters to other correspondents are included.

37. HEALEY, G. H. *Wordsworth's Pocket Notebook,* Ithaca, N. Y., Cornell University Press, 1942.

Contains lists of appointments, scraps of verse, and other matters, assigned to the years 1839–40, when Wordsworth visited London, Cambridge, and Oxford.

1944

38. DE SELINCOURT, ERNEST, ed. *The Poetical Works of William Wordsworth. Poems Founded on the Affections. Poems on the Naming of Places. Poems on the Fancy. Poems of the Imagination,* Oxford, The Clarendon Press, 1944.

Volume II of de Selincourt's edition of the poetry. Since his recent death, the work on the remaining volumes will be completed by Helen Darbishire. See *34*.

Rev. *TLS,* June 17, 1944, p. 294.

III. BIBLIOGRAPHY OF CRITICISM

1850

39. Masson, David. "Wordsworth," *North British Rev.*, xiii (1850), 473.

Reprinted in *Essays, Biographical and Critical,* Cambridge, Macmillan and Co., 1856; and in *Wordsworth, Shelley, Keats,* London, Macmillan and Co., 1874. This general essay remains of some interest in that it indicates how Wordsworth was evaluated at the time of his death.

1851

40. Wordsworth, Christopher. *Memoirs of William Wordsworth,* 2 vols., London, Edward Moxon, 1851.

The first full-length life to appear. The task was intrusted by the poet to his nephew, but the biography was not regarded as satisfactory, even at the time of its publication. Heavy stress is placed upon the more pious and sedate elements of Wordsworth, and much pertaining to the early life is passed over or suppressed. The work, however, is the primary source of some biographical material of value.

1864

41. Bagehot, Walter. "Wordsworth, Tennyson, and Browning; or Pure, Ornate, and Grotesque Art in English Poetry," *National Rev.,* xix (1864), 27.

Reprinted in *Literary Studies,* 2 vols., London, Longmans, Green and Co., 1879. Wordsworth's art is "pure," treating universals with intensity and strict economy of detail. The essay is illuminating.

42. Shairp, J. C. "Wordsworth, the Man and the Poet," *North British Rev.,* xli (1864), 1.

Revised and enlarged in *Studies in Poetry and Philosophy,* Edinburgh, Edmonston and Douglas, 1868. While not intending to "take the measure" of Wordsworth, Shairp points out the sources of delight to be found in the poetry. He distinguishes three epochs in Wordsworth's poetry, and discusses the nature of his art and his philosophy and natural religion. This is one of the better of the Victorian general essays on the poet.

1869

43. Clough, A. H. *Poems and Prose Remains,* 2 vols., London, Macmillan and Co., 1869.

Contains "Lecture on the Poetry of Wordsworth," notable chiefly as a delineation of Wordsworth's art in poetic style and diction.

44. Graves, R. P., *et al. Afternoon Lectures on Literature and Art,* Dublin, William McGee, 1869.

A collection of lectures delivered by various speakers at the Royal College of Science, Dublin, containing Graves's "Recollections of Wordsworth and the Lake Country." Graves was rector at Windermere, and his "Recollections" is one of the standard essays by a personal friend of the poet and of his family in the later years.

1871

45. Hutton, R. H. *Literary Essays,* London, Strahan, 1871.

Republished by Macmillan, 1888. Contains "The Genius of Wordsworth," an intricate and philosophic interpretation. The central point is Wordsworth's spiritual frugality, extracting much from the smallest objects contemplated.

1873

46. Shairp, J. C. "Wordsworth's Three Yarrows," *Good Words,* xiv (1873), 649.

Reprinted in *Aspects of Poetry,* Oxford, The Clarendon Press, 1881. This essay should be read by anyone studying these poems. It presents the occasion of their composition, Wordsworth's relations with Scott and Hogg, and sensitive comments on the scene and the spirit of the poems.

1874

47. Brooke, S. A. *Theology in the English Poets,* London, Henry S. King and Co., 1874.

Lectures delivered in 1872, V–XIII on Wordsworth. Of the several contributions of Stopford Brooke to the Wordsworthian bibliography, this book and *Naturalism in English Poetry* are the most significant. These lectures discuss the combined spiritual and material forces evident in Wordsworth's poetry. Much of the matter is based on a detailed reading of *The Prelude.*

48. PATER, WALTER. "Wordsworth," *Fortnightly Rev.,* xxi (1874), 455.

Reprinted in *Appreciations,* London, Macmillan and Co., 1889. While Pater treats with skill various aspects of Wordsworth's poetry, perhaps the most remarkable thing in this essay is his apprehension of Wordsworth's doctrine of the presence of life in the objects of nature, of man as part of nature, of the revival of the idea of the *anima mundi,* and of Wordsworth's chief aim, "in life and art alike, to be a certain deep emotion . . . an absolute sincerity of feeling and diction."

49. SHAIRP, J. C. "The White Doe of Rylstone," *Good Words,* xv (1874), 269.

Reprinted in *Aspects of Poetry,* Oxford, The Clarendon Press, 1881. Contrasts the narrative method with that of Scott, tells the history of the incident and summarizes the story of the poem, and interprets the spiritual aspect of Emily and the Doe.

1876

50. STEPHEN, LESLIE. "Wordsworth's Ethics," *Cornhill Magazine,* xxxiv (1876), 206.

Reprinted in *Hours in a Library,* Third Series, London, Smith, Elder and Co., 1879. One of the most important of the Victorian essays, this continues to be one of the best expositions of this aspect of Wordsworth's thought. By stressing the importance of Wordsworth's philosophy in measuring the significance of his poetry, Stephen provoked Matthew Arnold's well-known and influential essay, "Wordsworth," denying the importance of the poet's system of philosophy. See *3*.

1877

51. SHAIRP, J. C. *On Poetic Interpretation of Nature,* Edinburgh, David Douglas, 1877.

The last chapter is devoted to Wordsworth.

1878

52. DOWDEN, EDWARD. *Studies in Literature, 1789–1877,* London, C. Kegan Paul and Co., 1878.

Contains a good essay on "The Prose Works of Wordsworth," as well as comments on his relations to the French Revolution, and to both scientific and transcendental thought.

53. ———. "The Text of Wordsworth's Poems," *Contemporary Rev.*, xxxiii (1878), 734.

Reprinted in *Transcripts and Studies,* London, Kegan Paul, Trench and Co., 1888.

1880

54. Caird, Edward. "Wordsworth," *Fraser's Magazine,* ci (1880), 205.

Reprinted in *Essays on Literature and Philosophy,* 2 vols., Glasgow, James Maclehose and Sons, 1892. A well-rounded, general essay. The discussion of Wordsworth and Rousseau is of especial value.

55. De Vere, Aubrey. "The Genius and Passion of Wordsworth," *Month,* xxxviii (1880), 465; xxxix (1880), 1.

Republished in *Essays Chiefly on Poetry,* 2 vols., London, Macmillan and Co., 1887. De Vere was moved by Arnold's essay "Wordsworth" to write this and No. *61*. He reaffirms the philosophic and ethical value of Wordsworth's teaching, and points out that Wordsworth is not cold and passionless. *Essays Chiefly on Poetry* also reprints "The Wisdom and Truth of Wordsworth's Poetry" (see *61*), and "Recollections of Wordsworth," first published in Grosart's edition of the *Prose Works* (see *2*).

1881

56. Bedford, E. J. *Genealogical Memoranda Relating to the Family of Wordsworth,* London, Mitchell and Hughes (privately printed), 1881.

A rare item, the issue being limited to fifty copies.

57. Myers, F. W. H. *Wordsworth,* London, Macmillan and Co., 1881.

"English Men of Letters" series. Out-of-date in places as the story of Wordsworth's life and as an interpretation of him as a man, the book contains some good criticism of his poetry.

1882

58. Knight, W. A., ed. *Transactions of the Wordsworth Society,* No. 1–No. 8, 1882–87.

For a survey of the most valuable papers in the *Transactions, vide,* pp. 70–73. See *66*.

1884

59. BURROUGHS, JOHN. *Fresh Fields,* Boston, Houghton Mifflin Co., 1884.

Contains a chapter "In Wordsworth's Country," and numerous references to Wordsworth indicating his appeal to the naturalist. See *79, 147*.

60. COURTHOPE, W. J. "Wordsworth's Theory of Poetry," *The National Rev.,* Dec., 1884, pp. 512–27.

This article also forms a part of *The Liberal Movement in English Literature,* London, John Murray, 1885.

61. DE VERE, AUBREY. "The Wisdom and Truth of Wordsworth's Poetry," *Catholic World,* 1884.

Republished in *Essays Chiefly on Poetry,* 2 vols., London, Macmillan and Co., 1887. See 55.

62. SWINBURNE, A. C. "Wordsworth and Byron," *The Nineteenth Century,* xv (1884), 583; 764.

Reprinted in *Miscellanies,* London, Chatto and Windus, 1886. A defense of Wordsworth as a poet, rather than as a philosopher or teacher. A stimulating essay in which Swinburne's admiration for Wordsworth is far from unqualified. Swinburne has a fine ear for Wordsworth's verse.

1887

63. KNIGHT, W. A., ed. *Memorials of Coleorton,* 2 vols., Edinburgh, David Douglas, 1887.

Letters by the Wordsworths, Southey, and Scott to Sir George and Lady Beaumont, 1803–34. Contains introduction and notes.

1889

64. DE VERE, AUBREY. *Essays Chiefly Literary and Critical,* London, Macmillan and Co., 1889.

Contains the essay, "Personal Character of Wordsworth's Poetry," reprinted from *Transactions of the Wordsworth Society,* No. 5 (1883).

65. KNIGHT, W. A. *The Life of William Wordsworth,* 3 vols., Edinburgh, William Paterson, 1889.

Marked as Volumes IX, X, and XI of Knight's edition of *Poetical Works of William Wordsworth* (1882–86). Knight collected and preserved much indispensable biographical material and his *Life* did service in its day; but it has been superseded by more recent biographies.

66. KNIGHT, W. A., ed. *Wordsworthiana. A Selection from Papers Read to the Wordsworth Society,* London, Macmillan and Co., 1889.

A convenient collection of the most important papers, with some revisions. See *58*.

67. MINTO, WILLIAM. "Wordsworth's Great Failure," *The Nineteenth Century,* xxvi (1889), 434–51.

Wordsworth failed in his ambition to complete his great philosophical poem on man and nature because: (1) he was not a constructive thinker and could not carry through such a scheme of thought; (2) he made a mistake in proposing man as the hero of the poem, as most of his portraitures of people are failures; (3) he is best in his spontaneous verse, when he has thrown off the burden of his grand system of thought.

1890

68. BROOKE, S. A. *Dove Cottage, Wordsworth's Home from 1800–1808,* London, Macmillan and Co., 1890.

A description, with comments on the biographical interest of the cottage. See *158, 463*.

69. EWING, T. J. "Wordsworth's 'Ode on Intimations of Immortality,'" *N&Q,* April 12, 1890, pp. 297–98.

This opens a discussion of the interpretation of the line in stanza III: "The Winds come to me from the fields of sleep." See *N&Q,* Aug. 9, 1890, pp. 109–10 (two entries); Sept. 6, pp. 196–97; Sept. 27, pp. 258–59; Nov. 8, pp. 375–76 (three entries). See also *270*.

1891

70. BAYNE, THOMAS. "Wordsworth's 'Sonnet Composed upon Westminster Bridge; Sept. 3, 1802,'" *N&Q,* Jan. 17, 1891, p. 53.

The date given for this poem is corrected to July 30, 1802, from Dorothy's *Journals*. See *N&Q,* Nov. 8, 1890, p. 375; Dec. 13, 1890, p. 465.

71. BUSSIÈRE, GEORGES, AND ÉMILE LEGOUIS. *Le Général Michel Beaupuy,* Paris, 1891.

Beaupuy, more than any other man, influenced Wordsworth's revolutionary ideas during his residence in France. The book includes information on the Beaupuy family, the life of Michel, and his relation with Wordsworth.

72. GOSSE, E. W. *Gossip in a Library,* London, William Heinemann, 1891.

Contains the essay "Peter Bell and his Tormentors," discussing the unfavorable criticism of that poem, and conjecturing that Wordsworth long withheld its publication because it represents the extreme point of his literary theory of 1798. See also *276, 612, 635.*

73. GREEN, S. F. "John de Clapham," *N&Q,* Dec. 19, 1891, p. 488.

Sources of the details on John de Clapham in the second canto of *The White Doe of Rylstone.* See *N&Q,* Feb. 20, 1892, pp. 151–52.

74. TUTIN, J. R. *The Wordsworth Dictionary of Persons and Places,* Hull, J. R. Tutin, 1891.

Contains also a list of familiar quotations.

1892

75. TUTIN, J. R. *An Index to the Animal and Vegetable Kingdoms of Wordsworth,* Hull, J. R. Tutin, 1892.

A complete reference list.

76. WINTRINGHAM, W. H. *The Birds of Wordsworth,* London, Hutchinson and Co., 1892.

An ornithologist discusses the fifty-one species of birds mentioned by Wordsworth.

1893

77. MEUSCH, R.A.J. "Goethe and Wordsworth," *Publications of the English Goethe Society,* VII (Old Series, 1893), 85–107.

Both Goethe and Wordsworth wisely abandoned the extreme revolutionary view for a sober devotion to freedom achieved through law and control. The poets differ essentially in their views of nature. To Wordsworth, nature was sublime and above man. To Goethe it was beautiful, but inferior to man. The essay is vitiated by a narrow, Victorian conception of Wordsworth. See *91, 364, 457.*

1894

78. MINTO, WILLIAM. *The Literature of the Georgian Era,* Edinburgh, William Blackwood and Sons, 1894.

Contains three chapters devoted to the interpretation of Wordsworth's poetry and the influences upon him.

79. RAWNSLEY, H. D. *Literary Associations of the English Lakes,* 2 vols., Glasgow, James Maclehose and Sons, 1894.

The best known of the numerous books on the Lake district, written by the rector of Crosthwaite Church, Keswick. All the well-known literary figures associated with the district are included. See *59, 147.*

1895

80. SCUDDER, VIDA D. *The Life of the Spirit in Modern English Poets,* Boston, Houghton Mifflin and Co., 1895.

Contains a discussion of "Wordsworth and the New Democracy," tracing his influence on the social and political thought of the nineteenth century.

1896

81. LEGOUIS, ÉMILE. *La Jeunesse de William Wordsworth—1770–1798,* "Annales de l'Université de Lyon," G. Masson, Éditeur, Paris, 1896.

The original French edition of this important book, translated into English the following year by J. W. Matthews. See *86.*

82. REYNOLDS, MYRA. *The Treatment of Nature in English Poetry between Pope and Wordsworth,* Chicago, University of Chicago Press, 1896.

Revised second ed. 1909. A comprehensive study, tracing the evolution of the subject to its full expression in Wordsworth. The numerous references to Wordsworth are conveniently indexed. The conclusion reached is that while Wordsworth was the first poet to give adequate expression to the essential unity between man and nature, much preparation had been made for his responses to nature, and "most of his characteristic thoughts on Nature had received fairly explicit statement."

1897

83. BRANDES, G.M.C. *Hauptströmungen der Literatur des Neunzehnten Jahrhunderts,* Charlottenburg, H. Barsdorf, 1897.

Wordsworth is discussed as a leading exponent of naturalism in England.

84. Dowden, Edward. *The French Revolution and English Literature,* London, Kegan Paul, 1897.

Long a standard text, including figures from Godwin to Byron and Shelley. Much attention is devoted to Wordsworth. See *114*.

85. Herford, C. H. *The Age of Wordsworth,* London, G. Bell and Sons, 1897.

Often reprinted. Although out of date on some points, the book remains a helpful survey of the Romantic period. It contains a good sketch of the intellectual backgrounds. Bernbaum's *Guide Through the Romantic Movement* gives a more thorough discussion of the major figures, but Herford's inclusion of some of the minor names is valuable for quick reference.

86. Legouis, Émile. *The Early Life of William Wordsworth. 1770–1798,* London, J. M. Dent and Sons Ltd., 1897.

Translated from the French (1896) by J. W. Matthews. Reprinted, with new material, in 1921 and 1932. An epoch-making book, which has left its stamp on all subsequent biographies. With *The Prelude* as the basis, it interprets the life of the young Wordsworth in the light of the French Revolution and revolutionary philosophies. It presents a careful study of his boyhood, his residence in France, his return to England and moral crisis, recovery, and his achievement of 1798. The book is also valuable for interpretations of many poems. Although Harper's *Life* covers most of these facts and is more complete, Legouis' critical study remains one of the books of first importance. See *81*.

Rev. *TLS,* Sept. 15, 1921, p. 593.

87. Magnus, Laurie. *A Primer of Wordsworth,* London, Methuen and Co., 1897.

The book is designed to make "easy of access" the facts of Wordsworth's life and the aspects of his thought. Most of the poems and the prose receive brief comment and explanation. The concluding "Critical Essay," a joint discussion of Wordsworth and Tennyson, is perhaps the most interesting section of the book to the present-day reader. Both poets are said to have a common "criticism of life." They were both animated by the democratic idea, in choice of subject, in selection of language, and in social outlook. Bibliography.

88. Stephen, Leslie. "Wordsworth's Youth," *National Rev.,* Feb., 1897.

Reprinted in *Studies of a Biographer,* 2 vols., London, Duckworth and Co., 1898. The essay was inspired by Legouis' *The Early Life of William Wordsworth* and is perhaps the first significant result in the critical field of that important book. As interpretative criticism of Wordsworth, it is "modern" rather than "Victorian." But Stephen is not in full agreement with Legouis. His thesis is that Wordsworth renounced radicalism and the French Revolution because they came to represent "the harsh doctrinaire system of the economists."

89. WHITE, W. H., ed. *A Description of the Wordsworth and Coleridge Manuscripts in the Possession of Mr. T. Norton Longman,* London, Longmans, Green and Co., 1897.

Important MSS., now at Yale University. See *432*.

1898

90. WHITE, W. H. *An Examination of the Charge of Apostasy against Wordsworth,* London, Longmans, Green and Co., 1898.

Defends Wordsworth, arguing, by an examination of his poetry, that he did not in later life depart from his principles.

1899

91. HELLER, OTTO. "Goethe and Wordsworth," *MLN,* xiv (1899), 131–33.

A series of parallels between *Faust* I and *The Excursion* IV, mostly relating to pantheism and the love of nature. See *77, 364, 457*.

92. YARNALL, ELLIS. *Wordsworth and the Coleridges,* New York, The Macmillan Co., 1899.

Recollections of visits to Rydal Mount in 1849 and 1855. The book is often quoted in discussions of the elderly Wordsworth.

1900

93. BAYNE, THOMAS. "Young and Wordsworth," *N&Q,* Dec. 1, 1900, p. 426.

Compares Wordsworth's line in *Peter Bell,* "primrose by a river's brim," to a passage in Young's *Seven Characteristical Satires*. See also *N&Q,* Dec. 29, 1900, p. 510.

94. FISHER, L. A. "The First American Reprint of Wordsworth," *MLN,* xv (1900), 77–84.

A description of James Humphrey's reprint of *Lyrical Ballads,* Philadelphia, 1802.

95. MERRILL, KATHERINE. "Wordsworth's Realism," *MLN,* xv (1900), 147–62; 204–15.

Wordsworth's subject matter is realistic, but his treatment is imaginative and didactic. The first paper deals with his narratives, the second with his descriptive poetry.

1901

96. OEFTERING, W. E. *Wordsworth's und Byron's Nature-Dichtung,* Karlsruhe, Buchdruckerie von Ferd, 1901.

1902

97. ANON. "Wordsworth and Keats," *N&Q,* Oct. 11, 1902, p. 284.

Notes a similarity of thought in the eight successive lines of Wordsworth's sonnet addressed to Sir George Beaumont, beginning "Praised be the art," and the six successives lines of Keats's *Ode on a Grecian Urn,* beginning "Fair Youth." See *99*.

98. BROOKE, S. A. *Naturalism in English Poetry,* London, J. M. Dent and Sons Ltd., 1902.

Contains two lectures: "Wordsworth the Poet of Nature" and "Wordsworth: Shelley: Byron." In the first, Brooke points out that Wordsworth is near to pantheism in his idea of an infinite spirit in the universe. In the second, Brooke says that it is not Wordsworth's morality or philosophy that makes him a poet, but his passionate joy and his vital feeling.

99. FORD, C. L. "Wordsworth and Keats," *N&Q,* Nov. 15, 1902, p. 398.

The lines from Wordsworth's sonnet addressed to Sir George Beaumont, compared in a previous letter to Keats's *Ode on a Grecian Urn,* are a repetition of the thought of Wordsworth's poem, *Peele Castle in a Storm.* See *97*.

1903

100. ANON. "Delivered from the Galling Yoke of Time," *N&Q,* June 27, 1903, p. 511.

Queries whether any record exists of Wordsworth's reasons for reversing the doom of Laodamia. Refers to a five-page discussion of the matter in Archdeacon Hare's *Guesses at Truth.* See *102*.

101. COOPER, LANE. "Note on 'The Ancient Mariner,'" *Athenaeum,* Sept. 5, 1903, p. 328.

Suggests dates when Coleridge may have first heard l. 15 of

Wordsworth's *The Waterfall and the Eglantine.* Dowden had suggested this as a source of ll. 41–42 of *The Ancient Mariner.*

102. POTTS, R. A. "Delivered from the Galling Yoke of Time," *N&Q,* May 23, 1903, p. 412.

Comments on the revisions of this line from *Laodamia.* See *100.*

103. RALEIGH, WALTER. *Wordsworth,* London, Edward Arnold and Co., 1903.

One of the standard books of general criticism and interpretation of Wordsworth's poetry, presenting an able discussion of the essentials. Of especial interest is the chapter on "Poetic Diction."

Rev. *Athenaeum,* July 4, 1903, pp. 27–28.

1904

104. ANON. "Sadler's Wells Play alluded to by Wordsworth," *N&Q,* Jan. 2, 1904, p. 7.

Suggests that the play founded on the story of John Hatfield and Mary of Buttermere and presented at Sadler's Wells Theatre, to which Wordsworth alludes in *The Prelude,* Book VII, may have been *William and Susan,* announced for April 25, 1803. See *107, 108.*

105. COOPER, LANE. "Coleridge's 'Brother' in Wordsworth's 'Castle of Indolence' Stanzas," *Athenaeum,* March 12, 1904, p. 340.

"Noisy he was, and gamesome as a boy; His limbs would toss about him with delight" interpreted as a humorous reference to Coleridge hailing the donkey as a brother, tossing its heels "in gamesome play" *(To a Young Ass).* See *110.*

106. ———. "Raleigh's 'Wordsworth': A Note," *Athenaeum,* Jan. 2, 1904, pp. 16–17.

Cooper does not regard the poem *A Slumber Did My Spirit Seal* as a genuine "Lucy" poem.

107. DIBDIN, E. R. "Sadler's Wells Play alluded to by Wordsworth," *N&Q,* Feb. 13, 1904, p. 136.

Mary Lamb inaccurately refers to Charles Dibdin's operatic piece, "The New Burletta Spectacle Edward and Susan," as "Mary of Buttermere." See *104, 108.*

108. LUCAS, E. V. "Sadler's Wells Play alluded to by Wordsworth," *N&Q,* Jan. 30, 1904, p. 96.

Mary Lamb, in a letter to Dorothy Wordsworth, refers to a play at Sadler's Wells on "Mary of Buttermere." See *104, 107.*

109. POTTS, R. A. "The Editio Princeps of 'The Convict,' by W. Wordsworth," *Athenaeum,* Aug. 13, 1904, p. 209.

Prints from the *Morning Post,* Dec. 14, 1797. For the writer's correction in dating two of Coleridge's poems, see *Athenaeum,* Aug. 27, 1904, p. 272.

110. WHITE, W. H. "Coleridge's 'Brother' in Wordsworth's 'Castle of Indolence' Stanzas," *Athenaeum,* March 19, 1904, p. 372.

Calls attention to an error of interpretation in Cooper's letter. Also, White believes the lines pointed out by Cooper as referring to Coleridge should more probably be ascribed to William Calvert. See *105.* See *Athenaeum,* April 16, 1904, p. 500, for Cooper's reply.

1905

111. COOPER, LANE. "Wordsworth Sources. Bowles and Keate," *Athenaeum,* April 22, 1905, pp. 498–500.

In Wordsworth, as well as in Coleridge, there may be some influence of Bowles. There are also echoes of the travel writers, Keate and Bartram.

112. SMITH, N. C. "A Quotation in Wordsworth," *Athenaeum,* July 1, 1905, p. 19.

Two quotations (and adaptations) by Wordsworth from Fulke Greville, Lord Brooke.

1906

113. BOMIG, KARL. *William Wordsworth im Urteile seiner Zeit,* Borna Leipzig, Buchdruckerei Robert Noske, 1906.

A Leipzig dissertation on the subject of the critical attitude towards Wordsworth in his day.

114. CESTRE, CHARLES. *La Révolution Française et les Poètes Anglais (1789–1809),* Paris, Hachette et Cie., 1906.

A noteworthy interpretation. Wordsworth serves as a transmitter of eighteenth-century ideas into the nineteenth century, conveying them to the new generation with passion and feeling rather than as reasoned thought or as a system of practical reform. See *84.*

115. INGE, W. R. *Studies of English Mystics,* London, John Murray, 1906.

A chapter on Wordsworth discusses his philosophy of divine immanence, which is not to be mistaken for pantheism.

116. SMITH, E.C.M. "Seneca, Jonson, Daniel and Wordsworth," *MLR,* i (1906), 232.

The Excursion, IV, 330–31 introduces two lines from Daniel's *To the Lady Margaret, Countess of Cumberland.* Smith gives the source from Seneca; and also points out that Jonson's *Cynthia's Revels* i, 5, 30 has another turning of the same thought, probably also from Seneca.

1907

117. ANON. "Wadsworth as a Yorkshire Name," *N&Q,* June 29, 1907, p. 515.

States that "Wadsworth" is the name of a village near Hebden Bridge in Yorkshire, from which originally sprang the family bearing the name in its varying forms. See *122.*

118. BAYNE, THOMAS. "Wordsworth and Browning," *N&Q,* Dec. 14, 1907, p. 466.

This letter starts a discussion concerning the interpretation of Wordsworth's phrase "mighty Being" in *It is a Beauteous Evening.* See issues for Jan. 11, 1908, pp. 33–34 (two letters), Feb. 1, p. 93 (two letters), and March 28, pp. 257–58.

119. COOPER, LANE. "A Glance at Wordsworth's Reading," *MLN,* xxii (1907), 83–89; 110–17.

Revised in *Methods and Aims in the Study of Literature,* Boston, Ginn and Co., 1915. Reissued in *Cornell Studies in English,* XXXI, Ithaca, N. Y., Cornell University Press, 1940. Cooper effectively explodes the popular idea that Wordsworth was no reader, that there was little literary influence on his poetry, and that the dominant passion of his life owed nothing to books. His reading of Pope and Dryden is pointed out, and his "astounding" familiarity with the lesser English poets. Cooper gives prominence to Wordsworth's knowledge of books on travel and geography, suggesting that such books are of equal significance to the Romantic Movement as to the Renaissance.

120. ———. "Some Wordsworthian Similes," *JEGP,* vi (1907), 179–89.

Reprinted, with revisions, in *Aristotelian Papers,* Ithaca, N. Y.,

Cornell University Press, 1939. Cooper comments on Wordsworth's sense of affinities, his creative instinct of associating one thing with another. This trait is especially noteworthy in his similes that associate natural objects with man and his passions, or one object of nature with another. Cooper remarks that Wordsworth's imagery is not mere ornament, but holds a deep underlying truth to Wordsworth and to "the constitution of things as he saw it."

121. ———. "Wordsworth on Spelling Reform," *The Nation* (U.S.A.), lxxxv (1907), 301.

Attention is called to Wordsworth's statement, recorded in Christopher Wordsworth's *Memoirs,* concerning the failure of modern efforts to reform spelling.

122. Francis, J. C. "Wadsworth as a Yorkshire Name," *N&Q,* April 20, 1907, p. 308.

Reference to an appendix in Samuel Longfellow's life of his brother, citing variant forms of the name "Wadsworth," one of which is "Wordesworth." See *117*.

123. Rannie, D. W. *Wordsworth and His Circle,* London, Methuen and Co., 1907.

This book presents nothing new to the student of later Wordsworthian scholarship, and neglects Wordsworth's sojourn in France. But Rannie offers a suggestive discussion of Romanticism, and interesting information on Wordsworth's contemporaries and their relation to him.

124. Shawcross, J., ed. *Biographia Literaria,* 2 vols., Oxford, The Clarendon Press, 1907.

The standard edition. See *18*.

1908

125. Anon. "Wordsworth's Patriotic Poetry," *TLS,* Sept. 3, 1908, p. 281.

The article is based on the *Convention of Cintra* and the political and patriotic sonnets of 1802–11. It contains a summary of Wordsworth's political principles, with the conclusion that he never wavered. His patriotism was that of "reasoned consistency."

126. Cooper, Lane. "Literature on Wordsworth," *PMLA,* xxiii (1908), 119–27.

The paper offers a brief view of the leading contributors to

Wordsworthian scholarship at the turn of the century, and concludes with a list of subjects that should be investigated by scholars.

127. EAGLESTON, A. J. "Wordsworth, Coleridge, and the Spy," *The Nineteenth Century and After,* lxiv (1908), 300–10.

Letters from the archives of the Home Office confirm the statement in *Biographia Literaria* that a spy was sent to Somerset to watch Coleridge and Wordsworth. The facts of the case are presented.

128. LIENEMANN, KURT. *Die Belesenheit von William Wordsworth,* Berlin, Mayer and Müller, 1908.

A guide to Wordsworth's references to other authors, ancient and modern.

129. PAUL, H. W. "The Permanence of Wordsworth," *The Nineteenth Century and After,* lxiii (1908), 987–98.

Wordsworth appeals because of the inevitability of his poetry. He represents the "deepest moods of the deepest minds."

1909

130. BRADLEY, A. C. *English Poetry and German Philosophy in the Age of Wordsworth,* Manchester, The University Press, 1909.

Reprinted in *Miscellany,* London, Macmillan and Co., 1929. Contains a four-point comparison between Wordsworth and Hegel: (1) the greatness of the "mind" of man; (2) truth perceived through imagination; (3) some similarity in political outlook; (4) an optimistic philosophy which recognizes the fact of evil. See *296, 558.*

131. ———. *Oxford Lectures on Poetry,* London, Macmillan and Co., 1909.

Includes two lectures on Wordsworth of a general interpretative nature, with much cogent criticism. Bradley remedies the deficiencies of Arnold's essay. He draws together Wordsworth's penetration of commonplace life and affections; his impassioned nature, manifested in his frequent dealings with pain and distress and in his political interests; and the full scope of his "visionary power." The interpretations are well balanced, with excellent quotations. See *3.*

Rev. *TLS,* June 10, 1909, p. 209.

132. ———. "A Plagiarism by Wordsworth?" *TLS,* Jan. 14, 1909, p. 18.

The origin of the first line of *Ode to Duty* could be from *Paradise Lost,* IX, 651 ff., as well as from Hawkin's "Ode." See *135.*

133. COOPER, LANE. "The 'Forest Hermit' in Coleridge and Wordsworth," *MLN,* xxiv (1909), 33–36.

The numerous references to hermits in Wordsworth and Coleridge are stereotyped and conventional. They are "romantic" in their love of solitude and their forest dwellings, but they are in the tradition of Spenser, Milton, and Parnell.

134. DUNBAR, ALICE M. "Wordsworth's Use of Milton's Description of the Building of Pandemonium," *MLN,* xxiv (1909), 124.

Finds parallels in Wordsworth's poetry to Milton's phrase "rising like an exhalation."

135. THISELTON, A. E. "A Plagiarism by Wordsworth?" *TLS,* Jan. 7, 1909, p. 6.

"And daughter of the voice of God," William Hawkins, "Ode for Saint Cecilia's Day" (*Poems on Various Subjects,* 1781). Cf. first line of Wordsworth's *Ode to Duty.* See *132.*

1910

136. COOPER, LANE. "On Wordsworth's 'To Joanna,'" *Academy,* lxxviii (1910), 108–10.

A possible connection between Wordsworth's description of the echo of Joanna's laugh and Canto XXX of Drayton's *Polyolbion* and Frere's *King Arthur and his Roundtable.* See *156.*

137. ———. "Wordsworth's Conception of 'The Ancient Mariner,'" *Archiv für das Studium der neueren Sprachen und Literaturen,* cxxv (1910), 89–92.

Wordsworth's contribution to the poem has generally been underrated. He furnished the plot of the story and two of the most distinct descriptions of the Mariner (ll. 9–12: 226–27). Cooper also comments on Wordsworth's criticism that the Mariner is not sufficiently distinct in character; he points to a parallel portrait in the apparition of the man on the moonlit road in *The Prelude,* IV, 379 ff.

138. ———. "Wordsworth: Variant Readings," *N&Q,* Sept. 17, 1910, pp. 222–23.

Comment on Wordsworth's shift of a sonnet from *Memorials of a Tour on the Continent* to *Ecclesiastical Sonnets,* and on his use of *coral* as an adjective. See also "C.C.B.," "Wordsworth: Variant Readings," *N&Q,* Oct. 8, 1910, pp. 294–95; Thomas Bayne, "Wordsworth: Variant Readings," *N&Q,* Oct. 8, 1910, p. 294. For other variants, see Lane Cooper, "Wordsworth: The Cuckoo Clock," *N&Q,* Oct. 22, 1910, pp. 324–25; and Lane Cooper, "Wordsworth: Variant Readings," *N&Q,* Nov. 19, 1910, p. 416. Cf. Thomas Bayne, "Wordsworth: Variant Readings," *N&Q,* Dec. 10, 1910, p. 476.

139. Masson, Rosaline, "An 'Inspired Little Creature' and the Poet Wordsworth," *Fortnightly Rev.,* lxxxviii (New Series, Nov. 1, 1910), 874–89.

An account of Emmeline Fisher, granddaughter of William Cookson, Wordsworth's uncle. Wordsworth had praised her poetry when she was a child.

140. Mead, W. E. "Wordsworth's 'Maiden City,'" *MLN,* xxv (1910), 174–76.

This term for Venice occurs in Coryat's *Crudities* (1611). See *143, 145.*

141. More, P. E. *Shelburne Essays,* Seventh Series, Boston, Houghton Mifflin Co., 1910.

Contains an essay on "Wordsworth" occasioned by the appearance of Knight's edition of the letters. In addition to some unpleasant aspects of Wordsworth's personality that More touches on, he finds the poet lacks "native vitality," is weak in "the poetry of events," that *Tintern Abbey* is contradictory, and that its sentimental philosophy of nature proved unenduring, as Wordsworth's later life shows.

142. Smith, D. N., ed. *Jeffrey's Literary Criticism,* London, Henry Frowde, 1910.

A convenient collection, containing Jeffrey's principal criticism of Wordsworth.

1911

143. Belden, H. M. "Venice: The 'Maiden City,'" *MLN,* xxvi (1911), 31.

Sources of Wordsworth's term for Venice. See *140, 145.*

144. Cooper, Lane, ed. *A Concordance to the Poems of William Wordsworth,* The Concordance Society, London, Smith, Elder and Co., 1911.

The only complete concordance, of prime importance. See *206.*

Rev. *Athenaeum,* March 9, 1912, p. 278. *TLS,* Feb. 29, 1912, p. 81. Strunk, *MLN,* xxvii (1912), 81–84.

145. ———. "She Was a Maiden City," *MLN,* xxvi (1911), 199.

Sources of Wordsworth's term for Venice. See *140, 143.*

146. Mullinger, J. B. "Wordsworth: 'Quam nihil ad genium, Papiniane, tuum!' " *N&Q,* Oct. 21, 1911, p. 325.

The source of this quotation on title page of *Lyrical Ballads* (1805) is probably from Selden's "Address to the Reader," in Drayton's *Polyolbion* (1622). See *N&Q,* Dec. 30, 1911, p. 531.

147. Robertson, E. S. *Wordsworthshire,* London, Chatto and Windus, 1911.

A description of the Lake district with comments on its effect on Wordsworth, and a concordance of persons and places referred to in the poetry. See *59, 79.*

1912

148. Cooper, Lane. "The First Person in Wordsworth and Shakespeare," *N&Q,* Jan. 27, 1912, p. 65.

Some reviewers of the *Wordsworth Concordance* commented on Wordsworth's frequent use of the first personal pronoun. Cooper explains that this practice is natural in a poet who is lyrical and meditative.

149. Courtney, W. P. "Wordsworth's Friend Jones," *N&Q,* Sept. 14, 1912, pp. 211–12.

In reply to query about Wordsworth's Welsh friend, Robert Jones, the writer supplies biographical details. See also *N&Q,* June 1, 1912, p. 430, and July 20, p. 55. See *290, 532.*

150. Stewart, J. A., *et al. English Literature and the Classics,* Oxford, The Clarendon Press, 1912.

Nine lectures by different men. See J. A. Stewart, "Platonism in English Poetry," for fundamental observations on Wordsworth's "personal Platonism."

151. Harper, G. M. "Rousseau, Godwin, and Wordsworth," *Atlantic Monthly,* cix (1912), 639–50.

The influence of Rousseau on Wordsworth is said to be

stronger than that of any other man of letters. The distinctive elements of Rousseau's mode of thought are: (1) prevalence of reverie; (2) tendency to simplify, which leads to the revolutionary process of equalizing; (3) individualism. Wordsworth was forced to make a synthesis of the retrospective attitude of Rousseau and the forward-looking attitude of Godwin.

152. MINCHIN, H. C. "Browning and Wordsworth," *Fortnightly Rev.*, xci (NS, 1912), 813–24.

A general essay on the two poets, including Browning's opinions of Wordsworth and a list of his favorite Wordsworth poems.

153. SNEATH, E. H. *Wordsworth, Poet of Nature and Poet of Man,* Boston, Ginn and Co., 1912.

An interpretative biography, presenting the phases of Wordsworth's life, and stressing the aspects of his thought. The book embodies most of the conventional ideas concerning Wordsworth, but in some respects it lacks the benefits of more recent research.

1913

154. BEATTY, ARTHUR. "Wordsworth and Hartley," *The Nation* (N. Y.), xcvii (July 17, 1913), 51–54.

An early statement of Beatty's theory (fully developed in his *Wordsworth. His Doctrine and Art in their Historical Relations*) of the influence of Hartley's system of thought on Wordsworth after his rejection of Godwinism. See *242*.

155. COLERIDGE, E. H. "The Genesis of 'The Ancient Mariner,'" *Poetry Rev.*, ii (1913), 11–15.

The poem was not the product of an opiate dream, as is popularly supposed, but of Coleridge's own awareness and the suggestions of Wordsworth. See *198*.

156. COOPER, LANE. "Lamb on Wordsworth's 'To Joanna,'" *N&Q,* March 22, 1913, pp. 223–24.

Interest in the laugh of Joanna expressed in an anonymous contribution to *The Indicator* (1821), apparently by Lamb. See *136*.

157. KNIGHT, W. A. *Coleridge and Wordsworth in the West Country,* London, Elkin Mathews, 1913.

An account of the early association at Racedown, Bristol, and Alfoxden. Except for a description of the local background of the poems the book contains little not found in the standard biographies.

158. Lang, Andrew, ed. *Poet's Country. The Homes and Haunts of the Poets,* London, T. C. and E. C. Jack, 1913.

Contains a chapter, written by E. H. Coleridge, on the homes occupied by Wordsworth after his twenty-fifth year. See *68, 463.*

159. Rice, Richard. *Wordsworth's Mind,* "Indiana University Studies," I (XI), No. 7, Bloomington, University of Indiana Press, 1913.

The essay traces some Wordsworthian elements in the eighteenth century, which are a mark of the "new" poetry, and explains Wordsworth's mind in relation to Romanticism. Wordsworth brought back into poetry the power of forming ideas and images simultaneously. His poetic energy, like that of other Romanticists, sprang "from an emotional egotism that seeks its *milieu* of sympathy and expression in surrounding nature."

160. Roberts, E. C. "The Ascendency of Wordsworth," *Contemporary Rev.,* ciii (1913), 703–11.

Wordsworth's popularity grew slowly, but his simplicity and love of nature appeal to our age, and his religious philosophy "is not up-to-date, but . . . in the vanguard of progressive thought."

161. Spurgeon, Caroline F. E. *Mysticism in English Literature,* Cambridge, The University Press, 1913.

Wordsworth is discussed as a nature mystic. The book is recommended for its clear analysis of the types of mysticism.

1914

162. Bell, C. C. "Wordsworth on War," *TLS,* Dec. 31, 1914, p. 591.

Refers to Wordsworth's alterations of four lines of the *Thanksgiving Ode,* beginning "But thy most awful instrument," and substitutions from the *Ode, 1815.* Quotation from the poem had been made in the leading article, "Peace," *TLS,* Dec. 24, 1914, p. 577. See *170, 176.*

163. Boas, F. S. "Wordsworth's Patriotic Poems and Their Significance To-day," English Association, Pamphlet No. 30, Dec., 1914.

The application of Wordsworth's nationalism to the War.

164. HUDSON, W. H. *Wordsworth and His Poetry,* London, George G. Harrap and Co., 1914.

An interweaving of biography and poetry (with many poems quoted in full), to acquaint the reader with what he should know about Wordsworth, and what to look for in his poetry. The study compacts into brief space much sensitive interpretation, but the peaceful, retired, contemplative poet dominates the picture.

165. STORK, C. W. "The Influence of the Popular Ballad on Wordsworth and Coleridge," *PMLA,* xxix (1914), 299–326.

The influence of the ballad narrative method upon Wordsworth's conception of poetry is very slight. The narrative style of *Lyrical Ballads* is often flat because he cultivated the spirit of the diluted eighteenth-century versions. But ballad influences fall into a threefold classification: "(1) imitation of the eighteenth-century domestic ballad, usually built around trifling incidents of the poet's own experience; (2) ballads proper, impersonal poems with genuine story incident usually taken from tradition; (3) poems founded on old ballad ideas but given a totally new significance." Most of the influence on Coleridge pointed out by Stork is in *The Ancient Mariner.* See 537.

166. STRUNK, W. "Some Related Poems of Wordsworth and Coleridge," *MLN,* xxix (1914), 201–5.

Presents the probability that Wordsworth suggested to Coleridge the subject of *The Three Graves* and some of the details of its treatment. Attention is called to the related "curse" theme in *Goody Blake and Harry Gill* and *The Thorn.* Also, in *The Thorn,* Strunk sees the forerunner of *The Danish Boy* and *Hart-Leap Well.*

1915

167. ACLAND, A.H.D. "Wordsworth's Patriotic Poetry," *The Living Age,* lxvi (1915), 502–6.

Reprinted from *The Westminster Gazette* [1914?]. The essay is on Wordsworth's attitude toward the Napoleonic war and its relevancy to the struggle of 1915. Acland edited a selection of Wordsworth's poems, with introduction and notes, entitled *The Patriotic Poetry of William Wordsworth* (Oxford, The Clarendon Press, 1915).

168. ANON. "The War-Sonnets of Wordsworth," *TLS,* Feb. 4, 1915, p. 36.

The writer points out that none of the Romantic poets save

Wordsworth left anything enduring on the subject of the Napoleonic wars.

169. ———. "The England of English Poets," *TLS,* April 29, 1915, p. 141.
Leading article, based on de Selincourt's series of lectures *English Poets and the National Ideal.* Comments are made concerning Wordsworth's position in the national life. See *171, 172.*

170. BELL, C. C. "Wordsworth on War," *TLS,* Jan. 14, 1915, p. 14.
Why did Wordsworth first publish two separate odes on the same subject, then combine them into one, and afterwards separate them again? See *162, 176.*

171. DE SELINCOURT, ERNEST. *English Poets and the National Ideal,* London, Oxford University Press, 1915.
Shakespeare, Milton, and Wordsworth are the leading exponents of the ideal of nationality. In Shakespeare we have national independence; in Milton, liberty and the rights of the individual within the state; in Wordsworth, the combination of the two ideas, broadening into a policy towards which all humanity can strive. See *169, 172.*

172. ———. "English Poets and the National Ideal," *TLS,* May 6, 1915, p. 154.
Comments on an article in *TLS,* based on de Selincourt's book, and a brief statement of the object of the four lectures. See *169, 171.*

173. DICEY, A. V. "Wordsworth and the War," *The Nineteenth Century and After,* lxxvii (1915), 1041–60.
Gives in condensed form the attributes of Wordsworth the statesman as he confronted the Napoleonic wars. He was neither a Whig nor a Tory. He combined an early enthusiasm for the French Revolution with a historical perception learned from Burke, suiting well his keen eye for everyday facts. He denounced the tyranny of Napoleon, and likewise the moral degeneration of England herself. He was a believer in nationalism, the independence of each state, anticipating the better elements of the nationalism that was to grow up later in the century.

174. ———. "Wordsworth on the Revolution," *The Nineteenth Century and After,* lxxviii (1915), 870–91.
Discusses three objects of Wordsworth's revolutionary reminis-

cences in *The Prelude:* (1) the joy of the Revolutionary dawn; (2) the Massacres of September and the Reign of Terror; (3) the fall of Robespierre and the rise of Napoleon. *The Prelude* offers a sagacious commentary on the events.

175. GRAHAM, WALTER. "Wordsworth and Shelley," *N&Q,* Jan. 30, 1915, pp. 83–84.

Notes instances of close parallels in thought and expression between Wordsworth and Shelley: Wordsworth's *To a Cuckoo* and Shelley's *To a Skylark; Excursion,* IV, ll. 1206 ff., and *Mont Blanc,* l. 76; *Tintern Abbey,* ll. 90 ff., and *Hellas,* ll. 20 ff., and 102 ff.

176. KNIGHT, W. A., "Wordsworth on War," *TLS,* Jan. 7, 1915, p. 6.

Answers some questions raised by C. C. Bell concerning the *Ode, 1815,* and *Thanksgiving Ode.* Both were composed and published in 1816, but in subsequent reprintings the first and fourth stanzas of the former *Ode* became stanzas nine and twelve of the latter *Ode.* But in the 1842 edition of the *Poems,* Wordsworth returned to the original arrangement. See *162, 170.*

177. LOANE, G. G. "Wordsworth on Poetry," *TLS,* Nov. 11, 1915, p. 405.

Finds the germ of Wordsworth's "emotion recollected in tranquility" in Akenside's *Inscriptions,* No. VIII. Cf. *TLS,* Nov. 4, 1915, p. 393.

178. MASSON, ROSALINE. "Milton, Wordsworth, and the Angels," *The Englishwoman,* xiv (1915), 255–71.

A contrast between Milton and Wordsworth in their views and treatment of the women in the family.

179. STOCKLEY, W.F.P. " 'The Happy Warrior' and Nelson," *N&Q,* Feb. 27, 1915, pp. 162–64.

Reasons Wordsworth could not regard Nelson as the model warrior of the poem. There were no puritanical grounds, as has been supposed.

1916

180. COOKE, MARGARET. "Schiller's 'Robbers' in England," *MLR,* xi (1916), 156–75.

The influence of *Die Räuber,* from Henry Mackenzie's paper on the tragedy (1788) to Shelley's *Cenci.* Strong parallels are pointed out between the play and Wordsworth's *The Borderers.*

Its influence on Wordsworth's play was more deeply psychological than on Coleridge's *Remorse.*

181. COOPER, LANE. "Wordsworth's Translation of the Harmodius Hymn," *The Classical Weekly,* ix (1916), 109–10.

Attention is called to Wordsworth's version, which had been overlooked by Dr. Mierow in his collection of modern renderings of the Harmodius and Aristogiton Hymn *(Classical Weekly,* ix, 82–86). Wordsworth's poem was first published by Knight in the *Classical Review,* xv (Feb., 1901), 82, and is ascribed to the first decade of the nineteenth century. Cooper intimates the possibility of 1795–96 as the period of composition, when Wordsworth and Wrangham collaborated in an imitation of Juvenal.

182. HARPER, G. M. *William Wordsworth, His Life, Works, and Influence,* 2 vols., London, John Murray, 1916.

Written with accurate scholarship and ample research, this is the standard biography. Enlarging on Legouis' *The Early Life of William Wordsworth,* Harper devotes the larger proportion of the biography to the years up to 1815. While ample facts concerning the later years are given, some critics feel that Harper has laid too much stress on the early years and on the poet's republicanism and unorthodox thought. Besides a full account of the poet's life, his associates, and the currents of thought of the period, Harper presents many authoritative interpretations of the poetry. A revised and abridged edition appeared in one volume in 1929. This incorporates some valuable new matter, especially on the Annette Vallon story, but on the whole the omissions of the new edition offset its advantages.

Rev. *TLS,* Feb. 17, 1916, p. 79. Rawnsley, *Poetry Rev.,* vii (1916), 269–81. Vaughan, *MLR,* xi (1916), 482–96. Bailey, *Quarterly Rev.,* ccxxvi (July, 1916), 116. Davison, *Lond. Quarterly Rev.,* cxxvi (July, 1916), 1. Cooper, *JEGP,* xvi (1917), 476–81. Chew, *MLN,* xxxii (1917), 253–56. Palmer, *Harvard Theological Rev.,* x (1917), 84. *TLS,* July 25, 1929, p. 589 (3rd ed. abridged).

183. SIMPSON, PERCY. "Wordsworth's Punctuation," *TLS,* Jan. 6, 1916, p. 9.

In *TLS,* the reviewer of the Clarendon Press edition of *The Convention of Cintra* remarked that the punctuation should have been corrected and modernized. Simpson advocates printing the *Tract* as Wordsworth "passed it for the press." A flood of letters followed on Wordsworth's punctuation and proofreading. See *TLS,* Jan. 13, p. 21; Jan. 20, p. 33 (2 letters); Jan. 27, p. 45 (2 letters); Feb. 3, p. 57; Feb. 10, p. 69 (2 letters). See also *431.*

184. Thayer, Mary R. *The Influence of Horace on the Chief English Poets of the Nineteenth Century,* "Cornell Studies in English," II, New Haven, Conn., Yale University Press, 1916.

Contains a brief introductory sketch, and a list of forty-two passages from Wordsworth that show traces of Horace. See *512, 639.*

185. Wise, T. J. *A Bibliography of the Writings in Prose and Verse of William Wordsworth,* London, Richard Clay and Sons, Ltd. (for private circulation), 1916.

Still reliable for checking first editions, although the 1846 edition of the poem "To the Queen" is a forgery. See *339, 623.*

186. Wylie, Laura J. *Social Studies in English Literature,* Boston, Houghton Mifflin Co., 1916.

Contains the essay "The Social Philosophy of Wordsworth," tracing various aspects of Wordsworth's thought based on his conception of the new democracy and of the common man with his simple yet universal elements of character. The weakness of his social philosophy is said to be his distrust of the reason after the disillusionment of his French and Godwinian period. The essay fails to give sufficient development of Wordsworth's Revolutionary period, dismissing it as something from which he quickly recovered. The statement that he was a dreamy optimist in his early years is questionable.

1917

187. Barstow, Marjorie L. (Greenbie). *Wordsworth's Theory of Poetic Diction,* "Yale Studies in English," LVII, New Haven, Conn., Yale University Press, 1917.

A painstaking study of the early poetry, *Lyrical Ballads,* and the theory expressed in the Prefaces. Barstow presents an able discussion of eighteenth-century theories of poetry, the problems of Wordsworth's Prefaces, and the vocabulary of his poetry.

Rev. Bickersteth, *MLR,* xiii (1918), 351–53. Bright, *MLN,* xxxiii (1918), 186.

188. Dicey, A. V. *The Statesmanship of Wordsworth,* Oxford, The Clarendon Press, 1917.

The most authoritative analysis of Wordsworth's mature political views in the period of *The Convention of Cintra* and the *Poems Dedicated to National Independence and Liberty.* The emphasis is on his nationalism and its relation to later nineteenth-century policy. There is included a brief and less satisfactory summary of Wordsworth's earlier revolutionary ardor.

Rev. Davidson, *Lond. Quarterly Rev.,* cxxviii (1917), 272. Tupper, *MLN,* xxxiii (1918), 128. Previté-Orton, *MLR,* xiii (1918), 108–9.

189. PIERCE, F. E. "Hellenic Current in English Nineteenth-Century Poetry," *JEGP,* xvi (1917), 103–35.

Most of this essay is on Byron, Shelley, Keats, and the Victorians. But Pierce comments briefly on the Grecian aspect of *Laodamia* and *Dion,* and refers to three Wordsworthian sonnets on Greek themes.

190. PURVES, JOHN. "Wordsworth's 'Happy Warrior': A Seventeenth-Century Parallel," *MLR,* xii (1917), 202–3.

Cartwright's translation of Hugo Grotius' *Elegy on Arminius* presents in one passage a likeness in movement and thought to the *Happy Warrior.*

191. VANN, W. H. "Two Borrowings of Wordsworth," *MLN,* xxxii (1917), 314–15.

The two opening lines of Wordsworth's sonnet, "With how sad steps, O man," are from Sidney's *Astrophel and Stella.* The first line of *Ode to Duty* is perhaps suggested by *Paradise Lost,* IX, 651–53.

1918

192. ALLEN, B. S. "Reaction Against William Godwin," *MP,* xvi (1918), 225–43.

An account of the anti-Godwinian novels. Reference is also made to Wordsworth's *The Borderers.*

193. ANON. "National Self-Depreciation," *TLS,* Aug. 29, 1918, p. 397.

Shakespeare's confidence in the greatness of England lasted in literature until the time of Wordsworth and Coleridge. Coleridge sounded the note of national self-depreciation in 1798, and Wordsworth in his sonnet to Milton gave the theme a nobler expression.

194. BAKER, H. T. "Wordsworth and Annette," *North American Rev.,* ccvii (1918), 433–39.

An early comment on the discovery of Wordsworth's liaison. A brief application is made to several poems.

195. Baldwin, E. C. "Wordsworth and Hermes Trismegistus," *PMLA,* xxxiii (1918), 235–43.

Wordsworth's conceptions of the child, its pre-existence, original innocence, and powers of intuitive truth, are not from Plato, but are more closely related to "that strange blend of oriental mysticism and of Neo-Platonism known as the Hermetical books." The influence on Wordsworth came through Coleridge and Vaughan.

196. Beatty, Arthur. "Joseph Fawcett: 'The Art of War.' Its Relation to the Development of William Wordsworth," *University of Wisconsin Studies in Language and Literature,* No. 2, Madison, University of Wisconsin Press, 1918, pp. 224–69.

Wordsworth's opinions on war were influenced by Godwin and by Fawcett's poem. Beatty prints the poem with brief notes.

197. Bensley, Edward. "Wordsworth: Seneca," *N&Q,* Nov., 1918, p. 312.

The motto to *Ode to Duty* is taken from Seneca's *Epistles,* 120, 10.

198. Coleridge, E. H. "The Genesis of 'The Ancient Mariner,'" *Poetry Rev.,* ix (1918), 271–77.

Additional evidence of the influences and the keen mental awareness that produced the poem. See *155.*

199. Cooper, Lane. "Wordsworth's Knowledge of Plato," *MLN,* xxxiii (1918), 497–99.

Corrections of references in A. E. White's note, and valuable additional references that throw light on Wordsworth's acquaintance with Plato. See *203.*

200. Kirtlan, E.J.B. "Did Wordsworth Recant?" *Contemporary Rev.,* cxiv (1918), 87–89.

Presents a brief statement of Wordsworth's early democratic zeal. In the last twenty years of his life he may have lost much of his fire, and the creative spirit had spent itself; but there was a growing belief in the supremacy of the spirit.

201. Loane, G. G. "Notes on the N.E.D.: VI," *TLS,* Aug. 8, 1918, p. 373.

Notes on words taken from Wordsworth. See *208.*

202. PALMER, G. H. *Formative Types in English Poetry,* Boston, Houghton Mifflin Co., 1918.

Contains a discussion of Wordsworth as a leading Romanticist, who broke from the tradition of classicism and prepared the way for modern poetry.

203. WHITE, E. A. "Wordsworth's Knowledge of Plato," *MLN,* xxxiii (1918), 246–48.

Assumption that Wordsworth knew Plato on the basis of: (1) Platonism in his poetry; (2) his acquaintance with Coleridge; (3) the fact that the library of Rydal Mount contained several volumes of Plato's dialogues; and (4) the report of Christopher Wordsworth that the poet had praised the last scenes of the life of Socrates. See *198.*

1919

204. ANON. "Poets of the Village," *TLS,* July 10, 1919, p. 369.

Contains a contrast between Crabbe and Wordsworth.

205. BRITTEN, JAMES. "Wordsworth's Verses 'To a Lady,'" *TLS,* March 6, 1919, p. 126.

These verses were written for Jane W. Penfold's *Madiera Flowers, Fruits, and Ferns* (1845).

206. COOPER, LANE. "The Making and the Use of a Verbal Concordance," *The Sewanee Rev.,* xxvii (1919), 188–206.

Reprinted in *Evolution and Repentance,* Ithaca, N. Y., Cornell University Press, 1935. Cooper gives first an interesting account of the procedure he used in compiling his *Concordance to the Poems of William Wordsworth.* There follows an account of various aspects of Wordsworth's thought and art which are illuminated by a study of the words he used, such as are indexed in the *Concordance.* A fruitful essay, followed up in a manner by Miss Josephine Miles (see *616*).

207. GARROD, H. W. "A Misprint in the Text of Wordsworth?" *TLS,* May 1, 1919, p. 238.

Suggests emending: "Whether in matters various, properities" to "Whether in matter's various properties" (*The Prelude,* XI, l. 331).

208. LOANE, G. G. "Notes on the N.E.D.: XI," *TLS,* May 22, 1919, p. 280.

Notes on words taken from Wordsworth. See *201.*

209. MARSTON, AGNES. "Lewis Carroll and Wordsworth," *MLR,* xiv (1919), 214–16.

"A-sitting on a Gate" (from *Through the Looking-Glass)* is a parody of the last thirteen stanzas of *Resolution and Independence.* See *221.*

210. MEAD, MARIAN. "Wordsworth's Eye," *PMLA,* xxxiv (1919), 202–24.

Points out, through citation of many passages, Wordsworth's emphasis on his sense of sight. His physical sight is related to his philosophy in his power to observe natural objects, discovering in them an inward and vital spirit.

211. WHITFORD, R. C. "Another Lucy," *JEGP,* xviii (1919), 369–71.

Parallels between *Lucy Gray* and Christopher Anstey's "moralizing ballad" *The Farmer's Daughter* (1795). "The resemblance between the two poems is clear enough to make it seem entirely possible that, if Wordsworth did not borrow the name of Lucy from Christopher Anstey, at least both poets derived it from a common source."

1920

212. BROUGHTON, L. N. *The Theocritean Element in the Works of William Wordsworth,* Halle, Verlag von Max Niemeyer, 1920.

Wordsworth shows no profound influence of Theocritus and was not a pastoral poet by convention. But he returned to the realism of the original pastoral; and "the great difference between the pastorals of Theocritus and those of Wordsworth is a difference in local coloring, not in function, not in style, not in literary type."

Rev. Pease, *JEGP,* xx (1921), 412–14. Mustard, *PQ,* ii (1923), 77.

213. CAMPBELL, O. J. "Sentimental Morality in Wordsworth's Narrative Poetry," *University of Wisconsin Studies in Language and Literature,* No. 11, Madison, University of Wisconsin Press, 1920, pp. 21–57.

The first paper in a series. Campbell contends that much of Wordsworth's early narrative poetry was not prompted primarily by interest in social reform, but was composed in the eighteenth-century genre of "sentimental morality," whereby scenes of distress evoke tears and pity and moral sensibility. See *307, 308, 438, 567.*

Rev. Graves, *SAQ,* xx (Oct., 1921), 371.

214. Clutton-Brock, A. "The Problem of Wordsworth," *The London Mercury,* ii (1920), 700–10.

The paper consists of a miscellaneous assortment of critical remarks and quotations which attempts to distinguish the poet from the tiresome philosopher and moralist. Wordsworth's lack of passion is pointed out. He is not at his best as a philosopher, but as an impressionist.

215. Dunn, Esther C. "Innman's Portrait of Wordsworth," *Scribner's Magazine,* lxvii (1920), 251–56.

The American artist, Henry Innman, was sent by Henry Reed to Rydal Mount in 1844 to paint Wordsworth's portrait. This article tells the story, with sidelights on Wordsworth's life and character at this period.

216. Harper, G. M. *John Morley and Other Essays,* Princeton, N. J., Princeton University Press, 1920.

Contains the essays "Wordsworth at Blois" and "Wordsworth's Love Poetry." The former is an account of Harper's researches at Blois concerning Wordsworth's residence there.

217. Knowlton, E. C. "The Novelty of Wordsworth's 'Michael' as a Pastoral," *PMLA,* xxxv (1920), 432–46.

The realistic yet Biblical quality of *Michael,* and the absence of the conventional amorous element.

218. Lee, E. "William Wordsworth," *Poetry Rev.,* xi (1920), 66–69.

A commemoration of the one hundred fiftieth anniversary of Wordsworth's birth. His value to us today is in the beauty and high nobility that he represents.

219. Madariaga, S. De. *Shelley and Calderón and Other Essays on English and Spanish Poetry,* New York, E. P. Dutton and Co., 1920.

Contains an astutely written essay on Wordsworth, condemning him as provincial and more moralistic than poetic. This is one of the most powerful attacks on Wordsworth's poetry.

Rev. *TLS,* Dec. 9, 1920, p. 825. Cf. *TLS,* Dec. 16, 1920, p. 859.

220. Morison, William. "The Spirituality of Wordsworth," *Poetry Rev.,* xi (1920), 55–65.

Summarizes the recognized aspects of Wordsworth's philosophy of nature and man.

221. PORTER, G. R. "'Alice in Wonderland' and Wordsworth's 'Leech-Gatherer,'" *N&Q,* May 1, 1920, pp. 161–62.

The White Knight's song in Chapter VIII of *Through the Looking-Glass* is a parody of *Resolution and Independence.* See 209.

222. POTTS, ABBIE F. "Wordsworth and the Bramble," *JEGP,* xix (1920), 340–49.

C. B. Tinker in "The Poet, the Bramble, and Reconstruction" *(Atlantic Monthly,* cxxiv [1919], 124) says he can find but one reference to the bramble in Wordsworth and that somewhat contemptuous. Potts supplies many others and comments that the bramble is used "as the image for the deep and kindly sway of nature."

223. ———. "Wordsworth's 'Ecclesiastical Sonnets': Date of Composition," *N&Q,* April 3, 1920, pp. 81–83.

Gives dates of composition of numerous sonnets in the series.

224. ROBERTSON, J. L. "Burns at Morningside," *TLS,* Jan. 22, 1920, p. 51.

Echoes in *The Excursion* of Burns's elegy, "O Death, Thou Tyrant."

225. WORDSWORTH, G. G. "The Boyhood of Wordsworth," *Cornhill Magazine,* xlviii (1920), 410–20.

Reprinted in *Living Age,* cccv (1920), 471–78. Details from the unpublished memorandum book kept by Wordsworth's father, and some items from an expense ledger kept by Anne Tyson. Some points about the family property, business, and expenses are revealed. There are numerous items of interest regarding the education at Hawkshead of William and his brothers.

1921

226. ANON. "James Peake," *N&Q,* April 9, 1921, p. 299.

Supplies some details about Wordsworth's schoolmaster.

227. ———. "Note to Wordsworth's 'Prelude.' V, 26," *N&Q,* Feb. 5, 1921, p. 106.

The quotation by Wordsworth, "weep to have," is from Shakespeare's *Sonnets,* LXIV.

228. CAMPBELL, O. J. "Wordsworth Bandies Jests with Matthew," *MLN,* xxxvi (1921), 408–14.

The Tables Turned and related poems are not seriously philosophic, but are dramatized bit of waggishness with the madcap Matthew. A similar interpretation had been made by Lane Cooper in 1907 (see *119*). For a reply to Campbell's paper, see *254*.

229. DUNN, ESTHER C. "A Retrospect of Rydal Mount," *Scribner's Magazine,* lxix (1921), 549–55.

An account of the visit to Rydal Mount in 1854 of Henry Reed and Miss Bronson.

230. GRAHAM, WALTER. "The Politics of the Greater Romantic Poets," *PMLA,* xxxvi (1921), 60–78.

A survey, including Wordsworth, Coleridge, Southey, Byron, Scott, Shelley, and Keats. Graham maintains that the group were less interested in local or temporary political affairs than in "the permanent politics of human nature."

231. HARPER, G. M. *Wordsworth's French Daughter,* Princeton, N. J., Princeton University Press, 1921.

The book contains Harper's significant discoveries concerning Wordsworth's relations with Annette Vallon. It includes much material not in Harper's *Life.* See *248.*

Rev. *TLS,* Aug. 25, 1921, p. 545.

232. HUGHES, MERRITT. "The Humanism of Francis Jeffrey," *MLR,* xvi (1921), 243–51.

An analysis of Jeffrey's critical and ethical principles. His criticism of Wordsworth "is all honest, clear-eyed criticism; and it all springs from a conviction that Wordsworth was confounding life's plainest distinctions in the mystical mist with which he had surrounded himself for years in the solitude of the Cumberland hills." See *260, 291.*

233. LILLEY, J. P. "Wordsworth's Interpretation of Nature," *Hibbert Journal,* xix (1921), 532–50.

Largely a theological essay, interpreting Wordsworth as essentially a religious teacher, a mystic, who believed in the unity of nature, and in spirits or presiding powers sent from God and present in nature, ready to instruct and bless the receptive heart.

234. McDOWALL, ARTHUR. "Johnson and Wordsworth: A Contrast in Travel," *The London Mercury,* iii (1921), 269–78.

An entertainingly written essay, contrasting the tours of Scotland in *Journey to the Western Isles* and Dorothy Wordsworth's *Journal* of the 1803 tour. See *236.*

235. Morison, William. "Affinities in Wordsworth to Milton," *Poetry Rev.*, xii, No. 3 (May-June, 1921), 130–41.

The lives of the two poets were different, but their characters and genius were much alike. Both were austere and regarded their genius with gravity. Both were controversialists, and were concerned with human freedom. Milton's material, being mostly borrowed, was the richer; but Wordsworth's was more original and more frugal. Milton wrote more of ideal conceptions, while Wordsworth, working in the field of reality, wrote of the sublime in the common.

236. Roscoe, E. S. "Johnson and Wordsworth in the Highlands," *North American Rev.*, ccxiv (1921), 690–96.

A contrast between Johnson's tour of the Scottish highlands in 1773, and Wordsworth's tour in 1803. Characteristic traits of both men are pointed out. See *234*.

237. Strong, A. T. *Three Studies in Shelley and an Essay on Nature in Wordsworth and Meredith,* London, Oxford University Press, 1921.

Wordsworth and Meredith are called the two modern poets who have seen most deeply into nature's meaning. The varying aspects of the thought of each are presented. Fundamentally, Meredith believes in a rigid adherence to nature, by which the race is promoted, with little thought of immediate spiritual blessing for the individual. Nature remains a physical thing. Wordsworth differs in his spiritualization of nature and in the mystical communion he finds between man and nature.

238. Wells, J. E. "The Story of Wordsworth's 'Cintra,'" *SP,* xviii (1921), 15–76.

The complete details of the complicated story of the composition and publication of the tract, including lists of revisions and insertions and a description of several first editions now in America. There remains little doubt that De Quincey suffered unfair judgment from Wordsworth and others in his difficult and, on the whole, successful task as editor.

1922

239. Anon. "La Poesia di Wordsworth," *TLS,* March 9, 1922, p. 157.

Review of the work of Pietro Bardi, the first Italian book on Wordsworth, with translations of his poems.

240. ———. "The Laureates," *TLS,* Jan. 26, 1922, pp. 49–50.

Contains some comments on Wordsworth's *Installation Ode,* a duty performed as laureate.

241. BABENROTH, A. C. *English Childhood. Wordsworth's Treatment of Childhood in the Light of English Poetry from Prior to Crabbe,* New York, Columbia University Press, 1922.

A comparative discussion, introducing many writers. The last chapter is devoted primarily to Wordsworth who, more than any other, is the poet of childhood. His treatment is in harmony with that of the poets from Prior to Crabbe, but more extensive and observant. See *617, 654.*

242. BEATTY, ARTHUR. *William Wordsworth. His Doctrine and Art in Their Historical Relations,* "University of Wisconsin Studies in Language and Literature," No. 17, Madison, University of Wisconsin Press, 1922.

Revised edition, "University of Wisconsin Studies in Language and Literature," No. 24, 1927. The most complete analysis of Wordsworth's sensationalism and his indebtedness to this school of thought, especially to David Hartley. Beatty argues that Wordsworth's transcendentalism is not mystical, but is based on sensationalism. A book of first importance. See *154.*

Rev. *Lond. Quarterly Rev.,* July, 1923, pp. 123–24. Harper, *JEGP,* xxii (1923), 566–69. White, *SAQ,* xxiii (Apr., 1924), 186–88. Bright, *MLN,* xxxix (1924), 59–64. Herford, *MLR,* xix (1924), 113–17. Fehr, *Ang. Bbl.,* xxxvii (Dec., 1926), 355–58. Dodds, *RES,* iv (1928), 358–59 (2nd ed., 1927).

243. CERF, BARRY. "Wordsworth's Gospel of Nature," *PMLA,* xxxvii (1922), 615–38.

The essay, while tinctured with the neo-humanist point of view, is not a destructive attack on the poet. It attempts to discover his true value, and to discard the false. In so far as Wordsworth's gospel of nature is based on sensuousness and "wise passiveness," it is no true religion, which can be achieved only by intellectual vigor and intense effort of spirit. Nor is he a great nature poet, in the strict sense of the term. He proclaimed the virtue of unpolished diction; yet in point of style he is akin to Milton and Pope. He misunderstood his own genius. His true nature is conservative, not radical; he is introspective and self-searching, not sensuous; his interest is primarily man, not nature; and his religion is spiritual, not "natural." See *292.*

244. GARROD, H. W. "Punctuation in Wordsworth," *TLS,* May 4, 1922, p. 292.

Suggests correction in punctuation of *The Prelude,* I, 398–99 to read: "But huge and mighty forms that do not live, Like living men moved slowly through the mind."

245. ———. "Wordsworth's Lines to Hartley Coleridge," *TLS,* Sept. 7, 1922, p. 569.

Points out that the "Lines" could not have originally formed part of the *Ode on Intimations of Immortality* since the *Ode* was not begun until March 26, 1802, and the "Lines" were quoted by Coleridge as early as March 17, 1801 *(Anima Poetae,* p. 15). See *247.* Garrod also calls attention to several errors in the punctuation of *The Prelude.* See *250.*

246. GUTHRIE, ANNA M. B. *Wordsworth and Tolstoi and Other Papers,* Edinburgh, T. and A. Constable Ltd. (privately printed), 1922.

Although vastly dissimilar in many respects, Wordsworth and Tolstoi in common emphasize the return to the simple life and a recognition of nature.

247. HARPER, G. M. "Wordsworth's Lines to Hartley Coleridge," *TLS,* Aug. 31, 1922, p. 557.

The suggestion had previously been made that the "Lines" to Hartley Coleridge may have been originally part of the *Ode on Intimations of Immortality.* Harper suggests that they fit either before or after stanza VIII. See *245.*

248. LEGOUIS, ÉMILE. *William Wordsworth and Annette Vallon,* London, J. M. Dent and Sons Ltd., 1922.

Legouis, carrying on the research of Harper, presents here the fullest account of this episode in Wordsworth's life. The book presents in revised form two articles, "Le Roman de William Wordsworth: sa Liaison avec Annette Vallon" *(Revue des Deux Mondes,* April, May, 1922). See *231.*

Rev. *TLS,* Feb. 1, 1923, p. 69.

249. LEHMAN, B. H. "The Doctrine of Leadership in the Greater Romantic Poets," *PMLA,* xxxvii (1922), 639–61.

Wordsworth's conception of the great man reached its full maturity when *The Convention of Cintra* was written. "The terms of the great man theory are the essential terms of all of Wordsworth's teaching . . . Reason, Nature, Unbending Truth, Virtue, Duty."

250. LUCAS, F. L. "Wordsworth's Punctuation," *TLS,* Sept. 14, 1922, p. 585.

Disagrees with Garrod's suggestion for altering the punctuation of *The Prelude,* VIII, 619–20. See *245.*

251. MERRILL, L. R. "Vaughan's Influence Upon Wordsworth's Poetry," *MLN,* xxxvii (1922), 91–96.

Traces the resemblance between Vaughan's *Retreat* and Wordsworth's *Ode on Intimations of Immortality.* The *Ode* appears to be indebted also to other poems of Vaughan. Wordsworth's conception of nature, its life and ethical influence, and the active principle that animates all, are also suggested in Vaughan.

252. MORLEY, EDITH J., ed. *Blake, Coleridge, Wordsworth, Lamb, etc. Being Selections from the Remains of Henry Crabb Robinson,* Manchester, The University Press, 1922.

The letters and diaries of Crabb Robinson are a rich source of information concerning Wordsworth and other figures of the period.

Rev. *TLS,* Jan. 26, 1933, p. 55.

253. ———. "Wordsworth's French Daughter," *TLS,* Aug. 3, 1922, p. 507.

References to Caroline found in Crabb Robinson's unpublished "Remains." See *269, 272.*

254. PANCOAST, H. S. "Did Wordsworth Jest with Matthew?" *MLN,* xxxvii (1922), 279–83.

A refutation of the interpretation of O. J. Campbell in his paper "Wordsworth Bandies Jests with Matthew." Pancoast argues that Wordsworth was serious in these "Matthew" poems; and that Matthew is not a single, consistent character in all of them. He suggests an identification with Coleridge. See *228.*

255. SHERARD, R. H. "Wordsworth's Installation Ode," *TLS,* Feb. 16, 1922, p. 108.

Points out the part that Edward Quillinan played in its composition.

256. WILLIAMS, T. A. "Wordsworth, Mrs. Hemans, and Robert P. Graves," *London Mercury,* vi (1922), 395–401.

A collection of letters from Wordsworth concerning a clerical appointment for Graves.

1923

257. Adkins, N. F. "Wordsworth's 'Margaret; or the Ruined Cottage,'" *MLN,* xxxviii (1923), 460–66.

Calls attention to similarities between Wordsworth's poem and Saint-Pierre's *Paul et Virginie.* The writer concludes that they are sufficiently close to suggest at least a subconscious source.

258. Allen, B. S. "Analogues of Wordsworth's 'The Borderers,'" *PMLA,* xxxviii (1923), 267–77.

An account of numerous minor novels directed against Godwinism. "These books I think I am justified in regarding as analogues. They contain characters and situations that, in substance and treatment, cannot be distinguished from Wordsworth's work." They differ in that none of the writers was ever a disciple of Godwin.

259. Anon. "Lord Grey and 'The Prelude,'" *TLS,* June 7, 1923, p. 377.

Wordsworth is a poet to whom a statesman naturally turns, and Lord Grey is a true Wordsworthian in that he turned to nature for spiritual comfort. Wordsworth found in nature a creative power, which stimulated a like power in man. *The Prelude* is the supreme expression of this dim and unconscious reaction of all Englishmen.

260. Beatty, J. M. "Lord Jeffrey and Wordsworth," *PMLA,* xxxviii (1923), 221–35.

A defense of Jeffrey as a sane, common-sense critic, who upheld a principle of poetic decorum. His judgments of Wordsworth are in some instances similar to those of Coleridge, Hazlitt, and Irving Babbitt. He was unable to comprehend Wordsworth's mysticism, but only a mystic can. See *232, 291.*

261. Dunn, Esther C. "Notes on Wordsworth," *MLN,* xxxviii (1923), 246–47.

A letter from Moxon to Henry Reed regarding the latter's criticisms, which Wordsworth had acted upon in revising his poetry. Also, a letter from Wordsworth to Moxon, agreeing to Reed's substitutions.

262. Fausset, H. I'A. *Studies in Idealism,* London, J. M. Dent and Sons Ltd., 1923.

Contains a chapter on Wordsworth, described as an idealist, but one who reconciled rather than confused the actual and the ideal. "He would neither solace himself with abstractions, nor accept the easy vicious creed of ingenious naturalism." The nature of his visionary philosophy is described, and something of his relation to the Romantic background. The interpretations here are less extreme than some in Fausset's book, *The Lost Leader*. See *442*.

263. GARROD, H. W. *Wordsworth,* Oxford, The Clarendon Press, 1923.

Many vital points of Wordsworthian criticism are vigorously examined in this relatively short work, which established Garrod as one of the outstanding Wordsworth scholars. The emphasis in this collection of lectures and essays is on the poetry and its formative forces up to 1805.

Rev. *TLS,* Oct. 4, 1923, p. 648. F. V. Morley, *Lit. Rev.,* Nov. 3, 1923, p. 213. Shanks, *Merc.,* Nov., 1923, pp. 105–7. Fausset, *Bookman* (Lon.), Nov. 23, 1923, pp. 114–15. Ritchie, *Nation-Athen.,* Oct. 27, 1923, p. 466. Van Doren, *Nation,* Oct. 6, 1924, p. 326. Bernard, *Eng. Stud.,* lx (1926), 385–86. Raysor, *MLN,* xliii (1928), 265–66 (2nd ed.). Herscher, *Ang. Bbl.,* xxxix (July, 1928), 200–3.

264. GREY, EDWARD. "Wordsworth's 'Prelude,'" English Association, pamphlet No. 57, Dec., 1923.

A brief general commentary.

265. HARPER, G. M. "Eugénie de Guérin and Dorothy Wordsworth," *Atlantic Monthly,* cxxxi (1923), 649–57.

A journal, in the literary remains of this French woman, sister to the poet Maurice de Guérin, suggests an interesting comparison to the *Journals* of Dorothy Wordsworth.

266. ———. "The Wordsworth-Coleridge Combination," *The Sewanee Rev.,* xxxi (1923), 258–74.

Points out, with comment, certain aspects of the relationship that would bear further investigation. (1) Where did Wordsworth and Coleridge meet before the Racedown visit of June, 1797? (2) Was Wordsworth more intimately connected with the Pantisocratic scheme than is generally supposed? (3) What more can be learned of Wordsworth's and Coleridge's associations with Priestley, Godwin, and the group of English "Jacobins"? (4) What was the relation of Wordsworth and Coleridge to the doctrines of Godwin? (5) What was the "moral relationship" of William and Dorothy Wordsworth and Coleridge? (6) What were the strictly intellectual aspects of the "great partnership"?

267. HOLMES, JOHN. "William Wordsworth," *Freeman,* viii (1923), 60–62.

Not more than thirty or forty lines of the poetry that Wordsworth wrote after 1805 can be read with pleasure today. The human figures in his early poetry were illumined by "the far light of eternity," but when this power was withdrawn Wordsworth became dull and stupid. A comparison is made with Blake.

268. LEGOUIS, ÉMILE. *Wordsworth in a New Light,* Cambridge, Mass., Harvard University Press, 1923.

In this lecture, delivered at Harvard, Legouis recounts briefly the circumstances of Wordsworth's relations with Annette Vallon, and the reasons why he was forced to leave her and his child. Legouis points out that Wordsworth was a Georgian, not a Victorian, and this unhappy episode need not have affected the rest of his life as deeply as some have supposed.

Rev. Chew, *MP,* xxii (1924), 111–12.

269. ———. "Wordsworth's French Daughter," *TLS,* March 8, 1923, p. 159.

Defends Caroline's husband from the charge of attempting to blackmail Wordsworth, a conclusion drawn by Miss Morley from items in Crabb Robinson's unpublished "Remains." See *253, 272.*

270. MACNAGHTEN, HUGH. "Three Critical Suggestions," *TLS,* Dec. 6, 1923, p. 852.

Suggests an interpretation of the figure, "the fields of sleep," from the *Ode on Intimations of Immortality.* See also G. H. Clarke, *TLS,* April 17, 1924, p. 240; and C. C. Bell, *TLS,* May 22, 1924, p. 322. See *69.*

271. MOORE SMITH, G. C. "Wordsworth and George Herbert," *N&Q,* Jan. 13, 1923, p. 30.

In addition to the influence of Herbert's *Constancy* on *The Character of the Happy Warrior,* the writer suggests that Herbert's *Man's Medley* may have influenced some lines in *The Ode on Intimations of Immortality.* For disagreement on this point, see *N&Q,* Feb. 10, 1923, p. 113.

272. MORLEY, EDITH J. "Wordsworth's French Daughter," *TLS,* Feb. 15, 1923, p. 108.

Records in Crabb Robinson's unpublished "Remains" of appeals to Wordsworth for money, made by Caroline's husband. See *253, 269.*

273. Shackford, Martha H. "Wordsworth's Italy," *PMLA,* xxxviii (1923), 236–52.

The article draws together the fragments on the subject from Wordsworth's translations of Michael Angelo's sonnets and of Chiabrera's *Epitaphs,* and from his visits to Italy in 1790, 1820, and 1837.

274. ———. "Wordsworth's 'Michael,'" *The Sewanee Rev.,* xxxi (1923), 275–80.

A general interpretative essay, commenting on the poem's austere strength and simplicity akin to Greek tragedy, the immemorial relationship with nature, Michael's spiritual growth through suffering and disappointment, and the value Wordsworth associates with the individual man.

275. Snyder, F. B. "Wordsworth's Favorite Words," *JEGP,* xxii (1923), 253–56.

A list from the *Concordance* of forty-eight words, most frequently used by Wordsworth. Several conclusions are drawn. His vocabulary is predominantly Anglo-Saxon; that of the ordinary man; of one who lived much in the open; and of one who has achieved a quiet happiness.

276. Swaen, A.E.H. "Peter Bell," *Anglia,* xlvii (1923), 136–84.

Opinions regarding *Peter Bell,* and the parodies of it. Swaen reprints *Peter Bell, a Lyrical Ballad* (Reynolds), *The Dead Asses,* and another burlesque of Wordsworth, *The Baby's Debut.* See *72, 612, 635.*

277. Ternant, Andrew de. "Wordsworth's French Daughter," *TLS,* March 15, 1923, p. 180.

All the details of Wordsworth's French liaison were known to French literary circles in the early 1850's when a member of the Baudouin family sent letters and related documents to the Imperial Library. The papers were offered to Sainte-Beuve, who refused to use them because many of the family were still living. The writer learned this from his father, who was an assistant in the Library during that time.

278. Turner, A. M. "Wordsworth and Hartley Coleridge," *JEGP,* xxii (1923), 538–57.

Points out Hartley Coleridge's veneration for Wordsworth, and evidences of Wordsworth's influence on the style and subject matter of Hartley's poetry, an influence stronger than that of S.T.C.

279. ———. "Wordsworth's Influence on Thomas Campbell," *PMLA,* xxxviii (1923), 253–66.

Campbell was said not to have cared greatly for the "Lake Poets," and there is some doubt as to his actual opinion of Wordsworth. But the writer sees some Wordsworthian influence, such as his idyllic picture of Switzerland in *Theodric,* his attitude toward nature, his feeling for children, and his later simplicity of style.

1924

280. Anon. "Wordsworth's 'Prelude,'" *TLS,* June 12, 1924, p. 372.
Suggests rearrangement of lines, Book VII, ll. 159–67.

281. Colvin, Sidney. "Conclusions," *TLS,* Oct. 2, 1924, p. 612.

Remarks concerning the effective conclusion of Wordsworth's *The Yew Trees,* based on an appeal to the imagination through the weird and iterated sonority of vowel sounds. See the article "Conclusions," *TLS,* Sept. 25, 1924, p. 585.

282. Elton, Oliver. *Wordsworth,* London, Edward Arnold and Co., 1924.

Revised from the author's chapter on Wordsworth in *Survey of English Literature, 1780–1830.* The emphasis is on Wordsworth's art and on poetic interpretations, with less stress on biography and philosophy. Outstanding are the discussions of Wordsworth's sonnets, blank verse, and his theory and practice in regard to poetic diction.

283. Gingerich, S. F. *Essays in the Romantic Poets,* New York, Macmillan and Co., 1924.

The essay on Wordsworth gives one of the best discussions of the religious aspect of Wordsworth's philosophy. No one formula explains the poet's views. Gingerich believes critics have emphasized too strongly special aspects: pantheism, associationism, philosophic sensationalism. In this essay, Wordsworth's religion is traced from naturalism, to immanence, and to transcendence of the spirit.

284. Morley, Edith J. "A Manuscript Poem of Wordsworth," *MLR,* xix (1924), 211–14.

Found in Crabb Robinson's papers, in Wordsworth's hand, no date or title. Morley believes it to be a first draft of *To the*

Moon, Composed by the Seaside—On the Coast of Cumberland. She prints a facsimile of the MS. page, including deletions.

285. MORLEY, F. V., ed. *Dora Wordsworth, her Book,* London, Selwyn and Blount Ltd., 1924.

The story afforded by Dora's album, begun in 1830 and concluded by Sara Coleridge's entry a few months after Wordsworth's death. The album is used by Morley as a thread to hold together a miscellaneous collection of sidelights on Wordsworth and the family at Rydal Mount.

286. MORRIS, MURIEL. "A Note on Wordsworth and Vaughan," *MLN,* xxxix (1924), 187–88.

Parallels between *Ode to Duty* and Vaughan's *Misery* and *The Constellation;* and between Wordsworth's line "Or let me die!" *(The Rainbow)* and Vaughan's "Or let me die!" *(Anguish).*

287. MURRY, J. M. "Wordsworth and Coleridge," *The Adelphi,* i (1924), 923–26.

The comments were occasioned by the appearance of Garrod's *Wordsworth.* Murry suggests that the reason for the decay of vision in Coleridge and Wordsworth "was that each of these two men needed the other in order to believe in his own belief."

288. RICE, R. A. "Wordsworth Since 1916," *Smith College Studies in Modern Languages,* V, 1924, 31–66.

A survey of the trends in Wordsworthian criticism since the appearance of Harper's *Life,* with a selected bibliography. The essay is critical and interpretative. Consideration is given to the "two Wordsworths" as interpreted by Harper; to the discoveries concerning Annette Vallon and the effects of the episode on Wordsworth; to Wordsworth's importance as a political thinker; to the results of Beatty's study of Hartleian influences and Campbell's theory of sentimental morality; and to the attacks on Wordsworth as a poet, notably that of Madariaga.

289. WEATHERHEAD, L. D. "The Idea of Immortality in Wordsworth," *London Quarterly Rev.,* cxlii (1924), 185–97.

Contains a list of passages in which Wordsworth expresses orthodox views concerning immortality. But more prominent are the Platonic and Coleridgeon views in the *Ode on Intimations of Immortality.* Weatherhead attempts to confirm Wordsworth's serious acceptance of the doctrine of prenatal existence by supplying a number of quotations, from widely scattered poems, in which Wordsworth glorifies childhood.

290. Wright, Henry. "Wordsworth and Wales," *The Welsh Outlook,* xi (1924), 103 and 127.

Two papers on Wordsworth's friendship with Robert Jones, his visits to Wales, his treatment of British legend and history. See *149, 532.*

1925

291. Bald, R. C. "Francis Jeffrey as a Literary Critic," *The Nineteenth Century and After,* xcvii (1925), 201–5.

Jeffrey represents the type of Romanticist prior to the publication of *Lyrical Ballads*—that of Gray, Collins, and Goldsmith, but was not far enough advanced to understand the new developments of Wordsworth, Coleridge, and Lamb. See *232, 260.*

292. Beach, J. W. "Expostulation and Reply," *PMLA,* xl (1925), 346–61.

A reply to an article by Barry Cerf. Beach contends that Wordsworth's attitude toward nature is not a mere sensuous ecstasy; that his chief interest is in man and moral philosophy. Wordsworth seeks, in the spirit of Platonism, the One, the permanent. Nature, with her enduring laws, is a manifestation of this. Nor does Wordsworth lose man in nature; he sees the relationship of the two. See *243.*

293. De Selincourt, Ernest. "The Composition of 'The Prelude,'" *TLS,* March 19, 1925, p. 196.

A corroboration, correction, and expansion of Garrod's conclusions, in his *Wordsworth,* concerning the composition of *The Prelude.* De Selincourt bases his statements on a study of the five manuscripts, on the notebooks containing fragments of *The Prelude,* and on evidence from the *Letters.* He throws much light on the problem of dating specific parts of *The Prelude,* especially sections of the last three-quarters of the poem.

294. ———. "Notes in Correction of the Text of Wordsworth's 'Prelude,'" *RES,* i (1925), 151–58.

A series of corrections of the 1850 text, made from MS. "E" (the one of 1839, which was used by the printer), with reference also to earlier MSS. Mostly printer's errors.

295. Greenlaw, Edwin. "Modern English Romanticism," *SP,* xxii (1925), 538–50.

Devotes several pages to recent developments in the scholarship on Wordsworth, especially to Legouis' *Wordsworth in a New*

Light, Beatty's *William Wordsworth,* Pott's *Ecclesiastical Sonnets,* and Garrod's *Wordsworth.*

296. HERZBERG, M. J. "William Wordsworth and German Literature," *PMLA,* xl (1925), 302–45.

Wordsworth read little German in the original. He disliked Goethe. He is "almost the last writer of this age in England whom one would pick out as an instance of German influence." But three poets undoubtedly influenced him—Brun, Bürger, and Schiller. The German philosophers probably reached him through Coleridge. See *130, 558.*

297. KAUFMAN, P. "Defining Romanticism: A Survey and a Program," *MLN,* xl (1925), 193–204.

Chiefly bibliographical references.

298. MOORE, J. R. "Wordsworth's Unacknowledged Debt to Macpherson's 'Ossian,'" *PMLA,* xl (1925), 362–78.

Shows by an abundance of citations that Wordsworth was familiar with *Ossian* through Macpherson (whom he despised). Influence is also indicated in a list of parallel diction and phraseology.

299. MORLEY, EDITH J. "Blake and Wordsworth," *TLS,* May 28, 1925, p. 368.

Morley calls attention to errors in some of the readings in her book *Blake, Coleridge, Wordsworth, Lamb.*

300. STERNBERG, T. T. "Wordsworth's 'Happy Warrior' and Herbert's 'Constancy,'" *MLN,* xl (1925), 252–53.

Emerson, in his *Journals,* says *Constancy* must have suggested the *Happy Warrior.* E. K. Chambers has pointed out indebtedness to Vaughan's *Righteousness,* but this poem in its turn is modeled on *Constancy.* Sternberg believes Wordsworth's poem is a direct echo of Herbert.

301. WHITEHEAD, A. N. *Science and the Modern World,* New York, Macmillan Co., 1925.

Chapter V on "The Romantic Reaction" shows that Wordsworth's protest against the abstractions of science is still valid. By his insistence on the full concrete experience and his grasp of the whole of nature, he reaches a truth beyond scientific analysis. An authoritative discussion.

1926

302. ANON. "A Conversation with Wordsworth," *TLS,* May 27, 1926, p. 355.

In a conversation with Bonamy Price in 1844, Wordsworth spoke of grasping solid objects to make sure that matter existed outside the mind. There is a similar remark in a Fenwick Note (see L.R.M. Strachan, *TLS,* June 3, 1926, p. 374).

303. BARBER, H. "Wordsworth's 'Ode', and Personal Immortality," *The Adelphi,* iii (1926), 818–22.

Wordsworth offers little expectation of personal survival after death, but he emphasizes the more strongly the importance of man's present.

304. BARNARD, C. C. "Wordsworth and 'The Ancient Mariner,'" *Englische Studien,* lx (1926), 262–71.

Differences in Wordsworth's and Coleridge's accounts of the composition of the poem. The chief points are that Wordsworth relates the story of his early collaboration, which is not mentioned by Coleridge; and that Coleridge indicates that the poem was begun after the scheme for *Lyrical Ballads* had been proposed.

305. BERTRAM, ANTON. "Wordsworth's First Love," *TLS,* July 15, 1926, p. 480.

The writer disagrees with de Selincourt that Wordsworth's early love, suggested in passages in *The Prelude,* was Mary Hutchinson. See *315, 318, 321, 322, 377.*

306. BRINTON, C. C. *The Political Ideas of the English Romanticists,* Oxford University Press, Humphrey Milford, 1926.

Includes an analysis of the *Letter to the Bishop of Llandaff* and *The Convention of Cintra.* Wordsworth's nationalism and his opposition in later life to many reform measures in politics are noted.

307. CAMPBELL, O. J. AND PAUL MUESCHKE. "'Guilt and Sorrow': A Study in the Genesis of Wordsworth's Aesthetic," *MP,* xxiii (1926), 293–306.

The second paper in the series devoted to a study of the development of Wordsworth's aesthetic. In *Guilt and Sorrow* the authors see the "sentimental morality" which they have pointed out in his early narrative poetry, combined with the influence of the Gothic romances. They conclude that the poem is weak "because it is a piece of aesthetic patchwork, the product of two distinct and inharmonious artistic modes." See *213, 308, 438, 567.*

308. ———. " 'The Borderers' as a Document in the History of Wordsworth's Aesthetic Development," *MP,* xxiii (1926), 465–82.

The third paper of the series. The same forces are at work here that appeared earlier: "sentimental morality" and the aesthetic of terror. The play reflects Wordsworth's personal remorse, his effort to escape emotion and natural ties in Godwinism. In this he failed. He advanced to a new aesthetic concept. Its fundamentals are memory as an aesthetic principle, and the realization of the importance of feelings based on natural relationships. Not spasmodically, but by perceptible development Wordsworth was prepared for *Lyrical Ballads. See 213, 307, 438, 567.*

309. Cookson, H. E. "Wordsworth and Plato," *TLS,* Nov. 25, 1926, p. 868.

Presents evidence that Wordsworth read Plato and was therefore not only a "natural" Platonist, but a conscious one.

310. Cooper, F. G. "Source of Quotation Wanted," *N&Q,* April 17, 1926, pp. 286–87.

Concerning the deleted passage in *Peter Bell:* "Is it a party in a parlour," etc. Also letters on the same subject by L.R.M. Strachan, J. B. Wainewright, and E. Bensley, *loc. cit.* p. 287.

311. Darbishire, Helen. "Wordsworth's 'Prelude,' " *The Nineteenth Century and After,* xcix (1926), 718–31.

Written on the appearance of de Selincourt's variorum edition of *The Prelude.* Darbishire points out canceled passages and revisions which tone down the boldness of Wordsworth's religion of the senses and the mind as expressed in the 1805 text. "When his religious thought flowed into the channel of Anglican doctrine he had to retouch his autobiography, and incidentally tamper with its poetry, in the spirit of that doctrine." In addition to the value of this article as a commentary on Wordsworth's revisions, it presents a well-defined statement of the philosophy of Wordsworth's early period. See *316, 579, 597, 608.*

312. De Selincourt, Ernest, ed. "The Hitherto Unpublished Preface to Wordsworth's *Borderers," The Nineteenth Century and After,* c (1926), 723–41.

Reprinted in *Oxford Lectures on Poetry,* London, Oxford University Press, 1934. By far the most important contribution on

The Borderers. The Preface was composed, says de Selincourt, not later than the summer of 1800, and was lately discovered in a manuscript volume in Mary Hutchinson's hand, prefixed to a copy of the play as revised for the stage in 1797. The Preface is referred to in the F.N. dictated by Wordsworth in 1843, but it had long been regarded as lost.

313. DODDS, ANNIE E. (POWELL, A. E.). *The Romantic Theory of Poetry. An Examination in the Light of Croce's Aesthetic,* London, Edward Arnold and Co., 1926.

Besides references to Wordsworth in Chapter I ("The Romantic Ideal"), Chapter V is devoted to him. "Theory of Poetry" is interpreted in a broad sense, including Wordsworth's basic realism, his rational psychology and his mysticism, his conception of nature, his theory of imagination, and other matters. Frequent comparisons with Coleridge are drawn.

314. GARSTANG, WALTER. "Wordsworth's Interpretation of Nature," *Nature* (Supplement), Jan. 16, 1926, pp. 1–8.

An interesting paper emphasizing Wordsworth's scientific sympathies. Certain aspects of his personality are likened to Charles Darwin. Comment is made on Wordsworth's associationism, which the writer regards as only a "ladder by which Wordsworth climbed out of the morass of sentimental idealism back to the point of view of his early vision." Also mention is made of Wordsworth's interest in the interrelations between the living and the inanimate universe. Wordsworth's view of nature is compared to listening to the whole symphony; that of the pure scientist, to attending to the individual instruments. But Wordsworth's synthesis is equally truthful.

315. HARPER, G. M. "Wordsworth's 'Lucy,'" *TLS,* Nov. 11, 1926, p. 797.

Conjectures that the reference to an early love *(The Prelude,* XII, 261–66) is not to Mary Hutchinson, but to an unknown girl whom Wordsworth met during the summer of 1788, who died young and was later the subject of the "Lucy Poems." See *305, 318, 321, 322, 377.*

316. KING, HENRY. "Wordsworth's Decline," *The Adelphi,* iv (1926), 106–15.

Presents certain evidences of Wordsworth's decline in his revisions of the original text of *The Prelude.* See *311, 579, 597, 608.*

317. KNIGHT, ANNA N. "The Early Influences of William Wordsworth," *Poetry Rev.*, xvii (1926), 1–10.

An account of Wordsworth's early life and the people with whom he came in contact, including Annette Vallon.

318. LEGOUIS, ÉMILE. "Wordsworth's 'Lucy' Again," *TLS*, Dec. 9, 1926, p. 913.

Points out that Wordsworth never spoke at random, and when he says "Three years," etc. he means that the girl was three years old. She could have been a gypsy child, exposed early to the elements. See *305, 315, 321, 322, 377.*

319. MEYERSTEIN, E.H.W. "Wordsworth and Chatterton," *TLS*, Oct. 21, 1926, p. 722.

Parallels between *Resolution and Independence* and Chatterton's "An Excellent Balade of Charitie," the last of the Rowley *Poems*. They have the same theme and meter, and both start with a description of a sunny day.

320. MOORE, J. B. "Emerson on Wordsworth," *PMLA*, xli (1926), 179–92.

The numerous references to Wordsworth in Emerson's *Journals* and elsewhere show much interest, and a growing admiration from somewhat juvenile irritation to mature discrimination. But Moore maintains that Emerson's conception of nature was not largely derived from Wordsworth, as some critics suppose.

321. PENNINGTON, WALTER. "The 'Lucy' Poems," *MLN*, xli (1926), 314–16.

The Lucy of the five poems is simply Lucy Gray. This opinion is based on the fact that *Lucy Gray* and the "Lucy" poems were written at the same time at Goslar; and that the "Springs of Dove" are in Yorkshire, and Lucy Gray lived near Halifax. See *305, 315, 318, 322, 377.*

322. WORDSWORTH, G. G. "Wordsworth's First Love," *TLS*, July 22, 1926, p. 496.

Gordon Wordsworth, correcting Bertram, points out that Mary Hutchinson resided at Penrith until 1789. See *305, 315, 318, 321, 377.*

1927

323. BICKERSTETH, G. L. *Leopardi and Wordsworth*, London, Humphrey Milford, 1927.

Each was a great political poet, a great nature poet, and a great poetical theorist.

324. Blundon, E. C. "Wordsworthian Topics," *The Adelphi,* iv (1927), 559–60.

Two poems by Dr. Sneyd Davies (on King's College Chapel and "A Voyage to Tintern Abbey") that curiously suggest Wordsworth.

325. Casson, T. E. "Wordsworth and the 'Spectator,'" *RES,* iii (1927), 157–61.

Possible obligations of Wordsworth to the subject matter of *The Spectator,* and verbal parallels.

326. Dunn, S. G. "Newton and Wordsworth," *TLS,* Aug. 25, 1927, p. 576.

Suggests a connection between Newton's "ethereal spirits" and Wordsworth's natural mysticism, generally thought of as drawn from Neoplatonism. Newton's theory of "ethereal spirits" was in opposition to mechanistic philosophy.

327. Harper, G. M. "Did Wordsworth Defy the Guillotine?" *Quarterly Rev.,* ccxlviii (1927), 254–64.

Harper unfolds convincing evidence that Wordsworth returned to France for a brief time in the autumn of 1793, presumably in an effort to see Annette Vallon.

328. ———. "Wordsworth's 'Vast City,'" *MLN,* xlii (1927), 464–65.

An added point, confirming that this phrase in the opening of *The Prelude* refers to London, is Milton's reference to London as "this vast city" *(Areopagitica).*

329. Havens, R. D. "Wordsworth's 'Guilt and Sorrow,'" *RES,* iii (1927), 71–73.

Takes issue with Campbell and Mueschke in their statement that the poem is an "aesthetic patchwork," and their attempt to connect the woman's confession of guilt with Wordsworth's remorse for his desertion of Annette. Havens argues that the predominant feeling throughout the poem (including the first twenty-one stanzas) is pity, not terror. He suggests that the woman's confession of sin can be explained as one of the evil results of war and oppression. See *307*.

330. Hughes, Helen S. "Two Wordsworthian Chapbooks," *MP,* xxv (1927), 207–10.

A description of two chapbooks containing *We Are Seven,*

based on a version of the poem before the revisions of the 1815 reprint.

331. Knaplund, Paul. "Correspondence Relating to the Grant of a Civil List Pension to William Wordsworth, 1842," *MLN,* xlii (1927), 385–89.

Letters between Gladstone and Sir Robert Peele. Gladstone's final letter of recommendation throws much light on Wordsworth's straitened pecuniary circumstances as late as 1842.

332. Knowlton, E. C. "Wordsworth and Hugh Blair," *PQ,* vi (1927), 277–81.

Blair, popular eighteenth-century critic, urged that pastoral poetry should include anything pertaining to the human passions and human nature (save violence). Blair specifically mentioned "scenes of domestic felicity or disquiet" and "the attachment of friends and brothers." Wordsworth has done just this, although there is no evidence that Wordsworth had actually read Blair.

333. Maclean, Catherine M. *Dorothy and William Wordsworth,* Cambridge, The University Press, 1927.

A short biography, with critical comments on some of Wordsworth's verse and theory of diction, by a distinguished biographer and student of Wordsworth. The book is not so full as Maclean's *Dorothy Wordsworth, the Early Years* (1932).

Rev. *TLS,* June 9, 1927, p. 405. Dodds, *RES,* iv (1928), 359–60. Raysor, *MLN,* xliii (1928), 265–66. Janney, *PQ,* ix (1930), 413–14.

334. Morley, Edith J., ed. *Correspondence of Crabb Robinson with the Wordsworth Circle,* 2 vols., Oxford, The Clarendon Press, 1927.

Contains also letters not included in de Selincourt's edition of *The Letters of William and Dorothy Wordsworth.*

Rev. *TLS,* Nov. 3, 1927, p. 773. Batho, *MLR,* xxiii (1928), 363–65. King, *RES,* iv (1928), 361–65. Harper, *MLN,* xliii (1928), 538–42. Zeitlin, *JEGP,* xxix (1930), 290–93.

335. Munk, Elias. *William Wordsworth. Ein Beitrag zur Erforschung seiner reliogiösen Entwicklung,* Berlin, Verlag von Emil Eberling, 1927.

Emphasizes the numinous in Wordsworth's religious experience, which is regarded as stronger than Hartleian psychology.

336. RICHARDS, A. E. "The Day Book and Ledger of Wordsworth's Carpenter," *PQ,* vi (1927), 75-79.

Prints several pages of items from the ledger, which dates from 1808 to 1843. These details "may lend additional interest to Grasmere associations and to the reading of *The Brothers* and of the preface to *The Excursion.*"

337. THORPE, C. D. "Wordsworth and Keats—A Study in Personal and Critical Impression," *PMLA,* xlii (1927), 1010-26.

Intended as a preliminary survey, assembling many interesting references. The points that appear are Keats's early veneration for Wordsworth, his meetings with the elder poet, his repulsion and adverse criticism, and his continued admiration for much of Wordsworth's philosophy and poetry.

338. WISE, T. J. "Plagiarism in Bibliography," *TLS,* Oct. 27, 1927, p. 766.

Wise complains of bibliographers who have borrowed from him without acknowledgment, and refers to an unnamed American planning (in 1927) a bibliography of Wordsworth.

339. ———. *Two Lake Poets. A Catalogue of Printed Books, Manuscripts and Autograph Letters by William Wordsworth and Samuel Taylor Coleridge,* London, privately printed, 1927.

A catalogue of the Wordsworth and Coleridge titles in the Ashley Library, with full bibliographical descriptions. See *185, 432, 622.*

1928

340. CÉCILIA, J. L. "Wordsworth and Comte," *TLS,* March 22, 1928, p. 221.

Some points of resemblance between Wordsworth's thought and the philosophy of Comte.

341. COOPER, LANE. "Quotations by Wordsworth," *TLS,* June 28, 1928, p. 486.

Suggested sources for a number of lines quoted by Wordsworth. See *351.*

342. DE SELINCOURT, ERNEST. "Wordsworth's 'Prelude,'" *TLS,* Aug. 23, 1928, p. 605.

A list of errata in his edition of *The Prelude.*

343. FAIRCHILD, H. N. *The Noble Savage: A Study in Romantic Naturalism,* New York, Columbia University Press, 1928.

A study of primitivism and the idealization of the savage from early times, with strong emphasis on the Romantic treatment of the theme in the eighteenth and nineteenth centuries. Wordsworth is given special examination. Fairchild finds numerous traces of the convention in Wordsworth, but few of its fundamental aspects.

344. HARPER, G. M. "Was Wordsworth Ever a Mystic?" *Discovery,* ix (1928), 348–50.

Harper presents briefly the case that Wordsworth—in spite of the impression he may have given later in life— was not a mystic in his early and most productive years. He had too strong a sense of the prime significance and reality of the objective world.

345. KORTELING, JACOMINA. *Mysticism in Blake and Wordsworth,* Amsterdam, H. J. Paris, 1928.

Only Blake and Wordsworth among English writers can be strictly defined as mystics.

346. NEWTON, ANNABEL. *Wordsworth in Early American Criticism,* Chicago, University of Chicago Press, 1928.

The slow recognition in America of Wordsworth, and a bibliography of early American editions. See *447, 634.*

Rev. *TLS,* June 21, 1928, p. 466. Foerster, *SP,* xxvi (1929), 85–95.

347. PIERCE, F. E. "Wordsworth and Thomas Taylor," *PQ,* vii (1928), 60–64.

Argues that the Neoplatonism of the *Ode on Intimations of Immortality* was less likely drawn from Coleridge than from Thomas Taylor's *Works of Plato,* published in 1804. Pierce finds parallels between Taylor's editorial comments and lines in the *Ode.*

348. RADER, M. M. "The Transcendentalism of William Wordsworth," *MP,* xxvi (1928), 169–90.

The article points out another side of Wordsworth than that presented by Beatty in his *William Wordsworth,* and discredits the tendency to carry too far an interpretation of Wordsworth according to the school of sensationalism. Rader concludes that there is no direct proof of Wordsworth's adherence to Hartley; that the influence of Coleridge was in opposition to Hartleianism; that Coleridge regarded *The Prelude* and *Ode on Intimations of*

Immortality as non-Hartleian; and that Wordsworth voiced transcendental doctrines quite beyond the Hartleian conception.

349. REA, J. D. "Coleridge's Intimations of Immortality from Proclus," *MP,* xxvi (1928), 201–13.

Rea produces plausible evidence that stanzas V–VII (as well as I–IV) of Wordsworth's *Ode on the Intimations of Immortality* were written in the spring of 1802. Wordsworth had begun the *Ode* under the influence of Coleridge's dejection over the loss of the buoyancy of childhood (cf. *Ode on Dejection*). To Wordsworth's questions as to the cause of the change, Coleridge had suggested a philosophical answer might be found in Proclus. Thus were derived stanzas V–VII of Wordsworth's *Ode.* See *384, 425, 472, 489, 611.*

350. ROBERTSON, STUART. "Chaucer and Wordsworth," *MLN,* xliii (1928), 104–5.

In *Ecclesiastical Sonnets,* Part II, No. XXXI, Wordsworth quotes as Chaucer's (and holds up for admiration) the sole original line interpolated in his otherwise pure paraphrase of the "Prioress' Tale."

351. SMITH, N. C. "Untraced Quotations in Wordsworth," *TLS,* April 12, 1928, p. 272.

Requests the source of a number of quotations in Wordsworth. For reply, see *341.*

352. TURNBULL, J. M. "Wordsworth's Part in the Production of Lamb's 'Specimens,'" *N&Q,* Feb. 18, 1928, pp. 114–15.

Calls attention to a statement in a letter of Mary Lamb to Mrs. Clarkson (Dec. 23, 1806), that her brother plans to go through old plays collecting extracts for a collection of poetry that Wordsworth intends to publish.

1929

353. ANDERSON, MARION. "Untraced Quotations in Wordsworth," *TLS,* Aug. 22, 1929, p. 652.

The line from *The Sparrow's Nest,* "She gave me eyes; she gave me ears," is traced to ll. 3–4 of Charles Churchill's *Independence.*

354. BARRY, J.A.F. "The First Review of Wordsworth's Poetry," *MLN,* xliv (1929), 299–302.

There was a favorable review of *An Evening Walk* in a letter, signed "Peregrinator," in the *Gentleman's Magazine,* March, 1794. The letter was dated Sept. 6, 1793, a month before the unfavorable review in the *Monthly Review.* Barry raises several pertinent questions concerning this early review. See *388.*

355. BLUNDEN, E. C. *Nature in English Literature,* London, The Hogarth Press, 1929.

A broad treatment of the theme, including many English writers. Good reading, but of no particular value in the study of Wordsworth.

356. CHAPMAN, J. A. *Papers on Shelley, Wordsworth and Others,* London, Oxford University Press, 1929.

Includes a criticism of Wordsworth's theory of poetry expressed in the Preface to *Lyrical Ballads.*

357. COBBAN, ALFRED. *Edmund Burke and The Revolt against the Eighteenth Century. A Study of the Political and Social Thinking of Burke, Wordsworth, Coleridge and Southey,* London, George Allen and Unwin Ltd., 1929.

Contains a survey, in some detail, of the political thinking of Burke. A chapter is devoted to Wordsworth's change from the doctrine of the French Revolution to nationalism.

358. COOPER, LANE. "Matthew Arnold's Essay on Wordsworth," *The Bookman* (U.S.A.), lxix (1929), 479–84.

Reprinted in *Evolution and Repentance,* Ithaca, N. Y., Cornell University Press, 1935. A sharp criticism of Arnold's selections for the *Golden Treasury,* and his essay. Cooper points out that Arnold uses faulty, early texts of the poems. He misses the "Christian note" of Wordsworth, observed by Sainte-Beuve.

359. DINGLE, HERBERT. "The Analytical Approach to Wordsworth," *The Realist,* i, No. 3 (June, 1929), 142–59.

The central purpose of Wordsworth's life was to be happy. In nature he saw only what was familiar to him and what pleased him, closing his eyes to the unpleasant. He loved what was simple and fixed, and disregarded the "processes" of nature. Even in youth he was at heart an uncompromising Tory, and his "essential quietism" produced a "complete alienation from the impulse to reform."

360. FRASER, W. G. "'The Prelude,' Book VI, ll. 592–616," *TLS,* April 4, 1929, p. 276.

This passage was interpreted by Garrod as an imaginative

experience which took place on the tour of 1790. Fraser maintains that it occurred during the composition of the poem.

361. GARROD, H. W. *The Profession of Poetry and Other Lectures,* Oxford, The Clarendon Press, 1929.

Contains a lecture on the "Lucy" poems, pointing to the identification of Lucy with Dorothy.

362. HARRINGTON, JANETTE. "Wordsworth's 'Descriptive Sketches' and 'The Prelude,' Book VI," *PMLA,* xliv (1929), 1144–58.

Points out the variants in the accounts of the holiday tour of 1790, in *Descriptive Sketches, The Prelude,* and the Keswill letter. She concludes that in the two poems Wordsworth uses his material not to give an accurate account, but for a desired effect, and each source therefore represents the mood at the time of composition. See *387.*

363. HAVENS, R. D. "A Project of Wordsworth's," *RES,* v (1929), 320–22.

Two letters of Southey to the effect that Wordsworth and Spedding were organizing a county meeting to speak against the Convention of Cintra (letters dated Oct. 19, and Oct. 30, 1808).

364. HERFORD, C. H. "Goethe and Wordsworth," *Contemporary Rev.,* cxxxvi (1929), 465–75.

Reprinted in *Publications of the English Goethe Society,* VII (New Series, 1930), 8–31. Goethe, the "world-poet," and the "insular" Wordsworth are contrasted: their different form of idealism, their different understanding of a great national state. But in some points they are not far apart, such as both poets' Spinozistic vision of the transcendency of the mind of man in the universe. See *77, 91, 457.*

365. HUXLEY, A. L. "Wordsworth in the Tropics," *YR,* xviii (1929), 672–83.

Reprinted in *Do What You Will,* New York, Doubleday, Doran and Co., 1930. The essay points out that Wordsworth does not recognize the harsh and ruthless aspect of nature, and had he been brought up in the tropics his philosophy might have been different.

366. MABBOTT, T. O. "Landor on Chatterton and Wordsworth: Marginal Notes," *N&Q,* Mar. 9, 1929, pp. 168–69.

Landor's marginal comments, written in his copy of Howitt's *Homes and Haunts of the Most Eminent British Poets.*

367. MacGillivray, J. R. "Wordsworth and his Daughter," *TLS,* Sept. 5, 1929, p. 684.

A letter from Wordsworth to Daniel Stuart (April 7, 1817) throws light on the financial assistance that Wordsworth gave his daughter Caroline after her marriage. See *375, 389, 398, 412.*

368. Mead, Marian. *Four Studies in Wordsworth,* Menasha, Wis., George Banta Publishing Co., 1929.

A discussion of Wordsworth's visual ability, his sense of color, his ideas of landscape and architecture and other matters. Contains a collection of color words which are compared with those of Keats. Also an essay on *The Idiot Boy.*

369. Potts, Abbie F. "The Date of Wordsworth's First Meeting with Hazlitt," *MLN,* xliv (1929), 296–99.

Several scholars have accepted the latter part of May, 1798, or the early part of June as the date of Hazlitt's arrival at Nether Stowey. Potts corroborates this date on the evidence of the dates of the Bristol performances of Monk Lewis' *The Castle Spectre,* which Wordsworth described to Hazlitt.

370. ———. "Wordsworth and William Fleetwood's 'Sermons,'" *SP,* xxvi (1929), 444–56.

The moral and social ideas in numerous early poems of Wordsworth seem to reflect strongly sentiments expressed in a volume of *Sermons* by Fleetwood (published in 1705) to which Wordsworth makes reference. This goes to show that Wordsworth did not embody in these poems themes peculiar to the period of the French Revolution. It would indicate also his early sympathy for the Christian doctrine of submission, strongly emphasized by Fleetwood.

371. Stallknecht, N. P. "Wordsworth and Philosophy," *PMLA,* xliv (1929), 1116–43.

A learned contribution to the study of Wordsworth's mysticism. Its two phases: Spinozistic in *The Prelude* and poems until 1805; Kantian in the *Ode to Duty* and *The Excursion.* After 1814 his philosophy seems to have changed little. Stallknecht does not exclude the influence of other related philosophers.

372. TURNBULL, J. M. "Wordsworth's 'Flying Tailor,'" *TLS,* Oct. 24, 1929, p. 846.

There is a parody of *The Recluse* by this title in Hogg's *The Poetical Minor* (1816). The phrase may have its basis in a reference to Lamb's *On the Melancholy of Tailors,* a copy of which was sent to Wordsworth.

373. WORDSWORTH, G. G. *Some Notes on the Wordsworths of Peniston,* Ambleside, The St. Oswald Press (privately printed), 1929.

On Wordsworth's Yorkshire ancestry, dating from the fourteenth century. The family seem to have come from the village of Wadsworth.

1930

374. BAILEY, JOHN. "Wordsworth's 'Lucy,'" *TLS,* Jan. 30, 1930, p. 78.

Asks why Sir Arthur Quiller-Couch accepts as "well established" the identification of "Lucy" as Dorothy Wordsworth. See *394.*

375. BATHO, EDITH C. "Wordsworth and his Daughter," *TLS,* April 13, 1930, p. 298.

On the basis of a series of entries in the unpublished portions of Crabb Robinson's *Diary,* Batho finds evidence that up to 1836 Wordsworth gave his daughter Caroline nearly £1000; £600 before the settlement and £400 at the time of the settlement of 1835. See *367, 389, 398, 412.* See also Batho, *The Later Wordsworth,* pp. 390–95.

376. BERNBAUM, ERNEST. *Guide Through the Romantic Movement,* New York, Thomas Nelson and Sons, 1930.

An admirable brief survey, the only trustworthy handbook for the period. Contains general and individual bibliographies, and an excellent chapter on "History of the Study of the Subject."

377. BERTRAM, ANTON. "Wordsworth's 'Lucy,'" *TLS,* March 6, 1930, p. 190.

Additional evidence that Wordsworth experienced a love affair earlier than that with Mary Hutchinson. See *305, 315, 318, 321, 322.*

378. BIRKHOFF, BARBARA. *As Between Friends,* Cambridge, Mass., Harvard University Press, 1930.

"Radcliffe Honors Theses in English," No. 1. Criticisms of each other by Wordsworth, Coleridge, and Lamb, derived from their letters.

379. BROUGHTON, L. N. "W. A. Knight's First Interest in Wordsworth," *PQ*, ix (1930), 402–3.

On the flyleaf of *Voices of Nature*, an anthology containing some of Wordsworth's poetry edited by G. B. Cheever, Knight penciled ". . . the book which started me on a study of Wordsworth."

380. CLAYDON, W. A. "The Numinous in the Poetry of Wordsworth," *Hibbert Journal*, xxviii (1930), 601–15.

Presents the case of Wordsworth's mysticism. The imagination in Wordsworth is a faculty of divination, essentially religious. It is to be distinguished from a purely aesthetic experience.

381. CRAVER, A. W. "Wordsworth in France," *TLS*, May 29, 1930, p. 458.

Discredits the evidence in the letter to Mathews, cited by Harper as contributing to the theory that Wordsworth returned to France in the autumn of 1793. See *383, 390, 520.*

382. EMPSON, WILLIAM. *Seven Types of Ambiguity*, London, Chatto and Windus, 1930.

See pp. 191–94 for an interesting analysis of *Tintern Abbey*, ll. 88–102.

383. HARPER, G. M. "Wordsworth in France," *TLS*, May 1, 1930, p. 370.

Finds evidence in a letter to William Mathews to support the case (presented elsewhere by Harper) that Wordsworth returned to France in the autumn of 1793. See *381, 390, 520.*

384. HARTMAN, HERBERT. "The 'Intimations' of Wordsworth's 'Ode,'" *RES*, vi (1930), 129–48.

The influences that contributed to the composition of the *Ode*. Outstanding is the Neoplatonism derived from Coleridge's reading of Proclus (previously pointed out by Rea), and from Coleridge's acquaintance with Fénelon. Hartman also gives strong evidence for dating stanzas V–VI in 1802, not four years later as Wordsworth states in the Fenwick Note. There is also a discussion of the connection between Coleridge's *Dejection* and Wordsworth's *Ode*. Hartman also says that Wordsworth had been reading Ben Jonson on March 23, 1802, and suggests that this reading excited him to his first irregular Pindaric ode. See *349, 425, 472, 489, 611.*

385. HERFORD, C. H. *Wordsworth,* London, G. Routledge and Sons Ltd., 1930.

An authoritative biography and critical analysis of Wordsworth and his poetry. It is the most dependable book available for a general, brief survey. The period after 1815 is regarded as an "Aftermath" and is discussed briefly in one chapter.

Rev. *TLS,* Dec. 18, 1930, p. 1073. Chew, *YR,* xxi (1931), 207–10. Van Doren, *Nation,* Apr. 1, 1931, pp. 384–85. Lewis, *Merc.,* Feb., 1931, p. 387. Barnard, *Eng. Stud.,* lxvii (1932), 141–46.

386. HOLT, EDGAR. "William Wordsworth," *The Bookman* (London), lxxix (1930), 170–71.

A brief notice, calling attention especially to *The Prelude* and Wordsworth's opinions on the French Revolution. It is stated that he shows the broader principles of the love of humanity.

387. HOOKER, E. N. "'Descriptive Sketches' and 'The Prelude,' Book VI," *PMLA,* xlv (1930), 619–23.

Conclusions regarding these two accounts (and a third in the letter to Dorothy) of Wordsworth's visit to Switzerland in 1790. Hooker refutes the points made by Janette Harrington in her article. See *362.*

388. MACGILLIVRAY, J. R. "A Possible First Review of Wordsworth's Poetry," *MLN,* xlv (1930), 387–88.

Quotes the *Analytical Review* on *An Evening Walk* and *Descriptive Sketches,* March, 1793. This antedates the notices in the *Monthly Review* for Oct., 1793, and the notice written in Sept., 1793 (although not published until March, 1794) for the *Gentleman's Magazine.* See *354.*

389. ———. "Wordsworth and his Daughter," *TLS,* May 8, 1930, p. 394.

Identifies the "Mme Williams," to whom Wordsworth sent money in 1815, as Annette. See *367, 375, 398, 412.*

390. ———. "Wordsworth in France," *TLS,* June 12, 1930, p. 496.

Although doubting the use as evidence of the letter to Mathews, pointed out by Harper, the writer presents other points that lend plausibility to the theory that Wordsworth visited France in the autumn of 1793. See *383, 381, 520.*

391. ———. "Wordsworth's Journey from London to Orleans," *TLS,* April 24, 1930, p. 352.

Evidence to show that Wordsworth arrived in Paris Nov. 30, 1791, and in Orleans Dec. 6, 1791.

392. ———. "Wordsworth's 'The Borderers,'" *TLS,* Dec. 25, 1930, p. 1101.

External evidence that the Marmaduke of the play is to be identified with Wordsworth. This character was called Mortimer in the 1797 text. *The Convict,* signed by the pseudonym "Mortimer," appeared in the *Morning Post,* Dec. 14, 1797, the day before Wordsworth left London after the play's rejection.

393. POTTS, ABBIE F. "A Letter from Wordsworth to Thomas Powell," *MLN,* xlv (1930), 215–18.

Quotes an unpublished letter in the Morgan Library on the subject of Chaucer and Wordsworth's modernization.

394. QUILLER-COUCH, ARTHUR. "Wordsworth's 'Lucy,'" *TLS,* Feb. 13, 1930, p. 122.

"Well established" is too strong a phrase to use concerning the identification of "Lucy" with Dorothy Wordsworth, but except for the poetical assumption of Lucy's death, the poems seem to describe Dorothy. See *374.*

395. READ, HERBERT. *Wordsworth,* London, Jonathan Cape, 1930.

A series of lectures, interpreting with brilliance Wordsworth's life and poetry. Read is one of the strongest advocates of the theory that Wordsworth suffered a permanent poetic and spiritual collapse from his "betrayal" of Annette Vallon and the cause of the French Revolution.

Rev. *TLS,* Dec. 18, 1930, p. 1073. Watkins, *Merc.,* June, 1931, p. 181. Church, *Fort. Rev.,* cxxxv (1931), 127–28. Van Doren, *Nation,* cxxxii (1931), 384–85. Harper, *SRL,* Apr. 4, 1931, pp. 707–8. Blunden, *Spect.,* July 23, 1932, p. 126.

396. SCHUMACHER, ELISABETH. *Einheit und Totalität Bei Wordsworth, Unter Dem Gesichtspunkt Psychologischer Strukturtypologie,* Leipzig, Akademische Verlagsellschaft, M.B.H., 1930.

An account of Wordsworth's development, using the psychological apparatus of Deutschbein and Jaensch.

397. TUCKERMAN, UNA V. "Wordsworth's Plan for his Imitation of Juvenal," *MLN,* xlv (1930), 209–15.

"Evidently he intended to follow rather closely the parts of

Juvenal's *Eighth Satire* which deal with the superiority of humble worth over degenerate nobility," making use of the lives of Englishmen as Juvenal had of the lives of Romans. He was also following Dr. Johnson's *London* and *The Vanity of Human Wishes.*

398. WORDSWORTH, G. G. "Wordsworth and his Daughter," *TLS,* April 17, 1930, p. 336.

Further facts concerning Wordsworth's gifts to his daughter Caroline. See *367, 375, 389, 412.*

1931

399. BABBITT, IRVING. "The Primitivism of Wordsworth," *The Bookman,* (U.S.A.), lxxiv (1931), 1–10.

Babbitt's essay is one of the most vigorous attacks on Wordsworth's philosophy. He condemns Wordsworth's dislike of reasoning, his preference for characters whose minds and manners are unschooled. Babbitt's attack is directed against Wordsworth's theory of "wise passiveness." This, says Babbitt, is the fatal weakness of primitivism. Only by the exertion of the mind and the will does man reach higher levels.

400. BANERJEE, SRIKUMAR. *Critical Theories and Poetic Practice in the 'Lyrical Ballads,'* London, Williams and Norgate Ltd., 1931.

The question is discussed of whether Wordsworth intended to introduce into poetry the arrangement and order of prose as well as the vocabulary. Many confused points and inconsistencies in theory and practice are detected. A routine piece of investigation.

401. BRASH, W. B. "Wordsworth and his Teachers," *Holborn Rev.,* xxii (N.S., 1931), 321–30.

A brief review of the influence on Wordsworth of Annette, the French Revolution, Rousseau, Godwin, Coleridge, Dorothy Wordsworth, and the Lake district.

402. BREDE, ALEXANDER. "Theories of Poetic Diction in Wordsworth and Others and in Contemporary Poetry," *Papers of the Michigan Academy of Science, Arts, and Letters,* XIV (1930), Ann Arbor, University of Michigan Press, 1931, 537–65.

The essay includes a summary and interpretation of Wordsworth's views. The language of "ordinary men" in a state of passion is interpreted as simply the language Wordsworth himself might have used, not that of rustics or illiterates.

403. BROUGHTON, L. N., ed. *The Wordsworth Collection formed by Cynthia Morgan St. John,* Ithaca, N. Y., Cornell University Library, 1931.

This collection, now in the possession of Cornell University, is the largest in America. The catalogue is of great value for bibliographical reference. See *607*.

404. DE SELINCOURT, ERNEST. "Early Readings in 'The Prelude,'" *TLS,* Nov. 12, 1931, p. 886.

The last twenty pages of Dorothy Wordsworth's notebook, in which she wrote part of her diary, contain the earliest drafts of some passages from *The Prelude,* chiefly in Book I. They seem to date from the Gosler period. This newly discovered manuscript source de Selincourt calls "JJ," and lists its variant readings.

405. FAIRCHILD, H. N. *The Romantic Quest,* New York, Columbia University Press, 1931.

"*The Romantic Quest* is a book for students of some intellectual maturity, who, having already a bowing acquaintance with the writers of the age of Wordsworth, desire an interpretative analysis and synthesis of the chief tendencies of that period" (Preface). A stimulating book, written in a clear and easy style, with occasional original interpretations. Fairchild's comments on Wordsworth's relations to Rousseau and to Godwin are of especial interest.

406. FAUSSET, H. I'A. "Wordsworth's 'Borderers,'" *Adelphi,* ii (1931), 337–48.

The play is interpreted as an expression of remorse for the collapse of Wordsworth's belief in the French Revolution and for his desertion of Annette Vallon. He turns to the cold unsentimentalism of Godwin, but his attempt to escape his emotions breaks down in despair. The picture of good turning to evil is drawn from his own experience.

407. HALL, B. G. "Wordsworth Emendations," *TLS,* May 21, 1931, p. 408.

Suggests that the emendation in a line of the "Westminster Bridge" sonnet (written in ink in Sir William Rowan Hamilton's copy of the poems) was made by Wordsworth himself from, "Dear God! the very houses seem asleep," to "the very houses seem to be asleep."

408. Hooker, E. N. "Wordsworth's Letter to the Bishop of Llandaff," *SP,* xxviii (1931), 522–31.

The probable early date of the composition of the *Letter* (before or shortly after Feb., 1793) throws doubt on the probability of the influence of Fawcett's *Art of War* or of Godwin's *Political Justice.* But Hooker shows that the major points of the *Letter* appear also in Paine's *Rights of Man.* See *427*.

409. MacGillivray, J. R. "Wordsworth and J. P. Brissot," *TLS,* Jan. 29, 1931, p. 79.

Evidence that Wordsworth lived with Brissot after his return to Paris from Blois. His relationship with the Girondists was closer than has been believed.

410. Rader, M. M. "Presiding Ideas in Wordsworth's Poetry," *University of Washington Publications in Language and Literature,* VIII, No. 2, Seattle, University of Washington Press, 1931, 121–216.

A helpful survey of Wordsworth's philosophy. The emphasis is on his transcendentalism, but the earlier mechanistic philosophy is not neglected.

Rev. Batho, *RES,* ix (1933), 347–48. Rea, *MLN,* xlviii (1933), 66–67. Bernbaum, *JEGP,* xxxii (1933), 422–23.

411. Rea, J. D. "Hartley Coleridge and Wordsworth's Lucy," *SP,* xxviii (1931), 118–35.

Identifies Lucy with the infant Hartley Coleridge. Coleridge's poems on Hartley and his letters from Germany attribute to Hartley traits similar to Lucy's. These sources also contain imagery strikingly paralleled in the "Lucy" poems.

412. Weber, C. J. "Wordsworth and his Daughter," *TLS,* May 7, 1931, p. 367.

Further proof that the "Mme Williams," to whom Wordsworth sent money in 1815, was Annette. See *367, 375, 389, 398.*

1932

413. Addington, M. H. "Wordsworth and Henry Headley," *MLN,* xlvii (1932), 90.

Quotes a striking parallel between *The World is too Much With Us* and *An Invocation to Melancholy,* by Headley, a friend of Bowles, who published poems in 1785 and 1786.

414. ANDERS, HERMANN. *Die Bedeutung Wordsworthscher Gedankengänge für das Denken und Dichten von John Keats,* Breslau, Verlag von Trewndt und Granier, 1932.

The theory of Wordsworth's influence on Keats seems forced in some points, but the study is a painstaking piece of investigation.

Rev. Finney, *JEGP,* xxxii (1933), 421–22. *RES,* xi (1935), 375.

415. BALD, R. C., ed. *Literary Friendships in the Age of Wordsworth,* Cambridge, Cambridge University Press, 1932.

An anthology of biographical material from letters, journals, extracts from books, etc.

416. BULLAUGH, G. "The Origin of the Soul in English Poetry before Wordsworth," *N&Q,* April 23, 1932, pp. 290–94; April 30, pp. 308–11.

A survey up to Wordsworth's *Ode on Intimations of Immortality,* with the conclusion that at least three eighteenth-century poems anticipate Wordsworth's doctrine.

417. CHAPMAN, J. A. *Wordsworth and Literary Criticism,* Russell Lecture. London, Oxford University Press, 1932.

An essay on how to understand the spirit of poetry, based largely on Wordsworth's concept of the poet and poetry.

418. CHAPMAN, R. W. " 'Lyrical Ballads,' 1800," *Book Collector's Quarterly,* ii, No. 6 (Apr.-June, 1932), 25–26.

Description of a copy taken to pieces, and compared with several others.

419. EVANS, BERGEN, AND HESTER PINNEY. "Racedown and the Wordsworths," *RES,* vii (1932), 1–18.

An entertaining account of the Pinney family who owned Racedown at the time Wordsworth and Dorothy lived there.

420. FRASER, W. G. "The Preamble to 'The Prelude,' " *TLS,* Oct. 6, 1932, p. 711.

Discrepancies in date arising from Wordsworth's statement in the opening of *The Prelude,* Book VII. Fraser believes that the preamble to which Wordsworth here refers is not that of *The Prelude,* but of *The Recluse* of 1798.

421. KNIGHT, G. W. "Wordsworth's Vision of Immortality," *University of Toronto Quarterly,* i (1932), 216–35.

Immortality in the *Ode* does not imply a limited conception of life after death. It signifies the victory of life, first in terms of the child and second in visionary moments. Knight also defends the *Ode* against Coleridge's criticisms in *Biographia Literaria.*

422. MACDONALD, HUGH. "'Lyrical Ballads,'" *TLS,* March 17, 1932, p. 202.

A description of variants in some early editions and issues of *Lyrical Ballads.*

423. MACLEAN, CATHERINE M. *Dorothy Wordsworth, the Early Years,* London, Chatto and Windus, 1932.

Although the "fruit of close research," the author disclaims that this as a "book of research." It is by design a more popular biography than de Selincourt's; it is not as complete. But it is a sensitive and excellently written book which "attempts to find in the life of Dorothy a unity of design."

Rev. *TLS,* May 12, 1932, p. 347. Van Doren, *Nation,* cxxxiv (1932), 686–87. Gregory, *NR,* Oct. 12, 1932, pp. 240–41. De Selincourt, *Observer,* July 24, 1932. Keller, *Spect.,* May 21, 1932, pp. 735–36. Fausset, *Bookman* (Lon.), May, 1932, p. 110. Chase, *YR,* Winter 1933, pp. 402–3. Barnard, *Eng. Stud.,* lxix (1934), 128–30.

424. POTTS, ABBIE F. "The Spenserian and Miltonic Influence in Wordsworth's *Ode* and *Rainbow,*" *SP,* xxix (1932), 607–16.

Wordsworth and his sister read Spenser's *Prothalamion* April 25, 1802, and had been reading Spenser in November and December of the previous year. Potts points out evidences of Wordsworth's indebtedness to both the *Prothalamion* and the *Epithalamion* in his *Intimations Ode* and elsewhere. The Platonism in the *Ode* she believes came through Vaughan and the Platonic Hymns of Spenser. From a reading of *Paradise Lost,* Book XI on Feb. 2, 1802, Wordsworth was inspired with the idea of a covenant and the hope of regeneration, expressed in *The Rainbow* and the *Intimations Ode.*

425. REA, J. D. "'Intimations of Immortality' Again," *PQ,* xi (1932), 396–400.

Attention is called to some inconsistencies in the poem. The lambs, like the child, are spontaneous and happy, and would therefore also be immortal. Hence Wordsworth later substitutes the sense of the unreality of the world for spontaneity as evidence of pre-existence, thereby breaking the plan of the poem as it was conceived in the opening stanzas. Rea also presents other evidence pointing to the conclusion that the passage on the unreality of the world was an afterthought. See *349, 384, 472, 489, 611.*

426. ———. "Wordsworth's Intimations of Palingenesia," *RES,* viii (1932), 82–86.

A comment on stanza IX of the *Ode on Intimations of Immortality.* Wordsworth has in mind the stories that the alchemists could recreate plants and even animals from their ashes, so that they would glow with all their pristine beauty. References to this belief were made by both Southey and Coleridge.

427. ROBERTS, C. W. "The Influence of Godwin on Wordsworth's Letter to the Bishop of Llandaff," *SP,* xxix (1932), 588–606.

Roberts (in opposition to E. N. Hooker) sustains the contention for Godwinian influence, pushing forward the date of the composition of the *Letter* to at least June, 1793, and pointing out parallels between the *Letter* and Volume II of *Political Justice.* See *408.*

428. SAMPSON, GEORGE. "Shelley's 'Prometheus Unbound,'" *TLS,* Oct. 20, 1932, p. 762.

Shelley is doing in *Prometheus Unbound* what Wordsworth did in the *Ode on Intimations of Immortality,* but in reverse order: he maintains that perfection and heaven can be attained only through death. Both poets view life as an interlude between primal and ultimate perfection.

429. SMITH, ELSIE. *An Estimate of William Wordsworth by his Contemporaries, 1793–1822,* Oxford, Basil Blackwell, 1932.

A collection of many pieces of criticism from periodicals, diaries, and letters, conveniently assembled in one volume. All the major criticism for these dates is included, but much of it is excerpted. The author provides explanations and brief comments. A helpful book.

Rev. *TLS,* May 26, 1932, p. 388.

430. STALLKNECHT, N. P. "The Moral of 'The Ancient Mariner,'" *PMLA,* xlvii (1932), 559–69.

There is a philosophic moral, held in common by both Wordsworth and Coleridge. The shooting of the albatross represents the destruction by the reason of love, sentiment, etc. It represents Wordsworth's state when he abandoned nature and was dominated by reason. There follows the punishment of bitter loneliness, the condition of being forsaken by nature. Regeneration comes with the first gush of love. See *450.*

431. WELLS, J. E. "De Quincey's Punctuation of Wordsworth's 'Cintra,'" *TLS,* Nov. 3, 1932, p. 815.

A defense of De Quincey from an unjust critical tradition that his punctuation was responsible for the failure of the *Cintra* tract. See *183*.

432. ———. "Variants in the 'Lyrical Ballads' of 1798," *TLS,* June 23, 1932, p. 464.

A discussion of the variants as they were first described in Wise's *Two Lake Poets* and in White's *A Description of the Wordsworth and Coleridge Manuscripts.* See *339, 89*.

433. WILLIAMS, CHARLES. *The English Poetic Mind,* Oxford, The Clarendon Press, 1932.

Wordsworth occupies a prominent place in this study. An early chapter is devoted to *The Prelude,* not as a piece of biography, but as an expression of the poetic experience from which Williams draws material for his study of the poetic mind. Prominent in the study is the "crisis of utter overthrow and desolation," a state of "change and subversion" that comes into the poetic mind. The weakness of Wordsworth is in his inability to trust poetry fully in this crisis. He wrote of it after he had experienced it, substituting other aids than the pure poetic experience.

434. WORDSWORTH, G. G. "Wordsworth's Papers," *TLS,* Feb. 25, 1932, p. 137.

Denies the truth of the statement, in *Memoirs of Edward Clodd,* that Wordsworth's publishers destroyed a quantity of erotic poetry discovered among his papers after his death.

1933

435. ADAMS, M. R. "Joseph Fawcett and Wordsworth's Solitary," *PMLA,* xlviii (1933), 508–28.

An extended account of Fawcett, his writings and opinions. He retained an optimism and moral robustness, and unlike Wordsworth's Solitary, never withheld himself from mankind in hate and disgust.

436. BATHO, EDITH C. *The Later Wordsworth,* Cambridge, Cambridge University Press, 1933.

An influential book, that departs from the Legouis-Harper tradition. A painstaking examination of much evidence is presented to show that the "early" and the "later" Wordsworth are essentially one. Others have since followed Batho's lead in an effort to diminish the cleavage, made by critics, between Wordsworth's early and late years.

Rev. Garrod, *Observer,* Nov. 26, 1933. Blunden, *Spect.,* Dec. 29, 1933, p. 769. *N&Q,* Dec. 2, 1933, pp. 395–96. De Selincourt, *New Sts.,* Dec. 9, 1933, pp. 746, 748. E. J. Morley, *RES,* x (1934), 238–42. Grierson, *MLR,* xxix (1934), 199–208. *TLS,* Jan. 4, 1934, p. 9. Broughton, *YR,* Spring 1934, pp. 638–40. Harper, *SRL,* Mar. 31, 1934, p. 590.

437. Bush, Douglas. "Wordsworth and the Classics," *University of Toronto Quarterly,* ii (1933), 359–79.

Presents ample evidence of Wordsworth's reading of the classics. The essay includes: his fondness as a boy for Ovid; his use of Greek myths; the Virgilian influence on *Laodamia;* the classic self-control evident in some of his poetry; some comments on "the large body of classical allusions" in his later writings. See *513.*

438. Campbell, O. J. and Paul Mueschke. "Wordsworth's Aesthetic Development, 1795–1802," *University of Michigan Publications Language and Literature,* X, Ann Arbor, University of Michigan Press, 1933, 1–57.

The fourth paper in the series devoted to the subject. Sentimental morality, the tale of terror, and the ballad and conversational narrative forms are steps in Wordsworth's development. They gave objective expression to his personal emotional experience, and were vehicles for conveying fundamental passions. See *213, 307, 308, 567.*

Rev. Havens, *MLN,* li (1936), 389–93.

439. De Selincourt, Ernest. *Dorothy Wordsworth,* Oxford, The Clarendon Press, 1933.

The skill with which this is written, and the wealth of material from which it is drawn, would indicate that it is the definitive biography. Even one who is familiar with most of the facts rises from the reading of this book with a newly harmonized view of Dorothy, William, and the Wordsworth family and friends.

Rev. *TLS,* Nov. 30, 1933, p. 853. Blunden, *Spect.,* Dec. 29, 1933, p. 969. Garrod, *Observer,* Nov. 26, 1933. *N&Q,* Dec. 23, 1933, pp. 449–50. E. J. Morley, *RES,* x (1934), 235–38. Batho, *MLR,* xxix (1934), 462–64. F. V. Morley, *Crit.,* Apr., 1934, pp. 504–6. Broughton, *YR,* Spring 1934, pp. 638–40. Harper, *SRL,* Jan. 20, 1934, pp. 417, 422. Weber, *Ang. Bbl.,* xlvi (1935), 74–76. Beatty, *MLN,* li (1936), 182–84.

440. Dunn, S. G. "A Note on Wordsworth's Metaphysical System," *Essays and Studies by Members of the English Association,* XVIII, Oxford, The Clarendon Press, 1933, 74–109.

Although Wordsworth disavowed any "system" of philosophy in his poetry, he was attempting to explain the mind of man (composed of both sensory impressions and a creative energy) and its relation to the external world, and the relation of man and nature to God. The 1805 text of *The Prelude* and the poetry to 1806 or 1807 point towards pantheism. But the later poetry and the revisions of the 1805 text of *The Prelude* show an effort to reconcile his philosophy with the tenets of the Church of England. In this effort to achieve orthodoxy he is indebted to Newton's theory of motion. "The active principle, which subsists in all things and circulates from each to each, is *assigned* to every Form. In this way he avoids the identification of God with Nature, while providing an explanation of our feeling of participation in the life of Nature."

441. Eliot, T. S. *The Use of Poetry and the Use of Criticism,* Cambridge, Mass., Harvard University Press, 1933.

One of these lectures, delivered at Harvard, is devoted to "Wordsworth and Coleridge." The chief points discussed are Wordsworth's theory of poetic diction, and Coleridge's distinction between Fancy and Imagination. Eliot explains that we must recognize Wordsworth's social interest as animating his theory of diction.

442. Fausset, H. I'A. *The Lost Leader,* London, Jonathan Cape, 1933.

An interpretative biography, stressing Wordsworth's recantation in later life and his betrayal of his spiritual birthright. Much significance is placed upon his supposed failure to face the moral crisis of his liaison with Annette Vallon and his desertion of France. Fausset is in sharp opposition to Edith Batho, *The Later Wordsworth.* See 262.

Rev. *TLS,* Feb. 9, 1933, p. 89. De Selincourt, *Observer,* Jan. 29, 1933. Sparrow, *Spect.,* Feb. 3, 1933, p. 156. Kendon, *Fort. Rev.,* Mar., 1933, pp. 399–400. Church, *New Sts.,* Mar. 18, 1933, p. 359. Harper, *SRL,* May 13, 1933, pp. 587–88. Van Doren, *Nation,* Apr. 19, 1933, pp. 450–51. Chew, *YR,* Autumn 1934, pp. 205–8.

443. Fraser, W. G. "A Note on Wordsworth's 'Tintern Abbey,' Lines 66–83 and 'The Prelude' (1805–1806), Book XI, Lines 171–199," *RES,* ix (1933), 457–62.

Differs with de Selincourt, who interprets *The Prelude,* XI, 171–99 as an expression of the same experience related in *Tintern Abbey,* 66–83. Fraser argues that they refer to two different states of mind. He is also inclined to interpret "When first I came among these hills" as a reference to Wordsworth's visit to the Welsh hills in 1791, not to his visit to Tintern Abbey in 1793. See *458.*

444. GRIGGS, E. L. "Hazlitt's Estrangement from Coleridge and Wordsworth," *MLN,* xlviii (1933), 173–76.

Coleridge, Southey, and Wordsworth befriended Hazlitt when he visited the Lakes in 1803. He seems to have become involved in an amatory escapade, and was saved from a public ducking by Wordsworth and Coleridge. The latter speaks of his behavior with abhorrence, as endangering the local reputation of the Coleridge, Southey, and Wordsworth families.

445. HARPER, G. M. "The Crisis in Wordsworth's Life and Art," *Queen's Quarterly,* xl (1933), 1–13.

The death of Wordsworth's brother John and the poem *Peele Castle* stand at the crisis, before Wordsworth repudiated his natural religion, with the resultant loss of spontaneity and power. The article also contains remarks on Godwin, whose influence on Wordsworth Harper believes has been exaggerated in extent and duration.

446. HAYAKAWA, S. I. "Wordsworth's Letter to Mathetes," *University of Toronto Quarterly,* ii (1933), 533–44.

Wordsworth's instructions to youth in the *Letter* help explain the psychology of some of his poems. Passages are quoted from the poems that parallel the observations in the *Letter.*

447. HOWARD, LEON. "Wordsworth in America," *MLN,* xlviii (1933), 359–65.

Points to American interest in Wordsworth as early as 1800. Dennie published excerpts from *Lyrical Ballads* in the Philadelphia *Port Folio* beginning in 1801, but his enthusiasm cooled with the growing antipathy of the British critics. See *346, 634.*

448. MCADAM, E. L. "The Publication of 'Lyrical Ballads,' 1800," *Yale University Library Gazette,* viii (1933), 43–46.

Bibliographical detail of the printing and publication.

449. MAGNUS, LAURIE. "Wordsworth and his Biographers," *The Nineteenth Century and After,* cxiii (1933), 629–40.

The author maintains that none of Wordsworth's biographers

have seen him in the correct light. The Victorians suppressed the fire and activity of his youth. Legouis and Harper go to the opposite extreme in playing up his youthful republicanism and regarding his later life as a retreat and failure. Fausset's interpretation of the poet, haunted through life by the shame of his connection with Annette, is fallacious.

450. Nitchie, Elizabeth. "The Moral of 'The Ancient Mariner' Reconsidered," *PMLA,* xlviii (1933), 867–76.

The simple moral is that, after a horrible dream (the Mariner's narrative), one awakes to the wisdom of kindness and humanitarianism. A criticism of Stallknecht's interpretation is included. See *430*.

451. Purcell, J. M. "William Wordsworth and the Camden Society," *TLS,* Dec. 21, 1933, p. 909.

Wordsworth's name appears on the first list of members in 1839. His copies of the *Publications,* now in the Milwaukee Public Library, have no notes or marks. See *453, 467*.

452. Simons, H. "The Etiology of the Wordsworth Case," *Symposium,* iv (1933), 343–72.

Wordsworth's flight from France, and the lack of form in the majority of his poems, are evidence of a congenital want of self-discipline, which is the ultimate origin of his collapse as a poet.

453. Stamp, A. E. "William Wordsworth and the Camden Society," *TLS,* Dec. 28, 1933, p. 921.

The Milwaukee Public Library set of the *Camden Society Publications* (Wordsworth's copies) must be defective, since the Publice Record Office has a copy of Volume I with the list of members, and Wordsworth's name is not among them. He is listed for May 1, 1839, Volume V. See *451, 467*.

454. Thomas, Gilbert. "The Tragedy of Wordsworth," *London Quarterly and Holborn Rev.,* clviii (1933), 475–84.

The essay is mostly a summary of Fausset's interpretation, in *The Lost Leader,* of Wordsworth's failure to be "reborn" and pass into a life of "selfless love," because he tried to repudiate his guilt in connection with Annette Vallon.

455. Wells, J. E. "'Lyrical Ballads,' a Variant?" *RES,* ix (1933), 199–201.

Variants in the first issue of *Lyrical Ballads* of "wood" for "woods," p. 204, l. 56; and "though" for "thought," *loc. cit.,* l. 58.

1934

456. Collis, J. S. "Wordsworthian Pantheism," *Aryan Path,* v (1934), 716–20.

Wordsworth's pantheism was based on the senses, and could embrace only what was pleasing to the senses. This narrowed his spiritual world to what the senses could perceive as good. His tragic failure was that he could not "make the transition successfully from his intuitive faith in Nature to the conscious faith in which the intellect plays so great a part."

457. Fairley, Barker. "Goethe and Wordsworth," *Publications of the English Goethe Society,* X (New Series, 1934), 23–42.

The point of contrast between the two is that Wordsworth confused the past (memory) with the present, both in his feeling for Nature and his philosophy of the Child. He could never clearly separate the two. Goethe was the greater philosopher with a clear beginning, a fixed point to which he could refer everything and from which he could move and grow indefinitely. See *77, 91, 364.*

458. Gray, C. H. "Wordsworth's First Visit to Tintern Abbey," *PMLA,* xlix (1934), 123–33.

If Wordsworth's first visit to Tintern Abbey occurred five years before the composition of the poem, he could not have enjoyed the healthy youthful attitude toward nature that is generally assumed from the lines in which he described himself at that time. From his biography in *The Prelude* we know that this was a period of "degradation," troubled by disappointment and Godwinian rationalism. See *443.*

459. Hartman, Herbert. "Wordsworth's 'Lucy Poems,'" *PMLA,* xlix (1934), 134–42.

Draws together a number of points, from other scholars and from the writer's own research, on the "Lucy Poems." They were written in Germany when Wordsworth was experimenting with the Common Measure of the ballad; and the name "Lucy" was a neo-Arcadian commonplace, an eighteenth-century elegiac fiction.

460. Havens, R. D. "'Descriptive Sketches' and 'The Prelude,'" *ELH,* i (1934), 122–25.

Havens sets the date for Wordsworth's ascent of Mount Snowdon in 1791, not 1793 as de Selincourt believes. Similarities between the description in *The Prelude* of the Snowdon experience and the ascent of the Alps described in *Descriptive Sketches* indicate that the two passages in part refer to the same experience. *Descriptive Sketches* was begun in 1791, the year of the poet's first visit to Wales, and published early in 1793, before his second visit.

461. ———. "Wordsworth's Shipwrecked Geometrician," *ELH*, i (1934), 120–21.

Points out that the source of *The Prelude* (1805), VI, 160–74 is a passage from John Newton's *An Authentic Narrative* (1764). Here on a remote island Newton took refuge in Euclid. See *629*.

462. Leavis, F. R. "Revaluations, VI. Wordsworth," *Scrutiny*, iii (1934).

Reprinted in *Revaluation, Tradition and Development in English Poetry*, London, Chatto and Windus, 1936. Astute comments on several aspects of Wordsworth, including his lack of a consistent, explainable philosophy; his wisdom, his sanity and normalcy; his contrast to Shelley; and his transition from "natural piety" to orthodox piety. Also, there is a note on "Arnold, Wordsworth and the Georgians," an additional note on Shelley and Wordsworth, and an analysis of *Strange Fits of Passion Have I Known*.

463. Lomer, G. R. "Dove Cottage: Wordsworth's Home," *Dalhousie Rev.*, xiv (1934), 47–55.

A descriptive essay. See *68, 158*.

464. MacGillivray, J. R. "The Date of the Composition of 'The Borderers,'" *MLN*, xlix (1934), 104–11.

The date 1795–96, given by Wordsworth in his Preface, has generally been accepted. From data in the Wordsworth *Letters*, MacGillivray argues that the play was begun in the autumn of 1796 and finished in the following spring. Thus it is unlikely that Wordsworth wrote the play while still a disciple of Godwin.

465. McCorkell, E. J. *The Mysticism of Wordsworth*, "St. Michael's College Pamphlet," No. 4, Toronto, 1934.

466. McMaster, Helen. "Wordsworth's Copy of Vaughan," *TLS*, April 12, 1934, p. 262.

Requests information on Wordsworth's copy of the first edition of Vaughan's *Silex Scintillans*, as reported by Archbishop Trent. See *484*.

467. MORLEY, EDITH J. "Wordsworth and the Camden Society," *TLS,* Jan. 4, 1934, p. 12.

Refers to a letter in which Wordsworth thanked Crabb Robinson for the receipt of three volumes of the Society's *Publications.* It seems likely that Robinson was responsible for the poet's subscription. See *451, 453.*

468. MUESCHKE, PAUL AND E. L. GRIGGS. "Wordsworth As the Prototype of the Poet in Shelley's 'Alastor,'" *PMLA,* xlix (1934), 229–45.

At the time of the composition of *Alastor* Shelley was concerned over Wordsworth's "apostasy" and decay as a poet. Moreover, much in *Alastor* can in no way apply to Shelley. By a close interpretation of the poem's significant utterances, the authors attempt to show that it is an allegory on the decay of Wordsworth's poetic power. Thus stripped of "romantic embellishments," the poem becomes more intelligible and significant. See *PMLA,* li (1936), 302–12 for an attack on this interpretation by Marcel Kessel, who insists that *Alastor* is autobiographical, followed by a sharp reply from Mueschke and Griggs.

469. ROBERTS, C. W. "Wordsworth, 'The Philanthropist,' and 'Political Justice,'" *SP,* xxxi (1934), 84–91.

Points out Wordsworth's indebtedness to *Political Justice* for the idea he expressed in his letters to Mathews concerning the proposed periodical *The Philanthropist.* Wordsworth turned to Godwin as "a short cut to a liberal political creed." But his detestation of revolution probably displeased Mathews and the more radical London group who were interested in launching the journal.

470. SHERWOOD, MARGARET. *Undercurrents of Influence in English Romantic Poetry,* Cambridge, Mass., Harvard University Press, 1934.

A book of large importance, written with matured scholarship, tracing the variety of philosophic concepts as they appear in the poetry of the period. Two chapters are devoted to Wordsworth, on his philosophy, mysticism, and religion, with comments on his relationship to other thinkers. Of especial note is the account of the philosophic background, mostly in the seventeenth and eighteenth centuries, from which is derived the nineteenth-century concept of the oneness between man and nature, and the system of endless growth and becoming.

Rev. *TLS,* Apr. 18, 1935, p. 254. Zabel, *MP,* xxxii (1935), 440–41.

Maclean, *RES*, xii (1936), 226–28. Thomas, *MLR*, xxxi (1936), 436–37. Rinaker, *JEGP*, xxxv (1936), 296–300. Raysor, *MLN*, li (1936), 270–71.

471. SMITH, J. H. "Genesis of 'The Borderers,'" *PMLA*, xlix (1934), 922–30.

Wordsworth owes the picturesque and Gothic elements of the play to William Gilpin's *Observations Relative Chiefly to Picturesque Beauty* (1786), a description of Westmorland and Cumberland and the "borderers," or bandits, who formerly infested the region. Smith comments that the borrowed Gothic element of the play is its least sincere aspect, as Wordsworth lacked Coleridge's ability to assimilate foreign material.

472. STALLKNECHT, N. P. "The Doctrine of Coleridge's 'Dejection' and its Relation to Wordsworth's Philosophy," *PMLA*, xlix (1934), 196–207.

The central point of Wordsworth's and Coleridge's natural religion Stallknecht calls the "theory of imaginative love." Stallknecht writes: "They believed that creative and appreciative imagination engenders a love of man, and they did not hestitate to affirm that this love is a profoundly religious experience which owes its power to the mystical communion with a cosmic spirit." The paper concludes with a summary of Wordsworth's attitude toward the philosophy of *Dejection*. See *349, 384, 425, 489, 611.*

473. STROUT, A. L. "John Wilson, 'Champion' of Wordsworth," *MP*, xxxi (1934), 383–94.

Although the attitude of *Blackwood's* is regarded as favorable to Wordsworth, its pages also contain fierce invective against him. Not the least curious is the inconsistency of John Wilson, rightly regarded as a champion of Wordsworth. But, as Strout shows, it is Wilson who wrote both the attack on, and vindication of Wordsworth, occasioned by the poet's "Burns Letter."

474. ———. "William Wordsworth and John Wilson: A Review of their Relations between 1802 and 1817," *PMLA*, xlix (1934), 143–83.

Excellent, detailed account of Wilson drawn from many sources.

475. WEAVER, BENNETT. "Wordsworth's 'Prelude': An Intimation of Certain Problems in Criticism," *SP*, xxxi (1934), 534–40.

It is a mistake to look for exact biographical statements in *The Prelude* and to interpret the poem from them. Memory is the source material of the poem, and we are twice removed from factual accuracies. Also, Wordsworth is writing chiefly of inner experiences, matter difficult to put into accurate words.

476. Willey, Basil. *The Seventeenth Century Background,* London, Chatto and Windus, 1934.

An illuminating book on seventeenth-century thought and its bearings on poetry of various periods. In addition to numerous references to Wordsworth, a chapter is devoted to "Wordsworth and the Locke Tradition." It was Wordsworth's purpose to write of the visible, the "real" world of eye and ear, as clarified by the Locke tradition; not a cold inanimate world, but an active universe, capable of being molded and modified by the "plastic power" within him. In expressing this, the poet stands alone, without the aid of traditional mythology by which he might deal imaginatively with the world of eye and ear. This Wordsworth could do in his youth, but as he grew older imagination failed, and he drew on memory for his power. This reservoir inevitably failed him. He was living on his capital (Cf. Sperry, *Wordsworth's Anti-Climax,* p. 142).

Rev. *TLS,* Apr. 19, 1934, p. 269. Burgess, *Spect.,* Mar. 23, 1934, p. 466. Beachcroft, *Crit.,* July, 1934, pp. 692–96. Grierson, *Scrutiny,* Dec., 1934, p. 294.

477. ———. "Wordsworth's Beliefs," *Criterion,* xiii (1934), 232–51.

A fruitful article, giving a survey of Wordsworth's beliefs in relation to the era in which he lived. For Wordsworth there was no system of beliefs and symbols to serve as a mold into which he could pour the stuff of his experience. Wordsworth was "alone, seeking the visible world." His was an age that sought to separate truth from error, "to arrive at a 'true' world-picture by means of a critique of reality-conceptions." Wordsworth's poetry was scientific in that "his interest lay in the free relations between the mind of man and the universe."

1935

478. Anon. "Wordsworth and Lamb," *N&Q,* June 1, 1935, pp. 382–83.

The writer believes that Wordsworth was a victim of gossip in his reference to "strange characters" with whom Lamb consorted (F.N. to *Written after the Death of Charles Lamb*).

479. BISHOP, D. H. "Wordsworth's 'Hermitage' Racedown or Grasmere?" *SP*, xxxii (1935), 483–507.

Argues that the three-day journey from the city to the "chosen vale," described in the opening of *The Prelude*, does not refer to Racedown but to the journey with Coleridge and John from Temple Sowerby to Grasmere in October, 1799. See *504, 595*.

480. HARRIS, J. R. "Wordsworth's Lucy," *After-Glow Essays*, No. 8, London, University of London Press, 1935.

The study presents some evidence that might identify Lucy as a girl whom Wordsworth loved when he visited Robert Jones in Wales during his college vacations.

481. HARTSELL, E. H. "The Date of the 'Ode to Duty,'" *TLS*, May 30, 1935, p. 348.

Evidence that the *Ode to Duty* was written in September, 1804. See *490*.

482. MACLEAN, CATHERINE. "Letters of Dorothy Wordsworth," *TLS*, Sept. 12, 1935, p. 565.

In the British Museum there are six uncatalogued manuscript letters, from Dorothy to Mrs. Clarkson, which were not included in the de Selincourt edition.

483. ———. "A Wordsworth Letter," *TLS*, Oct. 3, 1935, p. 612.

Presents evidence for changing the date of Letter 180 (de Selincourt, *The Early Letters of William and Dorothy Wordsworth*) from 1804 to 1806.

484. MCMASTER, HELEN N. "Vaughan and Wordsworth," *RES*, xi (1935), 313–25.

An attempt to show that Wordsworth did not know Vaughan, or if he did it was late in life and there was no influence on him. McMaster discusses the matter of the revival of Vaughan in the nineteenth century, which was too late to influence Wordsworth's early poetry. She next traces and discredits the statements that Wordsworth owned a copy of *Silex Scintillans*. She also presents internal evidence against direct influence in the poems that have been regarded as indebted to Vaughan. See *466*.

485. MAYNARD, THEODORE. "Wordsworth's Exquisite Sister," *Catholic World*, cxli (1935), 523–32.

A sympathetically told sketch of Dorothy's life based on the biographies of Maclean and de Selincourt.

486. PATTON, C. H. *The Rediscovery of Wordsworth,* Boston, The Stratford Co., 1935.

Patton, who gave his distinguished Wordsworth collection to the Amherst College Library, writes a general interpretation of the poet, stressing his "rediscovered" place in our present-day world.

Rev. *TLS,* June 6, 1936, p. 475.

487. ROWLAND, BUFORD. "William Wordsworth and Mississippi Bonds," *The Journal of Southern History,* i (1935), 501–7.

An account of the default of the State of Mississippi to pay interest on bonds of the Planters' Bank. Members of the Wordsworth family owned some of these bonds, and Wordsworth wrote to Reed and others in indignation.

488. ———. "William Wordsworth and Pennsylvania State Bonds," *Pennsylvania Magazine of Hist. and Biog.,* lix (1935), 301–3.

Calls attention to Wordsworth's letters and poetry expressing his indignation over the depreciation in the 1840's of the bonds of the State of Pennsylvania, in which the poet's brother had invested.

489. SMITH, F. M. "The Relation of Coleridge's 'Ode on Dejection' to Wordsworth's 'Ode on Intimations of Immortality,' " *PMLA,* l (1935), 224–34.

Covers briefly the scholarly findings on the dates of the two poems, and accepts Rea's theory that the first 129 lines of Wordsworth's poem were composed in 1802. However, Smith believes that Coleridge's ode is in answer to Wordsworth's, not the reverse, showing this to be so in phrase after phrase. See *349, 384, 425, 472, 611.*

490. SMITH, N. C. "The Date of the 'Ode to Duty,' " *TLS,* June 20, 1935, p. 399.

Dates the poem early in 1804, sometime after January 14th. See *481.*

491. SPERRY, W. L. *Wordsworth's Anti-Climax,* "Harvard Studies in English," XIII, Cambridge, Mass., Harvard University Press, 1935.

An able discussion of Wordsworth's philosophy, religion, and politics. Sperry reviews the various causes to which Wordsworth's decline has been assigned, none of which he regards as wholly responsible. He believes that the ultimate weakness rests in Wordsworth's theory of aesthetics, which restricted his subject matter, being based too narrowly on retrospection. The chapter on Jeffrey and the quarterlies is a convenient survey.

Rev. Harper, *SRL,* Nov. 2, 1935, pp. 22–23. Harrold, *MP,* xxxiii (1935), 206–9. Sackville-West, *Spect.,* July 19, 1935, p. 102. Garrod, *Hibbert Journal,* xxxiii (1935), 635–36. Zeitlin, *JEGP,* xxxv (1936), 293–96. Havens, *MLN,* li (1936) 389–93. Elton, *MLR,* xxxi (1936), 434–35. Maclean, *RES,* xiii (1937), 113–16.

492. WATSON, H. F. "'The Borderers' and 'The Ancient Mariner,'" *TLS,* Dec. 28, 1935, p. 899.

Points to an influence of *The Borderers* upon *The Ancient Mariner,* particularly in the parallel of a long narrative of warning to a younger man, and the calm at sea resulting in lack of drinking water. See *495*.

493. WICKE, CLARA. *Die Tranzendentalpoesie Bei William Wordsworth,* Marburg, N. G. Elwert 'sche Verlagsbuchhandlung—G. Braun, 1935.

A treatment of Wordsworth's unfolding transcendental aesthetic through several periods between 1798 and 1820.

1936

494. BEACH, J. W. *The Concept of Nature in Nineteenth-Century English Poetry,* New York, Macmillan and Co., 1936.

A book of much learning and large scope, tracing the concept of nature from the time of Wordsworth to modern poetry, with a full account of the sources in the sixteenth, seventeenth, and eighteenth centuries. Besides many important references to Wordsworth throughout, pp. 110–208 are devoted almost exclusively to him. Beach's treatment of Wordsworth is marked by balance and sanity. He takes the middle ground between the extreme materialistic interpretation and the position of those critics who emphasize the religion and pure mysticism of the poet. He gives full emphasis to Wordsworth's early naturalism, and points out how this was abandoned as he yielded more and more to a theological faith. The book is of great value for an understanding of Wordsworth's philosophy, and it is rich in sources and analogues.

Rev. *TLS,* Dec. 12, 1936, p. 1031. Van Doren, *Nation,* Sept. 12, 1936, p. 314. Brown, *Univ. of Toronto Quart.,* vi (1936), 141–47. Knowlton, *SAQ,* Oct., 1936, pp. 457–59. *Journal of Phil.,* xxxiii (1936), 696–97. Ballman, *MLN,* lii (1936), 609–11. Harrold, *MP,* xxxi (1937), 401–2. Rice, *JEGP*, xxxvi (1937), 599–602. *Archiv*, clxxi (1937), 263–64.

495. BEATTY, ARTHUR. "'The Borderers' and 'The Ancient Mariner,'" *TLS*, Feb. 29, 1936, p. 184.

A possible common source for the passages on thirst in these two may be found in the seventh volume of *Harleian Miscellany*, pp. 285–93. Wordsworth follows this more closely than does Coleridge. See *492*.

496. BROOKS, B. G. "Wordsworth and Coleridge," *TLS*, Aug. 29, 1936, p. 700.

Objections to the method employed by Munby in determining the popularity of Wordsworth and Coleridge by means of current anthologies. See *506*.

497. ———. "Wordsworth and La Fontaine," *TLS*, July 25, 1936, p. 616.

Wordsworth's stated appreciation of the style of La Fontaine, and echoes of La Fontaine in several poems.

498. BURRA, PETER. *Wordsworth*, London, Duckworth, 1936.

"Great Lives" series. Brief biography, related in an interesting way.

499. DE SELINCOURT, ERNEST. *The Early Wordsworth*, English Association. Presidential Address, Oxford, University Press, 1936.

A significant paper concerning the early development of Wordsworth as a poet. It contains some unpublished juvenilia, parts of which were worked into later poems.

Rev. *TLS*, Jan. 9, 1937, p. 24. Beatty, *MLN*, liii (1938), 546.

500. EATON, H. A. "The Letters of De Quincey to Wordsworth," *ELH*, iii (1936), 15–30.

Eaton prints four letters, all that remain of those that De Quincey wrote to Wordsworth before they met at Dove Cottage in 1807. They are from typed copies made by Gordon Wordsworth, and only one has been printed before. They contain an interesting account of the growth of De Quincey's relations with Wordsworth.

501. EVANS, B. I. "Variants in Wordsworth's 'Poems' of 1807," *TLS*, June 13, 1936, p. 494.

The basis of the examination is the manuscript versions in the Beaumont collection.

502. Gilkyson, Claud. "Henry Reed, 1825. Wordsworth's American Editor," [Univ. of Penna.] *General Magazine and Historical Chronicle,* xxxviii (1936), 84–90; 163–72; 318–32; 355–71.

503. Havens, R. D. "Wordsworth's Adolescence," *MLN,* li (1936), 137–42.

The statements from *The Prelude,* "I was left alone," and "The props of my affections were removed," are interpreted as a reference not to his mother's death, but to his loss of sport as the motive of his attraction to nature. The physical and emotional alterations accompanying adolescence caused Wordsworth blindly to seek nature as a vague joy, and as an escape from the morbid tendencies of this period of life.

504. ———. "Wordsworth's 'Hermitage,' Some Considerations," *SP,* xxxiii (1936), 55–56.

Raises several objections to the attempt of D. H. Bishop to date the opening of *The Prelude* as late as 1799. See *479, 595.*

505. Martin, A. D. *The Religion of Wordsworth,* London, George Allen and Unwin Ltd., 1936.

The substance of two articles contributed to *The Holborn Rev.,* Jan., 1919, and Oct., 1931. This study is a liberal theological interpretation of the poet, with strong emphasis on the middle and late years. The subjects of nature, humanity, friendship, the Bible, and the "religion of gratitude" are discussed.

506. Munby, A.N.L. "Wordsworth and Coleridge. Early Appreciation in the North," *TLS,* Aug. 22, 1936, p. 684.

An analysis of a large number of verse anthologies of the early nineteenth century shows that Wordsworth and Coleridge enjoyed considerable popularity in the north of England, while in the south the Augustan tradition still continued. See *496.*

507. Patton, C. H., ed. *The Amherst Wordsworth Collection,* Amherst College, 1936.

A descriptive catalogue of Patton's Wordsworth collection, presented by him to the library of Amherst College. This, and the one at Cornell, are the two best collections in the United States. The catalogue is of prime service as a Wordsworth bibliography. Convenient summaries of the contents and special values of each title are provided. Contains index of authors, and a section on other Wordsworth collections.

508. Pottle, F. A. "Shelley and Wordsworth," *TLS,* June 20, 1936, p. 523.

Suggests that Shelley's *Ode to the West Wind* may have been influenced by Wordsworth's "Composed while the Author was engaged in writing a Tract occasioned by the Convention of Cintra" (published 1815).

1937

509. App, A. J. "How Six Famous Poets Were Treated," *Catholic World,* cxliv (1937), 582–89.

Adverse criticism by contemporaries of Wordsworth, Coleridge, Byron, Keats, Shelley, and Tennyson.

510. Bartlett, Phyllis. "Annette and Albertine," *The Sewanee Rev.,* xlv (1937), 12–23.

A comparison between Wordsworth and Proust, in an attempt to explain and justify Wordsworth's omission from *The Prelude* of his liaison with Annette. The experience was alien to him and did not produce creative suffering such as Proust underwent on account of Albertine.

511. Blyton, W. J. "Wordsworth's View of Europe in 1837," *National Rev.,* cix (1937), 640–47.

Observations arising from Wordsworth's tour of Europe in 1837. The writer contends that there was no definite dividing line between Wordsworth's early and late years, but an orderly spiritual and artistic evolution.

512. Brooks, B. G. "Wordsworth and the Horatian Spirit," *MLR,* xxxii (1937), 588–93.

There is a marked Horatian tendency in many poems of 1819–29, characterized by "formal construction and balance of subject matter, the courtly artificiality of language slightly tinged with learned allusion, the maintenance of the elegant conversational tone and the undercurrent of domestic or personal emotion which gives genuineness to the work." See *184, 639.*

513. Bush, Douglas. *Mythology and the Romantic Tradition in English Poetry,* "Harvard Studies in English," XVIII, Cambridge, Mass., Harvard University Press, 1937.

An authoritative book on the subject. The section on Wordsworth points to a greater significance in his Hellenism than is generally supposed. It "was he who recreated mythological poetry for the nineteenth century." See *437.*

Rev. *TLS,* June 19, 1937, p. 460. Stinchcomb, *Classical Weekly,* May 10, 1937, pp. 276–77. DeVane, *MP,* xxxv (1937), 211–13. Bacon, *SRL,* July 10, 1937, p. 7. Osgood, *MLN,* liii (1938), 439–41. *ELH,* v (1938), 7–8. Ashton, *Journal Amer. Folk-Lore,* li (1938), 108–11. Glunz, *Ang. Bbl.,* xlix (1938), 169–71.

514. Carritt, E. F. "Addison, Kant and Wordsworth," *Essays and Studies by Members of the English Association,* XXII, Oxford, The Clarendon Press, 1937, 26–36.

Traces the influence of Addison, Burke, and other eighteenth-century critics of aesthetics on Kant, whc in turn influenced the ideas of Coleridge and Wordsworth. The conception of imagination, of sublimity, and of beauty are the chief points discussed.

515. Casson, Edmund. "Wordsworth and Theocritus," *TLS,* Sept. 11, 1937, p. 656.

Suggests a parallel between Wordsworth's *Poet's Epitaph* and *Inscription* xix by Theocritus.

516. Christensen, Francis. "'And Yet I Knew a Maid,'" *TLS,* Sept. 25, 1937, p. 695.

Argues that *The Prelude,* XI, l. 199, refers to Mary Hutchinson, not Dorothy.

517. Grierson, H.J.G. *Milton and Wordsworth,* Cambridge, Cambridge University Press, 1937.

Only the last chapter deals directly with Wordsworth. His republicanism is broadly similar to Milton's; his sympathy with "poor human nature" is more intense. Wordsworth is essentially more the poet of joy and love, than of nature.

Rev. *TLS,* March 6, 1937, p. 166. Saurat, *RES,* xiv (1938), 225–28. Tillyard, *MLN,* liii (1938), 381.

518. Hamilton, Marie P. "Wordsworth's Relation to Coleridge's 'Osorio,'" *SP,* xxxiv (1937), 429–37.

Wordsworth is indebted to *Osorio* for the cave and waterfall in *The Idiot Boy.* Also the villain in *Ruth* is taken from the unfortunate hero of *The Foster Mother's Tale* (Osorio IV, 1, 170–234).

519. Harper, G. M. *Literary Appreciations,* Indianapolis, Ind., Bobbs-Merrill Co., 1937.

A group of mixed essays, including a paper on "Wordsworth's Poetical Technique." First Harper points out that Wordsworth's style altered with the changes in his mode of thought. There follows a discussion of the varieties of poetic forms used by Wordsworth: satire, epistle, inscription, long descriptive poem, poetical drama, song, story, elegy, ode, sonnet, short reflective poem, and long reflective poem.

520. LOGAN, J. V. "Wordsworth in France," *TLS,* Nov. 20, 1937, p. 891.

Points out Wordsworth's statement, in a letter to Lord Lonsdale (1820), that he had last visited Paris in 1792. But this statement need not invalidate the theory that Wordsworth visited France in the autumn of 1793. See *383, 381, 390.*

521. MABBOTT, T. O. "A Sonnet by Wordsworth," *N&Q,* Dec. 25, 1937, p. 455.

Reprints in full a sonnet by Wordsworth addressed to "A Picture by Luca Giordana." It appeared in the New York *Home Journal,* Oct. 2, 1847, and is mentioned, but not given in full, in the *Concordance to the Poems of Wordsworth.*

522. MONK, S. H. "Wordsworth's 'Unimaginable Touch of Time,'" *MLN,* lii (1937), 503–4.

Finds the source of this phrase in Milton's *Of Education.*

523. MORRIS, J. E. "Wordsworth's Copy of 'Modern Painters,'" *N&Q,* Nov. 20, 1937, p. 366.

Reference to the copy of *Modern Painters* presented to Wordsworth by W. Boxall. See 527.

524. SHEARER, EDNA A. AND J. T. LINDSAY. "Wordsworth and Coleridge Marginalia in a Copy of Richard Payne Knight's 'Analytical Inquiry into the Principles of Taste,'" *The Huntington Library Quarterly,* i (Oct., 1937), 63–99.

These marginalia were supposed to be by Coleridge. But experts at the Huntington Library have discovered that the handwriting is that of Wordsworth. It is suggested that Wordsworth may have written the notes, probably from Coleridge's dictation, to assist Coleridge, when he was ill, to prepare his lectures in 1808.

525. STALLKNECHT, N. P. "Nature and Imagination in Wordsworth's 'Meditation upon Mt. Snowdon,'" *PMLA,* lii (1937), 835–47.

A significant philosophic interpretation, showing how much further Wordsworth goes than sensationalism and associationism.

Imagination is described "as power objective in the world about us and not as a faculty limited to our minds." This power induces the aesthetic conception, whereby many objects merge into their proper interrelationship, in contrast to the scientific conception, which abstracts the particular from the whole. As to nature, it is an animate power, working upon both objects and the mind. It makes one object suffuse another, and conducts the mind from mere sense to ideal form.

526. ———. "Wordsworth's 'Ode to Duty' and the Schöne Seele," *PMLA,* lii (1937), 230–37.

Wordsworth's debt to Schiller's restatement of the Kantian ethical philosophy. Schiller's *schöne seele* combines the grace of temperamental or spontaneous virtue, with heroic self-command in the face of stern alternatives. Both these types of moral character appear in the *Ode,* and a third (in the rejected stanza) which combines the two (as does Schiller), conscience becoming a matter for free and happy choice of alternatives.

527. Strachan, L.R.M. "Wordsworth's Copy of 'Modern Painters,'" *N&Q,* Dec. 4, 1937, p. 409.

Discusses the relationships of Wordsworth, Ruskin, and W. Boxall, and their opinions of each other. See *523*.

528. Viebrock, Helmut. *Erlebnis und Gestaltung des Schönen in der Dichtung von Wordsworth (1798–1808),* Marburg-Lahn, Buchdruckerei Hermann Bauer, 1937.

An inaugural dissertation on the subject of Wordsworth's aesthetics.

529. Watson, H. F. "Historic Detail in 'The Borderers,'" *MLN,* lii (1937), 577–79.

Suggested identifications of the principal characters in the play with historical figures. "No far-reaching conclusions can be drawn from these bits of hypothesis, but in the aggregate they would seem to indicate that, despite the known influence of *Caleb Williams, Othello* and *Die Räuber,* Wordsworth did adapt for his purpose actual historical characters and incidents."

530. Weaver, Bennett. "Wordsworth's 'Prelude': The Poetic Function of Memory," *SP,* xxxiv (1937), 552–63.

The 1805 text of *The Prelude* exhibits the vital function of the poetic memory, which grew dim with the coming of age, as is seen by some of the later revisions. Memory, functioning poetically, is not confined to recording past facts. Poetic memory is creative, something more than recollection. By means of poetic memory, "the vitality of the mind assimilates all into the mind; and the poetry which results is of another truth than the truth of tabulation."

531. WILCOX, S. C. "The Source of Wordsworth's 'The Force of Prayer,'" *MLN,* lii (1937), 165–66.

Argues that Whitaker's *History of Craven* is not the source of the incident of the poem, since Wordsworth had evidently not read the *History* until a month after the composition of the poem. He must have heard the tradition while visiting Bolton, June, 1807.

532. WRIGHT, H. G. "Two Letters from Wordsworth to Robert Jones," *RES,* xiii (1937), 39–45.

Prints two unpublished letters to Wordsworth's Welsh friend, dated Oct. 29, 1833, and March 30 [1835]. See *149, 290.*

1938

533. ANON. "Wordsworth: 'The Light That Never Was,'" *N&Q,* Aug. 20, 1938, pp. 130–31.

Discusses the mood that produced these lines from *Peele Castle* in their original form, and Wordsworth's alteration of them in 1827.

534. ———. "Wordsworth: Sense of Smell," *N&Q,* Jan. 1, 1938, p. 12.

In answer to the query, did Wordsworth have a sense of smell, there follows a discussion in a series of letters: Jan. 15, pp. 48–49; Jan. 22, p. 68 (three letters); Feb. 12, p. 124.

535. ASHTON, HELEN. *William and Dorothy,* London, Collins, 1938.

A fictional biography.

536. BRADFORD, C. B. "Wordsworth's 'White Doe of Rylstone' and Related Poems," *MP,* xxxvi (1938), 59–70.

The White Doe, Song at the Feast of Brougham Castle, and *The Force of Prayer* show Wordsworth's bid for popularity in the antiquarian genre of poetry. The sources discussed are: Nicholson and Burn, *History of Westmorland and Cumberland;* Whitaker, *History of Craven;* and *Rising in the North,* a ballad published by Percy.

537. BREWSTER, PAUL G. "The Influence of the Popular Ballad on Wordsworth's Poetry," *SP,* xxxv (1938), 588–612.

A more detailed study than the earlier essay by Stork. Brewster (1) examines "the extent of Wordsworth's acquaintance with traditional balladry, ballad stories, and ballad collectors and imitators"; (2) treats "his use of the ballad stanza, and . . . his experiments with it"; (3) considers "the use by the poet of ballad themes and situations." See *165.*

538. BURGUM, E. B. "The Myth of Impartiality in the Teaching of Literature," *English Journal* (Col. ed.), xxvii (1938), 502–13.

In an interpretation of *Resolution and Independence* the view is expressed that Wordsworth was "the poet par excellence of the bourgeoisie in its heyday," and that "Wordsworth's deification of the peasant became for both wealthy and poor a kind of ancestor worship," offering compensation for a sense of guilt.

539. CHRISTENSEN, FRANCIS. "The Date of Wordsworth's 'The Birth of Love,'" *MLN,* liii (1938), 280–82.

On the testimony of Southey this translation of *L'Éducation de l'Amour* was written when Wordsworth was an undergraduate.

540. CURRY, KENNETH. "Uncollected Translations of Michaelangelo by Wordsworth and Southey," *RES,* xiv (1938), 193–99.

History of the contributions to Duppa's *Life and Works of Michel Angelo Buonarroti.* See *544.*

541. DANIEL, R. W. "The Publication of 'Lyrical Ballads,'" *MLR,* xxxiii (1938), 406–10.

Argues that *Lyrical Ballads* was never published by Cottle. He had not done so by Thursday, Sept. 13, "and by Tuesday at the latest the bargain with Arch had been concluded." Newspaper advertisements show that the London issue was published Oct. 4.

542. DE SELINCOURT, ERNEST. "Émile Legouis and Wordsworth," *Études Anglaises,* ii (1938), 258–63.

A review of Legouis' significant contributions to the study of Wordsworth, opening with a brief summary of the work of earlier biographers.

543. ———. "Our Noisy Years," *TLS,* Nov. 12, 1938, p. 725.

There is a possible source of this phrase, from *Ode on Intimations of Immortality,* in a notebook belonging to Dorothy Wordsworth in which she has copied "Passages from an address to Silence published in the *Weekly Entertainer.*" Among these passages is the following: "Eternity of calmness is thy joy / Immensity of space is thine abode / The rolling planets own thy sacred power / Our noisy years are moments of thy life."

544. EVANS, B. I. "Unacknowledged Sonnet by Wordsworth," *TLS,* March 12, 1938, p. 172.

Concerns the discovery of a manuscript copy of Wordsworth's translation of a sonnet for Duppa's *Life and Works of Michel Angelo Buonarroti.* See 540.

545. HARPER, G. M. "Émile Legouis," *Quarterly Rev.,* cclxx (1938), 15–27.

Harper's tribute to, and biographical sketch of, the eminent French Wordsworthian scholar.

546. HARTMAN, HERBERT. "Wordsworth's 'Lapland Night,'" *RES,* xiv (1938), 189–93.

The phrase is from Wordsworth's poem *To a Young Lady, Who Had Been Reproached for Taking Long Walks.* Its source may be Thomson's *Seasons,* or a footnote by Coleridge.

547. POTTER, G. R. "Wordsworth and the 'Traité Élémentaire de Chimie' of Lavoisier," *PQ,* xvii (1938), 312–16.

Wordsworth's lines against scientific dissection *(Excursion,* IV, 941 ff.) were possibly influenced by Lavoisier, whom he may have known through Sir Humphrey Davy.

548. SANDERLIN, G. "The Influence of Milton and Wordsworth on the Early Victorian Sonnet," *ELH,* v (1938), 225–51.

From 1825–50 the sonnets of Milton and Wordsworth were respected and imitated by English writers more than the Italian or Elizabethan sonnets. Wordsworth's *Ecclesiastical Sonnets* completely dominated the Victorian religious sonnets, especially among the Oxford group. Milton, more than Wordsworth, influenced the political sonnets. Wordsworth's influence was felt in the descriptive sonnet, especially the various "tour" sequences. Sanderlin explains the technical characteristics imitated by the Victorians, and points to the waning influence of the sonnets of Milton and Wordsworth after 1850.

549. SMITH, JAMES. "Wordsworth: A Preliminary Survey," *Scrutiny,* vii (1938), 33–55.

First are the pitfalls that must be avoided in reading Wordsworth's poetry: (1) much of it need not be taken seriously; (2)

rhetorical skill does not always produce genuine poetry; (3) the subject and meter often do not coalesce to produce an authentic experience and the poetry creates a false impression. There follows a summary account of the peaks of Wordsworth's poetry. Smith presents a philosophic discussion of Wordsworth's endeavor to find himself, the external world, and their relationship. Second, he discusses at length the problem of suffering as it appears in the poet's philosophy.

550. STROUT, A. L. "A Critic of Wordsworth," *TLS,* July 16, 1938, pp. 479–80.

"An Essay on the Theory and Writings of Wordsworth" (*Blackwood's,* Sept.-Dec., 1829) has been credited to John Wilson, but it was written by Chauncey H. Townshend, as is shown by his letter to B. R. Haydon, March 15, 1830.

551. ———. "De Quincey and Wordsworth," *N&Q,* June 11, 1938, p. 423.

The relationship between the two at the time De Quincey was editor of the *Westmorland Gazette.*

552. ———. "Thomas Clarkson as Champion of Brougham in 1818," *N&Q,* June 4, 1938, pp. 398–401.

Some further details regarding the Brougham campaign of 1818. Wordsworth and Coleridge applauded Clarkson's stand against slavery, but were at odds with him in his adherence to Brougham. See *553, 592, 596.*

553. ———. "Wordsworth versus Brougham," *N&Q,* May 28, 1938, pp. 381–83.

Wordsworth's opposition to the election of the Whig Brougham in 1818, and the latter's attack on him. See *552, 592, 596.*

554. SUTTON, DENYS. "Unpublished Letters from Sir George and Lady Beaumont to the Wordsworths," *N&Q,* Aug. 27, 1938, pp. 146–49.

Excerpts from letters written from 1803 to 1827. They contain references to Coleridge, literature and art, etc.

555. WEAVER, BENNETT. "Wordsworth: Forms and Images," *SP,* XXXV (1938), 433–45.

Wordsworth first reacted in a sensuous way to the physical qualities of the forms and images of nature. Later, they took on a spiritual meaning, pointing to the "eternal Beauty," their source. But beyond their ability to ennoble the heart, the forms "became the substances and solidities with which the creative power works." Yet they must neither be torn from their relationships (analytic reasoning), nor allowed to dominate the mind.

556. Wells, J. E. "'Lyrical Ballads,' 1800: Cancel Leaves," *PMLA,* liii (1938), 207–29.

Notes on cancel leaves and variant readings, based on a study of forty-five copies of Volume I, and fifty-two copies of Volume II.

557. ———. "Wordsworth's 'Lyrical Ballads,' 1820," *PQ,* xvii (1938), 398–402.

At least three copies of Volume II show the substitution of a title leaf dated 1820.

558. Willoughby, L. A. "Wordsworth and Germany," *German Studies Presented to Professor H. G. Fiedler,* Oxford, The Clarendon Press, 1938, pp. 432–58.

An essay on Wordsworth's visits to Germany, the extent of his knowledge of German writers, German influences and parallels, and his attitude toward Germany as a nation. See *130, 296.*

559. Winwar, Frances. *Farewell the Banner,* New York, Doubleday, Doran, and Co., 1938.

A popular study of Coleridge, and William and Dorothy Wordsworth.

1939

560. Anon. "Wordsworth and Greek," *N&Q,* Nov. 18, 1939, pp. 366–67.

Comments on the question whether Wordsworth knew Greek. This, and the notion that he was not a well-read man, are further discussed in *N&Q,* Dec. 16, 1939, p. 446; and March 9, 1940, pp. 172–73.

561. ———. "Wordsworth's Experience," *TLS,* July 22, 1939, p. 437.

It is affirmed that Arnold's attitude is "more faithful to the master than Professor Dover Wilson [*Leslie Stephen and Matthew Arnold as Critics of Wordsworth*] will allow."

562. ———. "Wordsworth's 'Stanzas' (1802)," *N&Q,* July 8, 1939, pp. 32–33.

Discusses the efforts made to identify passages describing Coleridge and those referring to Wordsworth, in the latter's

Stanzas written in My Pocket-Copy of Thomson's Castle of Indolence. The writer suggests that there is a slight mixing of the two characters with possibly a detail from a third person.

563. Beatty, Frederika. *William Wordsworth of Rydal Mount,* London, J. M. Dent and Sons Ltd., 1939.

Citations and quotations from many sources which give the picture of Wordsworth and his varied circle of friends during the last ten years of his life.

Rev. Sunday *Times* [London], July 30, 1939.

564. Casson, T. E. "The Vernal Wood," *TLS,* April 29, 1939, p. 250.

A parallel, from the writings of Saint Bernard, to Wordsworth's lines in *The Tables Turned.*

565. Eigerman, Hyman. "A Negligible Note in Literary Criticism," *English Journal* (Col. ed.), xxviii (1939), 58–60.

Points out a passage from Wordsworth's essay, *Of Legislation for the Poor,* which shows the social conservatism and literary objectives of "the great bourgeois artist."

566. Grant, A. J. "A Line in Wordsworth," *TLS,* Sept. 16, 1939, p. 539.

Asks for an explanation of a line from the *River Dudden Sonnets,* XXIV. See also Sept. 30, pp. 551 and 563.

567. Griggs, E. L., ed. *Wordsworth and Coleridge, Studies in Honor of George McLean Harper,* Princeton, N. J., Princeton University Press, 1939.

The volume contains the following essays: Émile Legouis, "Some Remarks on the Composition of the *Lyrical Ballads* of 1798"; R. D. Havens, "Solitude, Silence, and Loneliness in the Poetry of Wordsworth"; O. J. Campbell, "Wordsworth's Conception of the Esthetic Experience"; N. P. Stallknecht, "The Tragic Flaw in Wordsworth's Philosophy"; E. de Selincourt, "Wordsworth and His Daughter's Marriage"; L. N. Broughton, "An Imitation of Wordsworth"; M. R. Adams, "Helen Maria Williams and the French Revolution"; S. H. Monk, "Anna Seward and the Romantic Poets: A Study in Taste"; G.H.B. Coleridge, "Samuel Taylor Coleridge Discovers the Lake Country"; B. R. McElderry, Jr., "Coleridge's 'Preface' to *Christabel*"; E.L. Griggs, "An Early Defense of *Christabel*"; C. D. Thorpe, "Coleridge on the Sublime"; Edith J. Morley, "Coleridge in Germany (1799)"; J. D. Spaeth, "Professor Harper: An Appreciation"; and Evelyn Griggs, "Bibliography of the Works of George McLean Harper."

Rev. *TLS,* July 22, 1939, p. 369. Bernbaum, *College English* (1939), pp. 280–81. Snyder, *ELH,* vii (1940), 16–17. Bald, *MLN,* lv (1940), 466–69. Batho, *MLR,* xxxv (1940), 397–99. King, *RES,* xvi (1940), 239–42.

568. HOLMES, ELISABETH. "Some Sources of Wordsworth's Passages on Mythology," *MLN,* liv (1939), 127–29.

Several of the mythological passages in *The Excursion,* Book IV, are indebted to *Purchas His Pilgrimage* (1614), which was in Wordsworth's library.

569. MILLEY, H.J.W. "Some Notes on Coleridge's 'Eolian Harp,'" *MP,* xxxvi (1939), 359–75.

The advance in thought and style of *The Eolian Harp* over Coleridge's earlier verse cannot be attributed to Wordsworth's influence, since the two men had not met when the poem was composed, Aug. 20, 1795. But Wordsworth was influenced by Coleridge, as the similarities between the form and philosophy of the *Eolian Harp* and *Tintern Abbey* indicate. Also, *The Eolian Harp,* in its essential form, serves as "a perfect exposition of Wordsworth's theory of the conditions of poetical inspiration, as can be seen if the several points in Wordsworth's theory are taken in order and illustrated briefly by quotations from *The Eolian Harp."*

570. RAYSOR, T. M. "Coleridge's Criticism of Wordsworth," *PMLA,* liv (1939), 496–510.

A justification of Coleridge's criticism of Wordsworth in the *Biographia Literaria,* on the basis that Coleridge was correct in interpreting Wordsworth's phrase "language of poetry" to mean not merely vocabulary but style. The editors of the Oxford and of the Cambridge editions of the *Biographia,* Shawcross and Sampson, have invalidated Coleridge's criticism of this point by restricting Wordsworth's meaning to vocabulary.

571. THORPE, C. D. "The Imagination: Coleridge *Versus* Wordsworth," *PQ,* xviii (1939), 1–18.

The chief point of departure is Coleridge's denial of Wordsworth's statement *(Preface,* 1815) that the imagination as well as the fancy might be an associative power. Coleridge at this date discovered that he differed more than he had realized from Wordsworth on the subjects of Imagination and Fancy. He proposed to investigate the "seminal principle" of Imagination,

Wordsworth having only sketched "the branches with their *poetic* fruitage." Chapters IV–IX, and XII of *Biographia Literaria,* leading up to the definition of Imagination at the end of Chapter XIII, make clear why Coleridge believed that Wordsworth had been unable to give a satisfactory scientific psychological explanation.

572. WEAVER, BENNETT. "Wordsworth: The Growth of a Poet's Mind," *Papers of the Michigan Academy of Science, Arts, and Letters,* XXIV (1938), Part IV, Ann Arbor, University of Michigan Press, 1939, 109–22.

Between 1798 and 1805 Wordsworth slowly dropped sensism and acquired a mystical and spiritual philosophy. His attempt to fit an earlier sensational psychology into an explanation of his poetic insight resulted mostly in uninspired prose, and it is a mistake to dig out such passages of metaphysics and point to them as truly Wordsworthian.

573. WELLS, J. E. "'Lyrical Ballads,' 1800: A Paste-In," *Library,* 4th Series, xix (1938–39), 486–91 *(Transactions of the Bibliographical Society,* 2nd Series, xix).

Two specimens of a paste-in, supplying fifteen missing lines in *Michael.*

574. ———. "Printer's Bills for Coleridge's 'Friend' and Wordsworth's 'Cintra,'" *SP,* xxxvii (1939), 521–23.

An examination of bills and accounts (in the British Museum) between the printers and publishers, and Daniel Stuart, furnishes fresh proof of the generosity of Stuart, and shows that *Cintra* sold better than has generally been assumed.

575. WILSON, J. D. *Leslie Stephen and Matthew Arnold as Critics of Wordsworth,* Cambridge, Cambridge University Press, 1939.

A defense of Stephen's *Ethics of Wordsworth* against Arnold's attack on Wordsworth as a philosopher. Wilson presents no new points, but puts well the case of Wordsworth as a philosopher.

1940

576. BEACH, J. W. "Reason and Nature in Wordsworth," *Journal of the History of Ideas,* i (1940), 335–51.

A reply to the charges of Babbitt, More, and other "humanists" that Wordsworth repudiates reason, and confuses the natural order with the moral order. Beach examines closely the concepts associated with the words "reason" and "nature," giving sixteenth-, seventeenth-, and eighteenth-century precedents that influenced Wordsworth. "Nature," "reason," and "law" are all closely associated. But by reason Wordsworth means more than eighteenth-century rationalism, as his "higher reason" involves intuitive ethical insight. Beach argues further that Wordsworth does not confuse the "law for things" (nature) with the "law for man."

577. BERNBAUM, ERNEST. "Is Wordsworth's Nature-Poetry Antiquated?" *ELH,* vii (1940), 333–40.

A defense of Wordsworth against the accusation of Beach and Willey that his nature philosophy is unscientific in assuming a discernible purpose in nature. Bernbaum points out the modern conception of the organic similarity between man and nature; the scientific interest of the common in nature, rather than of the sport; the "dignity" of man, his rise by evolution to superiority above all other living forms; and the optimism as to man's place in nature and his future development. All of these matters are consonant with Wordsworth's fundamental views of nature.

578. BURGUM, E. B. "Wordsworth's Reform in Poetic Diction," *College English,* ii (1940), 207–16.

In his theory of poetry, Wordsworth abandoned the idealistic approach of the classical tradition. But Wordsworth's rustics and "selection of language really used by men" in reality only reflected middle-class modes of thought and speech.

579. BURTON, MARY E. "Wordsworth's Nature Philosophy as Revealed by his Revisions of 'The Prelude,'" *College English,* i (1940), 300–9.

"I find in these revisions no indication that Wordsworth is attempting to alter the fundamental philosophy of the early version and much proof that he is intensifying and reaffirming it." See *311, 316, 597, 608.*

580. CROFTS, J. *Wordsworth and the Seventeenth Century* (Warton Lecture in English Poetry), British Academy, 1940, London, Humphrey Milford, 1940.

An original and interesting lecture, pointing out that Wordsworth is more akin to the seventeenth century than to the eighteenth or nineteenth. Analogies are drawn with the religious writers, both to the poets and to the less known biographers of the seventeenth century.

581. DAS, P. K. "Cowley and Wordsworth's 'Skylark,'" *MLR,* xxxv (1940), 214.

Dowden pointed out a similarity between Wordsworth's poem and Hogg's "The Lark," but no editor has commented on the parallel in the concluding stanza of Cowley's "The Shortness of Life and Uncertainty of Riches."

582. EIGERMAN, HYMAN, ed. *The Poetry of Dorothy Wordsworth,* New York, Columbia University Press, 1940.

Passages from the *Journals* arranged to form stanzas of free verse.

583. EMPSON, WILLIAM. "Basic English and Wordsworth," *Kenyon Rev.,* ii (1940), 449–57.

An analysis of the lines in *The Prelude* describing Wordsworth's dedication to poetry. The 1805 version is put into "basic" English, and this in turn is compared to the 1850 text. The result of the experiment shows a more self-important Wordsworth in the later text.

584. LOGAN, J. V. "Wordsworth and the Pathetic Fallacy," *MLN,* lv (1940), 187–91.

Parallels between Ruskin's theory and Wordsworth's statements in the Prefaces, suggesting a Wordsworthian influence.

585. MARJARUM, E. W. "Wordsworth's View of the State of Ireland," *PMLA,* lv (1940), 608–11.

Presents evidence of the influence on Wordsworth of Spenser's *View of the Present State of Ireland,* and of histories of Ireland by Campion, Hanmer, and Marleburrough.

586. MEYERSTEIN, E.H.W. "'The Mad Monk' and Wordsworth," *TLS,* Sept. 7, 1940, p. 447.

The opening lines of Coleridge's *The Mad Monk* show verbal resemblances to the opening stanza of Wordsworth's *Ode on Intimations of Immortality.* There follows a series of letters stating that this resemblance had been pointed out by Garrod, and replying to a question raised by Meyerstein concerning the date of the *Ode.* See *TLS,* Oct. 12, p. 552; Nov. 2, p. 555; and Nov. 9, p. 567.

587. STROUT, A. L. "Wordsworth's Desiccation," *MLR,* xxxv (1940), 162–72.

Strout draws together evidence of Wordsworth's decline as he grew older, and assigns as one cause the poet's early poverty, which cut him off from travel and other kinds of stimulus that he craved.

588. WEAVER, BENNETT. "Wordsworth: The Aesthetic Intimation," *PQ,* xix (1940), 20–28.

Wordsworth cast off sensism so that "the senses are remanded to their due place and the system falls off like a dry shell." He reached a pure aesthetic consciousness which fulfills itself in the spiritual.

589. ———. "Wordsworth's 'Prelude': The Shaping Spirit," *SP,* xxxvii (1940), 75–87.

The successive books of *The Prelude* illustrate Wordsworth's rejection of sensism and his growing spiritual conception of himself as a poet. The imagination is the shaping spirit which directs the poem towards visionary truths.

590. ———. "Wordsworth: The Property of Fortitude," *SP,* xxxvii (1940), 610–31.

The paper is in answer to those critics who accuse Wordsworth of not facing the pain and tragedy in life. It summarizes the train of sorrows and disturbances that filled his life, and traces the appearance of pain and tragedy in his verse from 1795 to 1805.

591. WELLS, J. E. "Wordsworth and Church Building: 'Airey-Force Valley,'" *MLR,* xxxv (1940), 350–54.

Concerns Wordsworth's association with Joshua Watson, philanthropist and church supporter; his effort to secure a new church building at Cockermouth; and his High Church attitude. Also, there is included an unpublished early version of the poem *Airey-Force Valley,* found in a letter to Watson, and an account of the occasion of the poem's composition and date (1835).

592. ———. "Wordsworth and De Quincey in Westmorland Politics," *PMLA,* lv (1940), 1080–1128.

An account of the Brougham campaign in 1818 to unseat Lord Lowther. Wordsworth was actively opposed to Brougham. Texts and letters not hitherto published are included. See *552, 553, 596.*

593. WILLEY, BASIL. *The Eighteenth Century Background,* London, Chatto and Windus, 1940.

A companion book to the author's *The Seventeenth Century Background.* The central theme of this book is the ideas of nature. It is a splendid survey of the philosophers and men of letters of the period, of great benefit to students of Wordsworth and other Romantic poets. The final chapter is on Wordsworth's view of nature. It is chiefly concerned with an account of his period of revolutionary agitation, his Godwinism and moral crises, and his return to nature with its restorative effects upon him. Willey also discusses the values to the modern reader of Wordsworth's nature poetry. His experiences voiced in his poetry are more congenial to the modern mind than are his efforts to explain them and draw teachings from them. Of special note, also, are the sections in the book devoted to Hartley, Godwin, and Burke.

Rev. *TLS,* June 22, 1940, p. 302. Low, *RES,* xviii (1942), 118–21. Graham, *JEGP,* xli (1942), 246–48.

1941

594. ANGUS, D. R. "The Relationship of Wordsworth's 'Ode on the Intimations of Immortality' to Ruskin's Theory of the Infinite in Art," *MLR,* xxxvi (1941), 506–8.

The effects of light and distance that suggest infinity, prevalent in the *Ode,* are one of the *dicta* of Ruskin's *Modern Painters.*

595. BISHOP, D. H. "The Origin of 'The Prelude,' and the Composition of Books I and II," *SP,* xxxviii (1941), 494–520.

The poem did not originate at Alfoxden, but at Sockburn, after the return from Germany in 1799. The passages written in Germany, later revised and incorporated into *The Prelude,* were not originally intended as a part of a designed autobiography, the conception of which had not yet been formed. See *479, 504.*

596. BROUGHTON, L. N. "Wordsworth and De Quincey in Westmorland Politics, 1818: Addendum," *PMLA,* lvi (1941), 597.

Corroboration of the points in Well's article, with some bibliographical additions. See *552, 553, 592.*

597. BURTON, MARY E. "How Wordsworth Changed the Diction of 'The Prelude,'" *College English,* iii (1941), 12–24.

A classification of the changes in the later text. Burton draws the conclusion that they represent an orderly set of principles on which the poet in his later years revised to advantage. See *311, 316, 579, 608.*

598. HAVENS, R. D. *The Mind of a Poet. A Study of Wordsworth's Thought With Particular Reference to The Prelude,* Baltimore, The Johns Hopkins Press, 1941.

A monumental work, of first importance to the student. With the equipment of his own research and that of many other scholars, Havens presents the fullest and one of the most discriminating interpretations of Wordsworth's thought, emphasizing its transcendental aspect. The second section of the book is a line-by-line commentary on *The Prelude.* In conjunction with de Selincourt's notes in his variorum edition (Clarendon Press, 1926), these comments and explanations are of inestimable value to the student of that poem.

Rev. *TLS,* June 27, 1942, p. 318. Harper, *SRL,* Feb. 21, 1942, p. 9. Beach, *MLN,* lvii (1942), 473–76. Weaver, *ELH,* x (1943), 13–15. Darbishire, *RES,* xix (1943), 97–100. Meyer, *MLQ,* iv (1943), 120–22; 515–18. Bernbaum, *JEGP,* xlii (1943), 133–37. Wells, *PQ,* xxii (1943), 88–89. MacGillivray, *Univ. of Toronto Quart.,* xii (1943), 233–35.

599. KNIGHT, G. W. *The Starlit Dome: Studies in the Poetry of Vision,* London, Oxford University Press, 1941.

"The Wordsworthian Profundity," pp. 1–82. An interpretation of *The Prelude, The Borderers, Intimations Ode, The Excursion,* and many minor poems. Knight reveals the symbols and other means whereby Wordsworth penetrates the hidden intricacies of the mind and spirit.

600. LANG, VARLEY. "A Lost Acquaintance of Wordsworth," *ELH,* viii (1941), 214–15.

Chauncey Hare Townshend wrote an essay on the "Theory and Writings of Wordsworth" *(Blackwood's,* xxvii [1829]), by which he fell into disfavor with the poet.

601. MABBOTT, T. O. "Haydon's Letter Arranging for Keats to Meet Wordsworth," *N&Q,* May 10, 1941, pp. 328–29.

Haydon left two conflicting accounts of the meeting, one in the *Autobiography* and one in a letter to Monkhouse. The possibility that there were two meetings is discussed.

602. MEYERSTEIN, E.H.W. "Wordsworth and Coleridge," *TLS,* Nov. 29, 1941, p. 596.

Among the juvenilia in de Selincourt's edition of early poems is a fragment entitled *Beauty and Moonlight,* written about 1786. The writer points out that with but a few variants it is identical with the short early version of Coleridge's *Lewti.* There follows a series of letters in reference to this, pointing out a note of Southey's on *Lewti,* in which he said it was a school poem by Wordsworth corrected by Coleridge. See *TLS,* Dec. 6, 1941, p. 611; and Dec. 20, 1941, p. 643.

603. NOYES, RUSSELL. *Wordsworth and Jeffrey in Controversy,* "Indiana University Publications. Humanities Series," No. 5, Bloomington, University of Indiana Press, 1941.

Various aspects of this difficult problem are examined. Noyes concludes that Jeffrey's temperament, tastes, and moral outlook were honestly in opposition to Wordsworth's, but once in the fray Jeffrey was guilty of duplicity and unfair practices. Attention is called to Wordsworth's stubbornness, and the unhappy effect of the controversy upon him.

604. PARKER, W. M. "Wordsworth to John Scott," *TLS,* Dec. 27, 1941, p. 660.

This letter, dated 1816, to the editor of *The Champion* is here printed for the first time in its correct form from the original.

605. WELLS, J. E. "De Quincey and 'The Prelude,'" *PQ,* xx (1941), 1–24.

De Quincey's second article on Wordsworth *(Tait's Magazine,* 1839) draws exhaustively on the 1805 version of *The Prelude.* Either De Quincey had a remarkably accurate memory, or he was drawing on elaborate notes he may have made in 1814–15 for a series of articles that Wordsworth hoped he would write in defense of the latter's poetry.

606. WILLIAMS, CHARLES. "Blake and Wordsworth," *Dublin Rev.,* No. 417 (1941), 175–86.

Similarities between the *Prophetic Books* and *The Prelude.*

1942

607. BROUGHTON, L. N., ed. *The Wordsworth Collection . . . a Supplement to the Catalogue,* Ithaca, N. Y., Cornell University Press, 1942.

Titles added to the Cornell University Collection since the *Catalogue* was issued. See *403.*

608. BURTON, MARY E. *The One Wordsworth,* Chapel Hill, University of North Carolina Press, 1942.

By an examination of the revisions of *The Prelude,* Burton finds little evidence for the notion of the "two Wordsworths." On the contrary, not only are the revisions better poetry but they show the early and late Wordsworth consistent in essentials. She disagrees with the conclusions of de Selincourt and substantiates the interpretation of Batho. See *311, 316, 579, 597.*

Rev. Harper, *SRL,* Dec. 12, 1942, p. 6. Weaver, *JEGP,* xlii (1943), 282. Havens, *MLN,* lviii (1943), 563–64.

609. CAMERON, KENNETH. "Wordsworth, Bishop Doane and the Sonnets on the American Church," *History of the Protestant Episcopal Church,* xi (1942), 83–91.

From the letters and diary of Bishop Doane.

610. DANIEL, ROBERT. "Jeffrey and Wordsworth: The Shape of Persecution," *The Sewanee Rev.,* l (1942), 195–213.

Jeffrey did not attack Wordsworth because of the poet's politics or because Jeffrey was neoclassic and out of sympathy with the innovations in poetry. He was hostile to Wordsworth and the "Lake" poets for numerous ulterior motives, not the least of which was a desire to display his wit and power of satire and to popularize *The Edinburgh Review.*

611. DE SELINCOURT, ERNEST. "A Wordsworth Date," *TLS,* May 9, 1942, p. 240.

Presents evidence for the dates March, 1802, and March, 1804, for the beginning and completion of the *Ode on Intimations of Immortality.* See *349, 384, 425, 472, 489.*

612. JORDAN, J. E. "Wordsworth and 'The Witch of Atlas,'" *ELH,* ix (1942), 320–25.

Shelley's poem, with its absurdities of style, is intended as a mockery of *Peter Bell.* See *72, 276, 635.*

613. LOGAN, J. V. "England's Peril and Wordsworth," *The Sewanee Rev.,* l (1942), 446–56.

Wordsworth's *Poems Dedicated to National Independence and Liberty* are the basis of this essay. A parallel is drawn between England's battle against Napoleon for survival and her struggle in World War II. See *659.*

614. MACLEAN, N. F. "An Analysis of a Lyric Poem," *University Rev.,* viii (1942), 202–9.

A critical analysis of Wordsworth's *It is a Beauteous Evening.*

615. MCKILLOP, A. D. *The Poet as a Patriot: Shakespeare to Wordsworth,* "Rice Institute Pamphlets," xxix, No. 4 (1942), 309–36.

Includes a brief account of Wordsworth's patriotic verse of the decade beginning 1802. McKillop says that Wordsworth is the first to express "the historical imagination which was about to transform European literature."

616. Miles, Josephine. *Wordsworth and the Vocabulary of Emotion,* "University of California Publications in English," XII, No. 1, Berkeley, University of California Press, 1942.

A thorough investigation of the words used by Wordsworth denoting emotion, with tables of percentages and comparisons with other poets. Miles's admirable study opens up new and interesting critical possibilities.

Rev. Weaver, *ELH,* xi (1944), 21–22. Wellek, *MLN,* lviii (1943), 644–45. Baker, *PQ,* xxiii (1944), 94–95.

617. Ryan, C. T. "The Child in Wordsworth's Poetry," *South Atlantic Quarterly,* xli (1942), 192–97.

With the appearance of Rousseau and Romanticism, the child takes a new place in literature. Wordsworth exemplifies the new treatment of childhood in poetry. See *241, 654.*

618. Simpson, Percy. "An Emendation in the Text of Wordsworth," *RES,* xviii (1942), 228.

Suggests correcting "Graceful" to "Grateful" *(Excursion,* I, 43).

619. Stauffer, D. A. "Coöperative Criticism," *Kenyon Rev.,* iv (1942), 133–44.

Résumés of four interpretations of Wordsworth's *Ode on Intimations of Immortality,* read before the English Institute by Horace Gregory, Lionel Trilling, Cleanth Brooks, and Frederick Pottle, with observations on critical aims and methods. See *620.*

620. Trilling, Lionel. "Wordsworth's 'Ode: Intimations of Immortality,'" *English Institute Annual,* New York, Columbia University Press, 1942.

The essay attempts to banish the interpretation that the *Ode* is Wordsworth's farewell to his poetic powers. He lost the "visionary gleam," but rededicated his powers to "the philosophic mind." See *619.*

621. Wellesley, Dorothy, ed. *Wordsworth. English Poets in Pictures,* London, Collins, 1942.

Brief biography, appropriately illustrated.

622. Wells, J. E. "'Lyrical Ballads,' 1798," *TLS,* Jan. 17, 1942, p. 36.

Corrects error (originating in T. J. Wise's *Two Lake Poets)* of a cancel leaf G1 in *Lyrical Ballads,* London, 1798. See *339.*

623. ———. "Wordsworth's 'To the Queen, 1846,'" *PQ,* xxi (1942), 415–19.

History of the poem, written on the flyleaf of Wordsworth's presentation copy of *Poems* (1845) to Victoria. It was not known until printed by Grosart on the reverse of his Dedication leaf of the *Prose Works* (1876). The copy in the Ashley collection, dated Kendal, 1846, was forged between 1880 and 1893. See *185*.

624. West, Geoffrey. "Literary Detection," *TLS,* May 30, 1942, p. 271.

Protests the position, indicated by a review of Edmund Wilson's *The Wound and the Bow,* that "interpretation of Wordsworth's poetry is impossible without knowledge of the youthful love affair in France."

625. "Wordsworth's 'The World is Too Much With Us,'" *Explicator,* i, No. 1 (1942), 4.

Remarks by the editors on the integration of the poem; "nearly every image in the sestet fulfills an image in the last half of the octave."

1943

626. Anon. "Wordsworth's 'Three Years She Grew in Sun and Shower,'" *Explicator,* ii, No. 2 (1943), Q7.

Raises the question "is not Nature behaving very oddly in transforming her 'Child' into a 'Lady'?"

627. Cooper, Lane. *Experiments in Education,* "Cornell Studies in English," XXXIII, Ithaca, N. Y., Cornell University Press, 1943.

Contains the essay "Wordsworth on Scott." By drawing together Wordsworth's comments on Scott, Cooper reveals some of the former's critical opinions. He indicates the justice of Wordsworth's comments. See *633*.

628. Daniel, Robert. "Wordworth's 'Elegiac Stanzas,' 15–16," *Explicator,* ii, No. 1 (1943), 5.

Not without a conflict, as these stanzas show, Wordsworth was repudiating as a "fond illusion" the kind of writing these lines describe.

629. De Selincourt, E. "Note on 'The Prelude,' VI, 160–174 (1805), 142–154 (1850)," *RES,* xix (1943), 71–72.

The source of the shipwrecked geometrician is John Newton's *An Authentic Narrative*. See *461*.

630. "Dorothy Wordsworth: a Correction," *N&Q,* Jan. 16, 1943, p. 42.

The editors correct the dates of the last two entries of Dorothy Wordsworth's Alfoxden journal. She, William, and Coleridge left for Cheddar Wednesday, May 23, arriving May 24. N. C. Smith's review of de Selincourt's edition of Dorothy's *Journals* credits Catherine Maclean for noting the error.

631. GEEN, ELIZABETH. "The Concept of Grace in Wordsworth's Poetry," *PMLA,* lviii (1943), 689–715.

A close study of Wordsworth's use of the word "grace," which throws light on the changing theological views in the various periods of his life. The paper includes evidences of Wordsworth's pietism before 1798, his tendency towards pantheism and naturalism in 1798–1802, and his return to pietism and eventual orthodoxy. Geen concludes: "It is impossible to escape the conclusion that Wordsworth's naturalism is a deviation from his fundamental beliefs rather than their most genuine expression."

632. GIERASCH, WALTER. "Wordsworth's 'I Travelled among Unknown Men,'" *Explicator,* i, No. 8 (1943), 65.

The nostalgic patriotism of the first two stanzas develops into something more, a personal love theme.

633. GORDON, R. K. "Scott and Wordsworth's 'Lyrical Ballads,'" *Proceedings and Transactions of the Royal Society of Canada,* 3rd Series, XXXVII (1943), Sec. II, 113–19.

Scott's quotations from Wordsworth are mostly from *Lyrical Ballads.* He especially appreciated the poems dealing with the feelings and sentiments of old age. The author also points out Wordsworth's influences on Scott, especially in *Guy Mannering* and *The Antiquary.* See 627.

634. LEARY, LEWIS. "Wordsworth in America: Addenda," *MLN,* lviii (1943), 391–93.

Early recognition of Wordsworth in America. See *346, 447.*

635. MARSH, G. L. "The 'Peter Bell' Parodies of 1819," *MP,* xl (1943), 267–74.

A discussion of the neglected parodies, *Benjamin the Waggoner,* and *The Dead Asses, a Lyrical Poem.* See *72, 276, 612.*

636. MEYER, G. W. *Wordsworth's Formative Years,* "University of Michigan Publications Language and Literature," XX, Ann Arbor, University of Michigan Press, 1943.

A study of Wordsworth's formative forces to 1798. In contrast to Campbell and Mueschke, Meyer argues for the genuine social protest in Wordsworth's early poetry arising out of his own bitter experiences. Too much credence has been given the poet's own idealized account of his youth in *The Prelude.* In his discussions of the early poems, Meyer presents many suggestive points.

Rev. Weaver, *ELH,* xi (1944), 20. Wolf, *MLN,* lix (1944), 424–25. Batho, *MLR,* xxxix (1944), 199. *TLS,* Jan. 22, 1944, p. 42.

637. Miles, Josephine. "Wordsworth and 'Glitter,'" *SP,* xl (1943), 552–59.

The writer holds that there have been large assumptions and too much theorizing in the explanations of Wordsworth's poetic theory. We now have ample opportunity for a study of the words he used in his critical pronouncements. As a beginning, Miles gives generous samples of Wordsworth's choice of adjectives of derogation. By seeing exactly what he did not like, we can go far in arriving at what he liked. The list of major derogatory terms also has their counterparts.

638. Peek, Katherine M. *Wordsworth in England: Studies in the History of His Fame,* Bryn Mawr, Pa., 1943.

A compendium of English opinion of Wordsworth from the time of his contemporaries to the present. It is very full in recording the views of the Victorians, and is especially valuable in indicating Wordsworth's affinities to Victorian religious movements.

639. Prichard, J. P. "Aristotle, Horace, and Wordsworth," *Am. Philological Assoc. Trans. and Proc.,* lxxiv (1943), 72–91.

Wordsworth's debt to Aristotle and Horace was great, and he was aware of these writers as sources of many of his ideas. The article lists numerous points in common, including artistic imitation, poetic diction, conception of the poet and the purpose of poetry, etc. See *184, 512.*

640. Stearns, M. M. "Wordsworth's 'She Was a Phantom of Delight,'" *Explicator,* i, No. 8 (1943), 68.

States that J. L. Lowes interprets the word "machine" in the sense of "universe" (from Bartrams' *Travels),* not in the Elizabethan meaning of "body."

641. "Wordsworth's 'She Was a Phantom of Delight,'" *Explicator,* i, No. 6 (1943), 46.

The editors give an analysis of the structure of the poem.

1944

642. Anon. "Wordsworth in Italy," *N&Q,* Jan. 15, 1944, p. 48.
Comments from a letter of John Carlyle, 1837.

643. Boas, Louise S. "Coleridge's 'The Ancient Mariner,' Part IV," *Explicator,* ii, No. 7 (1944), 52.
"Coleridge was here at one with Wordsworth in the belief that man is a social being; that isolationism is a sin against humanity."

644. Boyd, John. "Wordsworth's Irish Tour," *Dublin Magazine,* xix (1944), 29–34.
Tour of 1829. The content of the essay is mostly from Wordsworth's letters, but there are also brief comments on Wordsworth's friendship with William Rowan Hamilton.

645. Curry, Kenneth. "Southey's Visit to Caroline Wordsworth Baudouin," *PMLA,* lix (1944), 599–602.
Prints an unpublished letter from Southey describing a visit to Wordsworth's French daughter in 1817. He also met Annette, the baby Dorothy, and Jean Baudouin. Southey's impressions are interesting.

646. Dudley, F. A. "Wordsworth's 'Three Years She Grew in Sun and Shower,'" *Explicator,* ii, No. 4 (1944), Q19.
Why "three years"?

647. Gierasch, Walter. "Wordsworth's 'London, 1802,'" *Explicator,* ii, No. 6 (1944), 42.
Defends the organization of the poem.

648. Houghton, Walter. "Wordsworth's 'She Was a Phantom of Delight,'" *Explicator,* iii, No. 3 (1944), 20.
Stanza one presents the first ecstatic impression of the subject, viewed as a woman. The greater values of the woman, as seen on nearer view, are presented in stanza two. In the third stanza the poet penetrates beyond the physical to the ideal character.

649. Housman, Laurence. "What Happened to Wordsworth?" *Atlantic Monthly,* clxxiv (Nov., 1944), 66–71.
Remarks on the reasons for Wordsworth's unpopularity: his pompous tone and failure to recognize when the spirit was not in him. But his theory of poetic diction has been influential, and when he is at his best he is great in his simplicity. He changed for the worse when his philosophy and poetic creed

ceased to be intuitive; when he compromised in theology and politics.

650. Kessel, Marcel. "Wordsworth's 'We Are Seven,'" *Explicator,* ii, No. 6 (1944), 43.

Suggests that it is inaccurate to interpret the poem as expressing Wordsworth's belief that children have intuitive knowledge.

651. McElderry, B. R., Jr. "Common Elements in Wordsworth's 'Preface' and Shelley's 'Defence of Poetry,'" *MLQ,* v (1944), 175–81.

There are many points in common in Wordsworth's and Shelley's essays on poetry, although scholars have overlooked the possibility of direct influence. McElderry points out and classifies the similarities.

652. Metzdorf, R. F. "A New Wordsworth Letter," *MLN,* lix (1944), 168–70.

An unpublished letter from Wordsworth to John Wilson Croker (Feb. 24, 1830), enclosing a comment, dictated by Sir Joshua Reynolds, concerning Boswell's diligence in authenticating data for his *Life of Johnson.*

653. Mounts, C. E. "The Place of Chaucer and Spenser in the Genesis of 'Peter Bell,'" *PQ,* xxiii (1944), 108–15.

Points out the analogy between Wordsworth's journey through the sky in his crescent boat, as related in *Peter Bell,* and Chaucer's flight with the eagle in the *Hous of Fame.* The journey and what seems to be an allusion to Spenser's "realm of Fairy" are Wordsworth's avowal that not even the example of Chaucer and Spenser will deter him from writing realistically of humble, daily life.

654. Niblett, W. R. "Wordsworth's Study of Childhood," *London Quarterly and Holborn Rev.* (Jan., 1944), pp. 44–50.

Wordsworth's ideas on how the child develops into the man, retaining his self-unity, and how the man must continue to recognize that part of the child that lives on in him. See *241, 617.*

655. Noyes, Russell. "Wordsworth and Burns," *PMLA,* lix (1944), 813–32.

A detailed study of a neglected subject. Noyes discusses Wordsworth's understanding and appreciation of Burns; the influence of the latter on Wordsworth from 1798 to 1805 (culminating in

The Waggoner, written in the spirit of *Tam o' Shanter* and *The Jolly Beggars);* and the circumstances of Wordsworth's defense of Burns in his *Letter to a Friend of Burns.*

656. PFEIFFER, K. G. "The Theme of Desertion in Wordsworth," *Research Studies of the State College of Washington,* xii (1944), 122–28.

An analysis of the peculiar characteristics of the seven poems dealing with desertion, written between 1793 and 1799. They represent Wordsworth's state of mind after his desertion of Annette. The writer concludes: (1) that the Vallon affair was an important cause of Wordsworth's period of depression; (2) that these poems give a truer insight into his state of mind during these years than does *The Prelude;* (3) that the temporary break with nature was in some part caused by the state of mind induced by the Vallon experience.

657. SCHUBERT, LELAND. "The Realism in Romanticism: Hugo and Wordsworth," *Studies in Speech and Drama in Honor of Alexander M. Drummond,* 1944, pp. 152–66.

658. SMITH, J. C. *A Study of Wordsworth,* Edinburgh, Oliver and Boyd Ltd., 1944.

Much that is familiar is repeated in this little book, but the chapters on "Dreams, Hallucinations, Reverie, Vision" and on "Theory of Poetry" are of especial interest. In the latter it is remarked that there has been too much emphasis placed on Wordsworth's theory of diction, and insufficient on the larger matters—the conceptions of poetry and the poet.

659. TILLETT, NETTIE S. "Poet of the Present Crisis," *The Sewanee Rev.,* lii (1944), 367–80.

Wordsworth, perhaps better than any contemporary speaker, voices the spirit of the present world crisis. The article is drawn from the sonnets of 1802–16, *The Character of the Happy Warrior,* and passages in *The Prelude* indicating Wordsworth's attitude toward the war with France. See *613.*

660. VINCENT, H. P., ed. *Letters of Dora Wordsworth,* Chicago, Packard and Co., 1944.

Correspondence between Dora and Maria Jane Jewsbury (1825–32). Most of the letters were unpublished previously.

661. WATTERS, R. E. "Wordsworth's 'Amaranthine Flower of Faith,'" *MLQ,* v (1944), 339–56.

Wordsworth passed from a reliance on nature and imagination to dependence on orthodox faith, which he believed was the final product of imagination. The stages of this development are described.

ABBREVIATIONS

The conventional abbreviations are used throughout the bibliography for titles of periodicals frequently cited. Many of the following abbreviations, however, occur only in lists of reviews.

Ang. Bbl.	*Anglia Bieblatt*
Archiv	*Archiv für das studium der neueren sprachen und literaturen* ("Herrigs's Archiv")
Col. Eng.	*College English*
Crit.	*Criterion*
ELH	*Journal of English Literary History*
Eng. Stud.	*Englische studien*
Fort. Rev.	*Fortnightly Review*
JEGP	*Journal of English and Germanic Philology*
Merc.	*London Mercury*
MLN	*Modern Language Notes*
MLQ	*Modern Language Quarterly*
MLR	*Modern Language Review*
MP	*Modern Philology*
Nation-Athen.	*Nation-Athenaeum*
NR	*New Republic*
New Sts.	*New Statesman*
N&Q	*Notes and Queries*
PMLA	*Publications of the Modern Language Association*
PQ	*Philological Quarterly*
RES	*Review of English Studies*
SAQ	*South Atlantic Quarterly*
Spect.	*Spectator*
SP	*Studies in Philology*
SRL	*Saturday Review of Literature*
TLS	*London Times Literary Supplement*
YR	*Yale Review*

INDEX

INDEX I

PROPER NAMES AND SELECTED SUBJECTS

Numerals in roman type refer to pages, those in italic to numbered items in the bibliography.

INDEX II

TITLES

Numerals in roman type refer to pages, those in italic to items in the bibliography.